Blank Page

First Printing
March 2025

Contending for the Faith
Commentary on the Epistle of Jude

Additional copies can be obtained from:

Disciple Maker Ministries
905 Golf Course Rd. N.W.
Hutchinson, MN 55350

612-750-5515

<u>LanceKetchum@msn.com</u>
<u>www.disciplemakerministries.org</u>

ISBN: 979-8-9921926-3-6

Table of Contents

IN APPRECIATION

A special THANK YOU to the members and friends of Shepherd's Fold Baptist Church of Hutchinson, Minnesota for their patience with me in the unfolding and development of the truths contained in this book. You have helped me to grow through these studies. God blessed in the many decisions that you made to the glory of God during the preaching of this series.

It has also been a blessing to see the increase of spiritual fruit through your lives as you began to implement the doctrine of Grace into the practice of your everyday lives. Praise God for many of you who have come to receive the gift of God's salvation through the preaching and teaching of the truths of God's wondrous Gospel.

I also want to thank Mrs. Julie Rydberg for her careful and meticulous proofreading of the manuscript. I pray our Lord will bless you in a special way for your generosity in giving many hours to this work.

To my wife, Patty – thank you for your patience in allowing me every free moment of our lives together for the last year to finish this work. You catered to my every need to allow me the time I needed. Your graciousness has exemplified all the truths defined by the doctrine of Grace. Your self-sacrificing love reveals the selflessness that manifests the Spirit-filled life. You are undoubtedly a living definition exemplifying the word "helpmeet."

Cover Designed by Mrs. Julie Rydberg

Jude
Contending for the Faith
Chapter One

The epistle of Jude was written in approximately A.D. 66. As Jude 1:1 informs us, he was the "brother of James." Both Jude and James were half-brothers of Jesus sharing the same mother (Galatians 1:19). Neither James nor Jude were Apostles. Therefore, Jude reminds believers to "remember ye the words which were spoken before of the apostles of our Lord Jesus Christ" in Jude verse seventeen. Although neither James nor Jude were Apostles, the words of the epistles bearing their names are still inspired of God.

"[1] Jude, the servant of Jesus Christ, and brother of James, to them that are sanctified by God the Father, and preserved in Jesus Christ, *and* called: [2] Mercy unto you, and peace, and love, be multiplied" (Jude 1-2).

James and Jude were quite common names among the Jews. There were three individuals named Jude or Judas mentioned in the Gospels. There were also three named James mentioned in the Gospel. One of these named James was an Apostle and the brother of John the Apostle. We are told these men were "the sons of Zebedee" (Matthew 4:21). We say all this so as not to confuse these people with one another.

Both the epistles of James and Jude are Jewish in their admonitions. James defines "faith" from the Hebrew definition of the word establishing that real faith *does what it professes to believe* (James 1:22). This was important because the Gentiles saw "the faith" from more of a philosophical mindset, thinking these truths were to be discussed and debated rather than as dogmatic commands from God to be understood and obeyed without question.

Jude takes this same direction as his brother James regarding faith but focuses upon the fact that real faith contends for "the faith" (Jude 3). In James, faith that professes belief but does not become "doers of the word" is branded as false faith (James 1:22). In Jude, people who profess faith in God's Words but who do not "contend for the faith" are branded as unfaithful.

Although Jude is considered more general in its application to Gentile Christians, the weight of its admonitions brings the pattern of the dogmatisms of Rabbinical Judaism into Christianity. Real faith contends "for the faith which was once delivered unto the saints" (Jude 3) for their guardianship and dogmatic preservation of the doctrines ("the faith") established by those inspired God-words. Faith that does not fight for those doctrines ("the faith") is *false faith*.

Unlike the philosophical faith of the Gentiles that resulted in endless debates but never *thus saith the Lord*, Jewish Christianity refused this early form of subjective relativism for dogmatic absolutism. In this kind of Christianity "the faith" was definable. "The faith" established definitive boundaries that when those boundaries were traversed the person traversing them moved into the arena of apostasy. Those people then must be opposed. These two brothers take a different approach to the same thing. James says if you do not live your beliefs, you deceive yourselves. Jude says if you do not fight to maintain "the faith, you deceive yourselves.

Therefore, the presence of the definite article "the" before the word "faith" in Jude 3 is critically important. The subject of contending in Jude's epistle is not mere belief. The subject of contending in Jude's epistle is *what* is to be believed.

"The faith" for which we are to contend is the teachings of Jesus Christ in the whole of Scripture beginning with the beginnings in Genesis 1:1 through the endings in Revelation 22:21. The last words of Jesus Christ in Revelation 22:18-19 are very sobering words. The believer should carefully consider the warnings of Jesus' two half-brothers James and Jude about what defines false faith.

"[18] For I testify unto every man that heareth the words of the prophecy of this book, If any man **shall add unto these things,** God shall add unto him the plagues that are written in this book: [19] And if any man **shall take away from the words of the book of this prophecy,** God shall take away his part out of the book of life, and out of the holy city, and *from* the things which are written in this book" (Revelation 22:18-19).

Jesus expects true believers indwelled by His Spirit to "rightly dividing the word of truth" (II Timothy 2:15). The phrase "word of truth" is synonymous with the words "the faith." "The faith" is only established when the "word of truth" is rightly divided. Therefore, "the faith" always opposes teachings that are the outcomes of wrongly dividing the "word of truth."

Already, by the time of the writing of I and II Corinthians, Galatians, Colossians, I Thessalonians, II Timothy, Hebrews, James, I and II Peter, Jude, and II and III John, Christianity was being overwhelmed with wrongly dividing the "word of truth." When the "word of truth" is wrongly divided the heresies created never end and keep birthing further divisions, moving people farther and farther away from "the faith."

The point is that the truth never changes. Secondly, "rightly" and wrongly divided truth does not divide itself. "The faith" requires a *carrier* to accurately divide and transport it from generation to generation. Wrongly divided truth equally demands someone to transport it and propagate it to another generation.

Therefore, "the faith" demands the faithful contend against those wrongly dividing "the word of truth." In other words, this struggle is ongoing and is a battle between real people against real people. Yet it is a spiritual battle empowered by God or empowered by the forces of "the mystery of inequity" (II Thessalonians 2:7). Those wanting to eliminate this *dynamic of tension* between those maintaining *historic faith,* and those opposing it by trying to establish some variations of *new faith* are by that very purpose opposing "the faith."

Early Christianity had professing converts from every variation of religious beliefs possible. Many Jewish believers corrupted "the faith" by integrating variations of legalism into Christianity. These were the Judaisers that Paul exposes in his epistles to Galatians and Hebrews. There were also Gnostics and Ascetics that came into Christianity professing faith in Christ but integrating variations of their beliefs into "the faith" thereby corrupting "the faith."

Paul addresses them and the legalists in his epistle to the Colossians. There were the *Antinomians* that professed faith in Christ but tried to redefine grace as a license to sin. Paul addresses their falsities in Romans 6:1-13 and in his epistle against carnality of I Corinthians.

However, those that refused correction just formed other sects of *Christianity,* morphing into thousands of what are called denominations of Christianity. The Bible word for these

denominations is the word "heresies." These new kinds of *Christianity* were not Christianity.

Jude's epistle addressing those that "contend for the faith" is to whom Jude's epistle is addressed. These faithful individuals are distinguished as "them that are sanctified by God the Father, and preserved in Jesus Christ, *and* called" (James 1). The word "sanctified" is translated from the Greek word *hagiázō* (hag-ee-ad'-zo), meaning *to make something sacred.*

That which is sanctified is set apart from the common to be used solely by and for God's purposes. "Sanctified" is in the *perfect tense* and *passive voice.* This means this person is *positionally* once for all for ever set apart to God's service by God. This is true of every genuinely "born again" Church Age believer. Maintaining that sanctified position becomes the responsibility of every believer through a partnership with the indwelling Spirit of Christ (Romans 6:1-13).

Partnering with the indwelling Spirit of Christ **to maintain practical sanctification is primary to being enabled to "earnestly contend for the faith which was once** {*one time or once for all*} **delivered unto the saints" (Jude 3).** The word "saints" in Jude 3 refers back "to them that are sanctified" in Jude 1.

"Them that are sanctified" are the "saints" (the *sanctified ones*). However, sanctification is contextually connected to a *vocational calling,* which is the priesthood of all believers. This vocational calling is then connected to a primary responsibility that "should earnestly contend for the faith which was once delivered unto the saints" (Jude 3). This is true of all believers in the Church Age. Every believer is responsible to "earnestly contend for the faith which was once delivered unto the saints" (Jude 3).

Failure to "earnestly contend for the faith which was once delivered unto the saints" is a *dereliction of duty.* Therefore, to "earnestly contend for the faith which was once delivered unto the saints" is primary to defining faithfulness. **One cannot compromise "the faith" and still claim faithfulness before God.** One cannot fail at laboring "in the word and doctrine" (I Timothy 5:17) and expect to be "rightly dividing the word of truth" (II Timothy 2:15). This work is not the work of lazy or careless people. Laboring "in the word and doctrine" (I Timothy 5:17) is developing the tools of the ministry that is done through the priesthood of the believer.

This therefore defines the primary purpose of every local church in "perfecting of the saints, for the work of the ministry, for the edifying of the body of Christ" (Ephesians 4:12). Teaching believer-priests the Word of God so that those believer-priests can minister to people outside the local church is the primary purpose for the existence of every local church. The "perfecting of the saints, for the work of the ministry" (Ephesians 4:12) is equipping believers to "earnestly contend for the faith which was once delivered unto the saints" and the "common salvation" of Jude 3. There is no room or tolerance in this for *lazy learners.*

The rebuke of *lazy learners* is addressed in the epistle to the Hebrews in the context of the new Melchizedekian priesthood of all believers in Hebrews chapter five. Hebrews 5:10-14 is a strong rebuke of *lazy learners.* The fact that *lazy learners* are tolerated at all is abominable to the commands given to Christians in Jude 3.

"¹⁰ Called of God an high priest after the order of Melchisedec. ¹¹ Of whom we have many things to say, and **hard to be uttered** *{hard to teach to slow learners not really invested in their moral obligations as priests}*, **seeing ye are dull of hearing** *{sluggish/lazy learners; it is hard to teach disinterested people}.* ¹² **For when for the time ye ought to be teachers** *{they had already had more than enough time to learn the things that would have kept them from being drawn back to the corruptions of the Mosaic Covent if they would have put in the effort}*, **ye have need that one teach you again which *be* the first principles of the oracles of God; and are become such as have need of milk, and not of strong meat** *{these are words of frustration}.* ¹³ **For every one that useth milk *is* unskilful in the word of righteousness: for he is a babe** *{these are words of strong rebuke to lazy learners}.* ¹⁴ But strong meat belongeth to them that are of full age, *even* those who by reason of use **have their senses** *{as a developed organism for perception}* **exercised** *{disciplined/trained}* **to discern** *{a term used to describe the wisdom-based developments necessary to make mature judicial judgments}* **both good and evil**" (Hebrews 5:10-14).

Any saint unperfected "for the work of the ministry" is a saint unprepared to "earnestly contend for the faith which was

once delivered unto the saints." The main reason most saints are unprepared and unperfected is because they are *lazy learners*. There is no excuse for any Christian within any local church understanding Ephesians 4:12 to be unperfected "for the work of the ministry" unless the pastor is not laboring in "word and in doctrine" or the individual has been a *lazy learner*. Neither excuses the outcome of being unperfected "for the work of the ministry," which work includes the acquired ability to "earnestly contend for the faith which was once delivered unto the saints."

"Preserved in Jesus Christ"

> "Jude, the servant of Jesus Christ, and brother of James, to them that are sanctified by God the Father, and preserved in Jesus Christ, *and* called" (Jude 1).

Two great abuses had already "crept in unawares" (Jude 4) into Christianity. These two abuses were very general in their scope but devastating in their outcomes. The first was to deny Jesus the sovereign authority to be Lord over both the Church and over individual lives. The Lordship of Jesus was reduced to a *title* without any meaning or understanding of the term.

The term Lord means sovereign authority to execute judgment even to the capital degree. Therefore, fear is connected to the term Lord especially when a person lives contrary to the His commands. Therefore, the term Lord was disconnected from the deity of Christ making it almost meaninglessly ambiguous.

The second great abuse was an outcome of the first. When the Lordship of Jesus is denied in practical application of the meaning of the term, the grace of the Lord is turned into licentiousness and an excuse for people to personally indulge and excuse their carnality.

The fact that Jesus *forgives sin* never means that Jesus *excuses sinfulness*. The notion that Jesus excuses sinfulness or carnality happens when the deity of Jesus is disconnected from the humanity of Jesus, thereby diminishing and dismantling His sovereign and judicial Lordship.

The word "preserved" in Jude 1 in connection with the words "in Jesus Christ" is *perfect tense* and *passive voice*. "Preserved" is translated from the Greek word *tēréō*, (tay-reh'-o) meaning *kept* or *guarded*. The *passive voice* in connection with the *perfect tense* means that God **has done** this preserving, not the believer. *Perfect tense* means this is something that God **has already done *once for all forever*.** The very nature of the gift of salvation is a salvation that IS a *once for all forever* gift that is "preserved" by God the moment a sinner receives that gift and is genuinely "born again" of the Spirit of God "in Christ."

The indubitable fact that salvation is a gift provided, completed, gifted, and preserved totally from the "Father's hand" is the substance of John 10:22-33. The "works that" Jesus did, including the Cross work securing salvation for sinners, He says He did "in my Father's name" (John 10:25). The words "in my Father's name" signify that the works Jesus did were done under the character, nature, and authority of His "Father's name."

The second surety is that the promises that God offers are connected to the "works" Jesus "finished," which are connected to the power in the hands of Jesus and His Father. The point of the text is that salvation is a gift from God totally disconnected from human performance or participation other than faith in a "finished" gift, not just a "finished" work of redemption.

Secondly, the gift of salvation includes the fact that God has already preserved every "born again" believer in the New Creation "in Jesus Christ." This preservation is an act of *God's hand* and is totally disconnected from any aspect of human performance. IF a person is "born again," that person HAS BEEN preserved in his/her New Creation "in Jesus Christ." "If" is a valid question for people who profess faith in Christ but who habitually live in sin and deny His Lordship over their choices.

"22 And it was at Jerusalem the feast of the dedication, and it was winter. 23 And Jesus walked in the temple in Solomon's porch. 24 Then came the Jews round about him, and said unto him, How long dost thou make us to doubt? If thou be the Christ, tell us plainly. 25 Jesus answered them, I told you, and ye believed not: **the works that I do in my Father's name**, they bear witness of me. 26 But ye believe not, because ye are not of my sheep, as I said unto you. 27 My sheep hear my voice, and I know them, and they follow me: 28 And **I give unto them eternal life; and they shall never perish, neither shall any *man* pluck them <u>out of</u>**

<u>my hand</u>. [29] My Father, which gave *them* me, is greater than all; and no *man* is able to pluck *them* <u>out of my Father's hand</u>. [30] I and *my* Father are one. [31] Then the Jews took up stones again to stone him. [32] Jesus answered them, Many good works have I shewed you from my Father; for which of those works do ye stone me? [33] The Jews answered him, saying, For a good work we stone thee not; but for blasphemy; and because that thou, being a man, makest thyself God" (John 10:22-33).

"In Jesus Christ" (Jude 1) is the *New Genesis* with Jesus as the new *Federal Head* and the "last Adam," Who succeeded where the first Adam failed. Anytime the words "in Jesus Christ" or any derivative of that term is used, it refers to the *New Creation* into which the "born again" believer is delivered (*birthed*). The point of the word "preserved" in this context is that this is a *once for all forever* act of God that cannot be altered. Since it is an act of God, no person can alter this New Creation. Based upon the immutable promises of God, what God promises is positionally as sure as already done.

God cannot break His promises. The gift of salvation and the believer's preservation in the New Creation "in Jesus Christ" is **as good as done** in the plan and purposes of God. This is the meaning of the statement that Jesus Christ is "the Lamb slain from the foundation of the world" (Revelation 13:8). This fact was part of God's plan **BEFORE** the first creation began and the surety of this promise in God's eternal plan of the ages consummates itself in the creation of a New Heaven/Earth after the Kingdom age. Therefore, the surety of this preservation lays in the immutable promises of God. This fact is the substance of the *perfect tense* and *passive voice* in the words "preserved in Jesus Christ" in Jude 1.

This *eternal security* of the already completed preservation of a believer's position "in Jesus Christ" is the subject of II Corinthians chapter five. Although the whole of II Corinthians chapter five is about this 'new creation" of which the "born again" believer is a "new creature," the *once for all forever* nature of this act of God in the gift of salvation is found in the words "become new" in II Corinthians 5:17.

The word "become" is *perfect tense* and the word "new" is from the Greek word *kainos* (kahee-nos'), meaning something of *a new kind* not just *a new something of the old kind.* In other words, the "new creation" is NOT just a redo of the first creation to be like it was before the fall but without sin. However, the *perfect tense* of the word "become" means this is a *once for all forever* reality that is already finished in the heart and mind of God.

> "[1] For **we know** {*perfect tense, i.e. with perfect surety based upon the objective facts of God's promises in His inspired Words*} that if our earthly house of *this* tabernacle were dissolved, **we have** {*already*} a building of God, an house not made with hands, **eternal** {*that which has always been and will always be*} **in the heavens** {*the New Creation*}. [2] For in this we groan, earnestly desiring to be clothed upon with our house which is from heaven: [3] If so be that being clothed we shall not be found naked. [4] For we that are in *this* tabernacle do groan, being burdened: not for that we would be unclothed, but clothed upon, **that mortality might be swallowed up of life. [5] Now he that hath wrought us for the selfsame thing *is* God, who also hath given unto us the earnest of the Spirit**" (II Corinthians 5:1-5).

The words "God, who also hath given unto us the earnest of the Spirit" define God's *signature of fidelity* upon His promise of the fullness of His promises in the New Creation beginning with giving a sinner the gift of salvation. The indwelling presence of the Spirit of Christ is God's signature "seal" of promise upon a believer's soul. The promise is that what God begins in the salvation of a believer's soul will continue in every aspect of salvation until that believer is finally delivered into the New Heaven/Earth.

The statement of II Corinthians 5:5 is simply an extension of what was already stated in II Corinthians 1:22. The point is that God put His Seal upon the believer as a person, not upon a piece of paper. **The Seal upon your person is His Person!** The *perfect tense* of the words "preserved in Jesus Christ" in Jude 1 is that every truly "born again" believer is already *signed, sealed,* and *delivered* into the New Creation. Understanding this fact is part of understanding the gift of salvation that is given by God to believers.

> "[20] For all the promises of God in him *are* yea, and in him Amen, unto the glory of God by us. [21] Now he which stablisheth us with you in Christ, and hath anointed us, *is* God; [22] **Who hath also sealed us, and given the earnest of the Spirit in our hearts**" (II Corinthians 1:20-22).

"Being confident of this very thing, that he which hath begun a good work in you will perform *it* until the day of Jesus Christ:" (Philippians 1:6).

One of the most basic forms of false faith is the outcome of misunderstanding theologically connected terms such as "the Lord Jesus Christ." This phrase is used twenty-seven different times in the New Testament books. Each term in the phrase "the Lord Jesus" and "Christ" is connected to considerable meaning that cannot be disconnected.

However, when the meaning of these three terms "the Lord Jesus Christ" are not understood individually, their connected meaning loses context, and a false faith is created because real faith is established on the objective facts that comes from these terms and the understanding of those terms. Understanding all three terms in their connectivity is necessary to understanding the Gospel that comes from these three terms.

In other words, understanding each of these terms in "the Lord Jesus Christ" is necessary to understanding the doctrine of salvation, the New Birth, and the New Creation founded in these three terms. Failure to understand the meaning of these three terms results in a lot of false professions of faith in that genuine faith is then disconnected to the objective facts defined by understanding these three terms.

The believer cannot "confess with thy mouth the Lord Jesus, and shalt believe in thine heart that God hath raised him from the dead" (Romans 10:9) if he does not understand the meaning of the terms "the Lord Jesus Christ." **When Bible terms are emptied of their objective meaning, faith in those terms is empty faith and therefore vain faith.**

"The Lord Jesus Christ"

The three words "Lord Jesus Christ" are interconnected and essentials to understanding "the faith" for which all believers are to "contend." Understanding these three words are also connected to understanding the Gospel and what defines saving faith of the "common salvation." The point here is the question: can we "contend for the faith" that defines the saving faith of the "common salvation" if we allow the theological meaning of the words "the Lord Jesus Christ" to be reduced or emptied?

The fact is that the twenty-first century has very few professing Christians who understand the theological meaning, and therefore the theological significance, of the words "the Lord Jesus Christ." For most part, the theological meaning of the words "the Lord Jesus Christ" was lost over a hundred and fifty years ago to most people within *Liberal Christianity.*

Therefore, contending "for the faith" that defines the saving faith of the "common salvation" must now be done mainly within what still calls itself *Christianity* but is without any understanding of the terms that makeup true Christianity. Contending "for the faith" that defines the saving faith of the "common salvation" must once again fill these words with their God-intended meaning to restore the theological significance within the terms "the Lord Jesus Christ."

"[3] Beloved, when I gave all diligence to write unto you of the **common salvation**, it was needful for me to write unto you, and exhort *you* that ye should earnestly contend for the faith which was once delivered unto the saints. [4] For there are certain men crept in unawares, who were before of old ordained to this condemnation, ungodly men, turning the grace of our God into lasciviousness, and **denying the only Lord God, and our Lord Jesus Christ**" (Jude 3-4).

"Lord"

The word "Lord" in Romans 10:9 and 13 is *kýrios* (koo'-ree-os). However, Romans 10:13 is a partial quote of Joel 2:32, where "LORD" is the Hebrew Jehovah. **Jesus is Jehovah incarnate in human flesh.** When a believer confesses with His "mouth the Lord Jesus," he is *publicly agreeing* with holy Scripture and proclaiming faith in understanding the fact that Jesus is Jehovah incarnate in human flesh. Therefore, the believer understands that Jesus in human flesh is still Jehovah and still retains His judicial sovereignty over His creation while in human flesh.

Confessing Jesus as Lord understands the connection of the sovereign authoritarian Lordship of Jesus over the believer's life. This understanding brings the believer under subjection to the authority of the Lord Jesus Christ. **One cannot confess Jesus to be Lord and reject voluntary subordination to His authority. Such rejection is a false confession.**

Also, the term "Lord" connects saving faith to the deity of Jesus Christ. He is "the Lord Jesus Christ." No one can "contend for the faith" that defines the saving faith of the "common salvation" by disconnecting the Gospel from the deity of Jesus Christ.

The main substance of the incarnation of Jesus Christ is that Jehovah became human. The term "Lord," meaning *Jehovah*, loses most of its *Soteriological substance* when that meaning is disconnected from the term "Jesus" as the human Name of the incarnate Jehovah. **These terms and their meaning cannot be disconnected.**

"Jesus"

The name Jesus is the humanity of Jesus connected to Jehovah as the Savior and Redeemer. The name Jesus simply means *Jehovah saves*. Jesus is the Greek derivative of the Hebrew *Y^ehôwshûwa'* (yeh-ho-shoo'-ah), which simply means *the eternal self-existent one.* Jehovah is the Hebrew *tetragrammaton* (JHVH).

The Name Jesus connects our faith *in Jesus* as the incarnate Jehovah and as the eternal Savior. The four letters JHVH are intended to be unpronounceable because they reflect the incomprehensible character, nature, and attributes of God in the three tenses of the verb "to be" (*I am, I was, I shall be*) communicated in Revelation 1:8, 11, 21:6, and 22:18.

> "I am Alpha and Omega, the beginning and the ending, saith the Lord, **which is, and which was, and which is to come**, the Almighty" (Revelation 1:8).

> "Saying, I am Alpha and Omega, **the first and the last:**" (Revelation 1:11a).

The human Name Jesus connects us to the blood of kinsman redemption. God required the sacrifice of the blood of a perfect, sinless human to pay the price to redeem lost human souls. God requires blood to redeem blood and flesh to redeem flesh. Angels have neither blood nor flesh and therefore cannot be redeemed by the Blood of Jesus. This is the significance of the *kinsman redeemer*.

"[15] And for this **cause he is the mediator of the new testament**, that by means of death, **for the redemption of the transgressions** *that were* **under the first testament**, they which are called might receive the promise of eternal inheritance. [16] For where a testament *is*, there must also of necessity be the death of the testator. [17] For a testament *is* of force after men are dead: otherwise it is of no strength at all while the testator liveth. [18] **Whereupon neither the first** *testament* **was dedicated without blood.** [19] For when Moses had spoken every precept to all the people according to the law, he took the blood of calves and of goats, with water, and scarlet wool, and hyssop, and sprinkled both the book, and all the people, [20] Saying, **This** *is* **the blood of the testament which God hath enjoined unto you.** [21] Moreover he sprinkled with blood both the tabernacle, and all the vessels of the ministry. [22] **And almost all things are by the law purged with blood; and without shedding of blood is no remission.** [23] *It was* **therefore necessary** that the patterns of things in the heavens should be purified with these; but **the heavenly things themselves with better sacrifices than these.** [24] For Christ is not entered into the holy places made with hands, *which are* the figures of the true; but into heaven itself, now to **appear in the presence of God for us**: [25] Nor yet that he should offer himself often, as the high priest entereth into the holy place every year with blood of others; [26] For then must he often have suffered since the foundation of the world: but **now once in the end of the world hath he appeared to put away sin by the sacrifice of himself.** [27] And as it is appointed unto men once to die, but after this the judgment: [28] So **Christ was once offered** to bear the sins of many; and unto them that look for him shall he appear the second time without sin unto salvation" (Hebrews 9:15-28).

Progenitor and Primogenitor of the New Covenant and New Creation

Jesus was the "firstborn" human into the New Creation upon His glorification. **Therefore, the Name of Jesus is at the top of the family tree genealogy of "the regeneration."** Jesus is both the progenitor of the New Creation and holds the position of the Lord of the New Creation (Primogenitor). **Jesus is the Name of the Savior's connection to the "first Adam" of humanity of the fallen creation and the Name of the sinless human Who became "last Adam" of humanity and the first Adam the New Creation.**

God required a perfect Adamic sinless *flesh and blood* offering to deliver us out from the Adamic condemnation of *flesh and blood.* The transition of redemption in "the regeneration" is from *flesh and blood* to becoming *spiritual beings* no longer limited by *flesh and blood,* which includes sickness, aging, and death. How many people do you know, who call themselves Christians, understand these facts of the Gospel of the "Lord Jesus Christ"? Paul calls this "the unsearchable riches of Christ" in Ephesians 3:8.

"[35] But some *man* will say, How are the dead raised up? and **with what body do they come?** [36] *Thou* fool, **that which thou sowest is not quickened, except it die**: [37] And that which thou sowest, **thou sowest not that body that shall be,** but bare grain, it may chance of wheat, or of some other *grain*: [38] But God giveth it a body as it hath pleased him, and to every seed his own body. [39] All flesh *is* not the same flesh: but *there is* one *kind of* flesh of men, another flesh of beasts, another of fishes, *and* another of birds. [40] *There are* also celestial bodies, and bodies terrestrial: but the glory of the celestial *is* one, and the *glory* of the terrestrial *is* another. [41] *There is* one glory of the sun, and another glory of the moon, and another glory of the stars: for *one* star differeth from *another* star in glory. [42] **So also *is* the resurrection of the dead.** It is sown in corruption; it is raised in incorruption: [43] It is sown in dishonour; it is raised in glory: it is sown in weakness; it is raised in power: [44] **It is <u>sown a natural body</u>; it is <u>raised a spiritual body</u>. There is a natural body, and there is a spiritual body.** [45] And so it is written, **The first man Adam was made a living soul; the last Adam *was made* a quickening spirit.** [46] Howbeit **that *was* <u>not first which is spiritual</u>, but that which is natural; and afterward that which is spiritual.** [47] The first man *is* of the earth, earthy: the second man *is* the Lord from heaven. [48] **As *is* the earthy, such *are* they also that are earthy: and as *is* the heavenly, such *are* they also that are heavenly.** [49] And as we have borne the image of the earthy, we shall also bear the image of the heavenly. [50] Now this I say, brethren, **that <u>flesh and blood</u> cannot inherit the kingdom of God**; neither doth corruption inherit incorruption" (I Corinthians 15:35-50).

"[1] For this cause I Paul, the prisoner of Jesus Christ for you Gentiles, [2] If ye have heard of **the dispensation of the grace of God** which is given me to you-ward: [3] How that by revelation **he made known unto me the mystery**; (as I wrote afore in few words, [4] Whereby, when ye read, ye may understand my knowledge in the mystery of Christ) [5] Which in other ages was not made known unto the sons of men, as it is now revealed unto his holy apostles and prophets by the Spirit; [6] That the Gentiles should be fellowheirs, and **of the same body, and partakers of his promise in Christ by the gospel**: [7] Whereof I was made a minister, according to the gift of the grace of God given unto me by the effectual working of his power. [8] Unto me, who am less than the least of all saints, is this grace given, **that I should preach among the Gentiles the unsearchable riches of Christ**; [9] And **to make all *men* see what *is* the fellowship of the mystery**, which from the beginning of the world hath been hid in God, who created all things **by Jesus Christ**: [10] To the intent that now unto the principalities and powers in heavenly *places* might be known by the church the manifold wisdom of God, [11] **According to the eternal purpose which he purposed in Christ Jesus our Lord**: [12] In whom we have boldness and access with confidence by the faith of him" (Ephesians 3:1-12).

"Christ"

The word "Christ" is the Greek form of the Hebrew word "Messiah." Messiah is simply the promised Redeemer of Genesis 3:15. Jesus Christ would redeem the souls of lost humans through faith **AND** redeem humanity's lost dominion through incarnation, living a sinless life, dying to pay the penalty of sin, and to be resurrected from the dead. Then He was gloried into "the regeneration" thereby opening a "door" into "the regeneration" for "whosoever will." Faith in Jesus as "the Christ" connects the believer to the *Promised One* and all the eternal promises of God inherent in Jesus' accomplished works of redemption.

"And I will put enmity between thee and the woman, and between thy seed and her seed; it shall bruise thy head, and thou shalt bruise his heel" (Genesis 3:15).

"[13] Christ hath redeemed us from the curse of the law, being made a curse for us: for it is written, Cursed *is* every one that hangeth on a tree: [14] That the blessing of Abraham might come on the Gentiles through Jesus Christ; **that we might receive the promise of the Spirit through faith**. [15] Brethren, I speak after the manner of men; Though *it be* but a man's covenant, yet *if it be* confirmed, no man disannulleth, or addeth thereto. [16] Now to Abraham and his seed were the promises made. He saith **not**, And to seeds, as of many; but as of one, And **to thy seed, which is <u>Christ</u>**. [17] And this I say, *that* the covenant, that was confirmed before of God in Christ, the law, which was four hundred and thirty years after, cannot disannul, that it should make the promise of none effect. [18] For **if the inheritance *be* of the law, *it is* no more of promise: but God gave *it* to Abraham by promise**" (Galatians 3:13-18).

Like the Jews by the time of the first advent of Jesus, the word "Messiah" had been almost emptied of it meaning by the scholars of Rabbinical Judaism. This is equally true of the term "Christ" by the modern scholars of *Christianity*. The term "Messiah" came to mean deliverance from Roman bondage into an "under the sun" *Rabbinically ruled* kingdom on Earth that would be Jewish.

Their misunderstanding of both the terms "Messiah" and "kingdom" reduced the meaning of these terms to mere physical transitions in world governance. For them, there was no grand spiritual transformation involved. This is always what happens when we allow theological terms to be disconnected from their theological meanings. This is equally true of *Kingdom Constructionism* in the perverted theology of modern *Reformed Theology*.

People tend to think of the term "Christ" as Jesus' last name. However, when we empty the word "Christ" of its meaning, we disconnect the meaning of the word "Christian" from being followers of the teachings of Christ. To follow Christ and His teachings begins with obeying the Gospel.

To obey the Gospel is to repent of sin and "dead works," to believe in the propitiation of God's wrath upon all sin, to believe God will gift to the believing sinner His righteousness through the indwelling of His Holy Spirit, to confess Jesus is Jehovah incarnate in human flesh, and call on the Name of the "Lord" Jesus the Christ to be saved or "born again" out of the cursed creation and into the new creation.

"[3] We are bound to thank God always for you, brethren, as it is meet, because that your faith groweth exceedingly, and the charity of every one of you all toward each other aboundeth; [4] So that we ourselves glory in you in the churches of God **for your patience and faith in all your persecutions and tribulations that ye endure**: [5] *Which is* a manifest token of the righteous judgment of God, that ye may be counted worthy of the kingdom of God, for which ye also suffer: [6] Seeing *it is* a righteous thing with God to recompense tribulation to them that trouble you; [7] And to you who are troubled rest with us, **when the Lord Jesus shall be revealed from heaven with his mighty angels, [8] In flaming fire taking vengeance on them that know not God, and that obey not the gospel of our Lord Jesus Christ**: [9] Who shall be punished with everlasting destruction from the presence of the Lord, and from the glory of his power; [10] When he shall come **to be glorified in his saints**, and to be admired in all them that believe (because our testimony among you was believed) in that day" (II Thessalonians 1:5-10).

The term "Christ" connects the "born again" believer to all the prophetic promises of God in the humanity of "Jesus" and in His deity in the term "Lord." The One Who makes the promises is the One Who keeps the promises. Therefore, the Promised One of Genesis 3:15 is Jehovah incarnate through the "seed" of the woman. The Abrahamic Covenant was just a restatement of the Adamic Covenant of Genesis 3:15. The promised "seed" of Genesis 3:15 was God's promised solution to sin as the dividing line of condemnation between the Edenic Covenant of Genesis 2:16 and the Adamic Covenant of Genesis 3:16-19.

"[1] Now I say, *That* the heir, as long as he is a child, differeth nothing from a servant, though he be lord of all; [2] But is under tutors and governors until the time appointed of the father. [3] **Even so we**, when we were children, were in bondage under the elements of the world: [4] But when the fulness of the time was come, God sent forth his Son, made of a woman, made under the law, [5] To redeem them that were under the law, that we might receive the adoption of sons. [6] And because ye are sons, God hath sent forth the Spirit of his Son into your hearts, crying, Abba, Father. [7] **Wherefore thou art no more a servant, but a son; and if a son, then an heir of God through Christ**" (Galatians 4:1-7).

Kingdom Constructionism **has taken the terms "Christ" and the "Church" to be forms of** *cultural evolution* **with the goal of ushering in a** *utopian society* **on Earth where the principles and teachings of Christ will become** *cultural norms.* Of course, the teaching of Christ will need to be radically redefined and reduced to adapt to cultural norms and political correctness of the *Social Gospel.* For this *social evolution* to be accomplished, this evolving culture demands that Christ evolve as well. Dogmatism *must* be changed by a fluid adaption of understanding the *evolving Christ.* The old dogmatisms must be eradicated beginning with redefining *Christ.* This is all corruption of the terms "the Lord Jesus Christ."

These are the things that happen when true Christians allow terms to be emptied of meaning. Very quickly those terms take on new meaning until they take on meaning abhorrent to their original intent. This is what has happened to the terms "the Lord Jesus Christ." A radically different and wholly abhorrent world view has been created by emptying these terms of their theological meaning.

However, the deceivers did not leave those terms empty. The deceivers began to fill these terms with completely new meaning and new expectations of their "Lord Jesus Christ." Therefore, true Christians and false *Christians* use the same terms but with totally different meanings and different world views.

"To them that are sanctified by God the Father" (Jude 1)

Just as it is essential to understand the practical meaning of the theological significance of the words "the Lord Jesus Christ," it is equally essential that we understand the practical meaning of the theological significance of the words "to them that are sanctified by God the Father."

An epistle is a letter, and a letter is always addressed to someone. Those to whom a letter is addressed often defines the objective of the *directive purpose* for writing the letter. Only certain people can do what the epistle of Jude gives directions to do. The people to whom this letter is addressed and to whom the commands of this letter apply are "to them that are sanctified by God the Father" (Jude 1).

The word "sanctified" both defines the group of those commanded and the qualifications for fulfilling the objective of the commands given. The word "sanctified" is translated from the Greek word *hagiázō* (hag-ee-ad'-zo), which means *to make holy, or to ceremonially purify.*

Sanctification is always connected to purified preparation of a believer to either worship God or do some service for God. Serving God *from the heart* is always the purest form of worship. In fact, we might go so far as to say worship apart from sanctification is vain worship. Service without sanctification will always be fruitless service, hopeless of God's blessing upon that service. Jews would understand "sanctified" to mean all that is necessary to prepare something or someone for worship or service to God.

However, in Jude 1 sanctification is done "by God the Father." The word "sanctified" in Jude 1 is also a *perfect, passive, participle* (compare Romans 5:1-2). This means what God has done in positional sanctification, He has done *once for all forever*. However, **there are three levels of sanctification in the Bible: positional, practical, and ultimately perfect (glorification).**

1. Positional sanctification in the gift of salvation is known as *justification.* **This positional sanctification is what makes a sinner a** *saint* **before God.** All "born again" believers are saints positionally in the eyes of God. God makes sinners saints in the gift of the indwelling Holy Spirit, Who is the righteousness of Jesus Christ imparted to the believing sinner in the gift of salvation (II Peter 1:4). This initiates all true believers into the New Covenant Melchizedekian Priesthood with Jesus Christ as the High Priest. Perfect sanctification is the *once for all forever* act of God whereby every sinner is made a saint and set apart from the common to particularly serve God as a believer-priest under the headship of our High Priest Jesus Christ. **This is saving grace.**

"[1] Simon Peter, a servant and an apostle of Jesus Christ, to them that have **obtained like precious faith** {*living faith, not saving faith*} **with us** <u>**through the righteousness**</u> **of God and our Saviour Jesus Christ** {*this 'righteousness' is justification and the impartation of the indwelling Spirit of Christ; Grandville Sharp's Rule here means 'God' and 'Jesus' are one*}: [2] **Grace and peace be multiplied** {*this is the enabling of God's grace*} unto **you through the knowledge** {*epignosis, complete, personal, and intimate knowledge that accompanies theanthropic union, this is relational knowledge*} of God, and of Jesus our Lord, [3] **According as his divine power** {*in the indwelling and enable Spirit of Christ*} **hath given** {*perfect, passive*} **unto us all things that** *pertain* **unto life and godliness,** <u>**through**</u> the **knowledge** {*epignosis, complete, personal, and intimate knowledge that accompanies theanthropic union, this is relational knowledge*} of him that hath **called us** {*vocationally*} **to glory and virtue**: [4] Whereby are given unto us exceeding great and precious promises: that **by these ye might be partakers** {*sharer, associate, partner*} **of the divine nature**, having escaped the corruption that is in the world through lust" (II Peter 1:1-4).

"[1] Therefore **being justified** {*aorist, passive*} by faith, we have peace with God through our Lord Jesus Christ: [2] By whom also **we have** {*perfect, active*} <u>**access**</u> **by faith into this grace** {*positional sanctification of the priesthood of all believers transitions that believer into the potential for practical sanctification through the enabling of the indwelling Christ*} **wherein we stand** {*perfect, active*}, and rejoice in **hope of the glory of God** {*glorification of the believer by God*}" (Romans 5:1-2).

2. Practical sanctification is the potential of living the Christ-life through "fellowship" (working partnership) with the Lord Jesus Christ as the believer-priest fully yields or surrenders his/her will

to the will of Jesus Christ and is supernaturally enabled by the indwelling Christ to live the will of Christ. This is enabling grace. God cannot answer prayer, accept worship, or use service from a saint that is not positionally sanctified. **Practical sanctification prepares a sinner to live as a saint (*a sanctified one*) during the Church Age while still living in a body of flesh and while retaining a sin nature.** Sainthood does not automatically generate *saintly lives*.

Saintly lives are always sanctified lives. Full surrender is essential to living sanctified lives. No one will be enabled to "rightly divide the word of truth" (II Timothy 2:15) or be enabled to "earnestly contend for the faith" (Jude 3) apart from full surrender to the indwelling Christ and His supernatural enabling. Water baptism is intended to be the time of a believer's education into the obligations and outcomes of practical sanctification.

Spirit baptism connects every believer to the headship of Christ and therefore to the Church of which Christ is "head." Water baptism is intended to physically reflect the believer's understanding of that connection to Christ and His Church with the responsibilities of that connection first to Christ and to other believers to which we connect ourselves in that "fellowship."

Practical sanctification is NOT will-power sanctification. Although practical sanctification requires a volitional choice involving the human will, that *free will* cannot empower the believer to be victorious over the *will/wants/lusts* of his fallen, sinful nature. In fact, the "flesh" ("old man") is powerless to generate spirituality or God-kind righteousness. Neither is practical sanctification automatic. Practical sanctification is accomplished through synergism with the indwelling Spirit of Christ.

The choice to be enabled by the indwelling Spirit of Christ *must come from the heart*, not just the will of a believer. When the will engages the human heart in wanting what God offers in the potential of sanctification, God will enable the fully yielded believer to say no to the sinful lusts of the "old man." Therefore, the practical understanding of practical sanctification and enabling is not fleeing to a *strong will* of a *weak fallen nature* but rather yielding to the enabling strength of the Spirit of the indwelling Christ. This is the substance of Romans 6:1-14. Practical sanctification is necessary before God can consecrate a believer to the service for which he is sanctified.

"[1] What shall we say then? Shall we continue in sin, that grace may abound? [2] God forbid. How shall we, that are dead to sin, live any longer therein? [3] Know ye not, that so many of us **as were baptized** {*Spirit baptism*} **into Jesus Christ** {*'the regeneration'*} were {*Spirit*} baptized into his death? [4] Therefore we are buried with him by {*Spirit*} baptism into death: that like as Christ was raised up from the dead by the glory of the Father, **even so** {*now transitioning from position to practice*} **we also should walk in newness of life**. [5] For **if we have** {*perfect tense*} **been planted together** {*with Christ by Spirit baptism*} in **the likeness** {*buried under water in water baptism*} **of his death**, we **shall be also** *in the likeness* of *his* **resurrection** {*raised out of the water/grave in water baptism, the practical must correspond with the spiritual*}: [6] Knowing this, that our old man is crucified with *him*, that the body of sin might be destroyed, **that henceforth we should not serve sin** {*now transitioning from position to practice*}. [7] For he that is dead is freed from sin. [8] Now if we be dead with Christ, we believe that we shall also live with him: [9] Knowing that Christ being raised from the dead dieth no more; death hath no more dominion over him. [10] For in that he died, he died unto sin once: but **in that he liveth, he liveth unto God**. [11] <u>Likewise</u> reckon ye also yourselves to **be dead indeed unto sin, but alive unto God through Jesus Christ our Lord** {*the practical likeness of water baptism portraying Spirit baptism*}. [12] Let not sin therefore reign in your mortal body, that ye should obey it in the lusts thereof. [13] Neither yield ye your members *as* instruments of unrighteousness unto sin: but yield yourselves unto God, as those that are alive from the dead, and your members *as* instruments of righteousness unto God. [14] **For sin** {*the fallen nature*} **shall not have dominion** {*Lordship*} over you: for ye are **not under the law** {*which condemns to death*}, but **under grace** {*the Lordship of the indwelling Christ, which enables the Christ-life*}" (Romans 6:1-14).

3. Perfect sanctification is the believer's glorification, the annihilation of the believer's sin nature, and the creation of a new glorified body from the dust the body of the "old man." This will happen at the time of the believer's resurrection if he/she has died, or translation if he/she is still living at the time of Christ's coming in the air for His Bride just before the beginning of the seven-year Tribulation on Earth. We have looked at this with some depth already from I Corinthians 15:35-50. Reiteration in I Corinthians 15:42-50 should suffice here.

I Corinthians 15:44 details that perfect/ultimate sanctification (glorification) involves a completely new and different type of "body." Therefore, perfect/ultimate sanctification involves a completely different kind of existence. This change of body takes place before a new kind of real estate is created in which these glorified beings shall live for one-thousand years.

"[42] **So also *is* the resurrection of the dead.** It is sown in corruption; it is raised in incorruption: [43] It is sown in dishonour; it is raised in glory: it is sown in weakness; it is raised in power: [44] **It is <u>sown a natural body</u>; it is <u>raised a spiritual body</u>. There is a natural body, and there is a spiritual body.** [45] And so it is written, **The first man Adam was made a living soul; the last Adam *was made* a quickening spirit.** [46] Howbeit **that *was* <u>not first which is spiritual</u>, but that which is natural; and afterward that which is spiritual.** [47] The first man *is* of the earth, earthy: the second man *is* the Lord from heaven. [48] **As *is* the earthy, such *are* they also that are earthy: and as *is* the heavenly, such *are* they also that are heavenly.** [49] And as we have borne the image of the earthy, we shall also bear the image of the heavenly. [50] Now this I say, brethren, **that <u>flesh and blood cannot inherit the kingdom of God</u>**; neither doth corruption inherit incorruption" (I Corinthians 15:35-50).

Glorification is the believer's actual entrance into "the regeneration." "The regeneration" unfolds like a flower opening its petals to the early morning sun. The first phase is the indwelling of the Spirit of Christ, which indwelling connects us spiritually to that new destiny and Whose indwelling is God's seal upon the surety of that promised eternal destiny. However, the last phase of "the regeneration" is God's creating a new Heaven/Earth wherein He will eternally dwell with His redeemed.

"[1] And I saw a **new** {*kainós*; *new of a different kind*} heaven and a **new** {*kainós*; *new of a different kind*} earth: for the first heaven and the first earth were passed away; and there was no more sea. [2] And I John saw the holy city, **new** {*kainós*; *new of a different kind*} Jerusalem, coming down from God out of heaven, prepared as a bride adorned for her husband. [3] And I heard a great voice out of heaven saying, **Behold, the tabernacle of God *is* with men, and he will dwell with them, and they shall be his people, and God himself shall be with them, *and be* their God.** [4] And God shall wipe away all tears from their eyes; and there shall be no more death, neither sorrow, nor crying, neither shall there be any more pain: **for the former things are passed away** {*'no more curse,' Revelation 22:3*}. [5] And he that sat upon the throne said, Behold, I make all things **new** {*kainós*; *new of a different kind*}" (Revelation 21:1-5).

"Called of God"

"Jude, the servant of Jesus Christ, and brother of James, to them that are sanctified by God the Father, and preserved in Jesus Christ, *and* **called**" (Jude 1).

Not only is the epistle of Jude written "to them that are sanctified" and to them "preserved in Jesus Christ," it is also addressed to the "called." **God's calling is His divine appointment of His redeemed to priestly servanthood**. In Jude 1, the term just ends with the statement: "called." Paul uses a similar statement in Romans 1:7 and I Corinthians 1:2 which provide more specificity.

"To all that be in Rome, beloved of God, **called *to be* saints**: Grace to you and peace from God our Father, and the Lord Jesus Christ" (Romans 1:7).

"Unto the church of God which is at Corinth, to them that are sanctified in Christ Jesus, **called *to be* saints**, with all that in every place call upon the name of Jesus Christ our Lord, both theirs and ours" (I Corinthians 1:2).

In both these verses the words *"to be"* are italicized and therefore added for clarification of intent. **The words *"to be"* are intended to objectify intent that connects the noun "saints" to what**

is involved in that term. "Saints" is translated from the Greek word *hágios* (hag'-ee-os). The word "saints" simply means *set apart to holy or sacred service to God.* That service is the *ministry* in the priesthood of all Church Age believers to which all Church Age believers are vocationally "called." Therefore, although the italicized words *"to be"* are not in the Greek text, they are accurately supplied to objectify intent or purpose that connects the word to ministry. In other words, believers are not just positionally "called saints." **They have a job description.**

The point here is that all believers have a responsibility of ministry within this position as "saints" for which they will be held accountable by God. *Being* "saints" is what defines faithfulness as a Christian. *Being* "saints" involves both doing what believers are separated from the world to do and maintaining their sanctity before God by "rightly dividing the word of truth" and being "doers of the Word and not hearers only."

According to Jude 3 *being* "saints" involves every believer-priest with the responsibility to "earnestly contend for the faith which was once delivered unto the saints." If the command to "earnestly contend for the faith which was once delivered unto the saints" of Jude 3 is disconnected from the word "called" in Jude 1, the objective of moral and ethical responsibility of the word "called" is completely lost. Thereby, the word *faithful* is also emptied of its intended meaning.

Although the words "called *to be* saints" in Romans 1:7 and I Corinthians 1:2 are representative of the intent of Jude 1 and is accurate; to understand the *specificity of the objective* it is best to find this in another text that deals with this specificity in detail. Ephesians chapter four does this. However, Ephesians chapter four should never be removed from the context established in Ephesians chapter one. **Every pronoun in Ephesians chapter one referring to believers is plural.** This is evident in the KJV, but not all other English translations.

The plurality of the pronouns is important because the *election* ("chosen," Ephesians 4:4) of Ephesians chapter one is the *election* of the Church *corporately* to be a new priesthood. **It is not the *election* of individuals to be saved. Election (*calling*) is *vocational* (Ephesians 4:1), not *salvational*.**

1. The Church is an incorporation of "saints" (sanctified priests) as "born again" believers faithful to the commands of Jesus Christ (vs.1).

2. The Church is distinct from the nation of Israel and her blessings are eternal and spiritual rather than temporal and earthly (vs. 3).

3. The Church is chosen corporately "in Christ," her High Priest, as a new, spiritual Priesthood before "the foundation of the world" (i.e., not an afterthought, but a *before creation thought*, vs. 4).

4. This whole new priesthood, that is "saved by grace through faith," is predestined to glorification (vs. 5). This is the meaning of the word "adoption" – translated from the Greek *huiothesia* (hwee-oth-es-ee'-ah). The word means the placement or position of the sons of God. This cannot be understood apart from the placement of the "firstborn" as the typical priesthood now fulfilled in the Church as the priesthood of all believers in the "church of the firstborn" (Hebrews 12:23).

5. This new priesthood is "accepted" (positionally sanctified and consecrated) in Christ, "the beloved" (vs. 6-9).

6. The Church is embryonically what all believers of all ages will be in "the regeneration" in the New Heaven/Earth – a kingdom of glorified priests (vs. 10-14).

7. Paul's prayer is for the *enabling power* of the indwelling *Christ-life* of the believer's High Priest to be realized, actuated, and released in and through the local church as the "body" of Christ (vs. 15-23).

Ephesians chapter four spells out the specificity of the responsibilities of the meaning of "called *to be* saints" in considerable detail. Ephesians chapter four is the *job description* of the priesthood of all believers.

1. Believers are exhorted to walk worthy of their vocational election as priests before God by living in *theanthropic unity* with God and with one another (vs. 1-6).

2. The *Christ-life* is the primary *gift* in the gift of salvation given to all believers in the indwelling Holy Spirit (v. 7).

3. Christ has also given local churches gifted men to administrate, lead, and disciple/mature believers in the doctrines of Jesus Christ for their preparation for "the work of the ministry" – winning souls, baptizing those saved and bringing them into formal accountability for their discipleship within a local church context, and teaching them to live the *Christ-life* (vs. 8-16). This "work of the ministry" is the "vocation" of ALL believer-priests.

4. The admonition is against the believer-priest living in selfishness, against worldly thinking, against living in doctrinal and practical ignorance of the *Christ-life* and living without compassion for the lost around them by being preoccupied with the pleasures of life and the pursuit of materialistic goals (vs. 17-19).

5. The admonition is to "put on" the *Christ-life* and allow Christ to live His self-sacrificing life through your body (vs. 20-24).

6. The admonition is to "put off" the "old man" and all his selfish, carnal tendencies (vs. 25-29).

7. The admonition is that selfish, carnal living grieves the indwelling Spirit of God (v. 30).

8. Some practical examples of selfish carnality that must be "put away" are given in v. 31.

9. Some practical examples of selfless spirituality that exemplify the *Christ-life* are given in v. 32.

Jude 3 is another detail of the job description of all believer-priests. Jude 3 describes a major part of the "work of the ministry" (Ephesians 4:12) to which all believer-priests are to be *perfected* to accomplish.

"Beloved, when I gave all diligence to write unto you of the common salvation, **it was needful for me to write unto you, and exhort** *you* **that ye should earnestly contend for the faith** which was once delivered unto the saints" (Jude 3).

After Paul's similar instruction in I Corinthians 1:2 to Jude 1, he goes on in I Corinthians chapter one and lays the foundation for his rebuke. He does so in the next fourteen chapters regarding the failure of the Corinthian believer-priests to live sanctified lives thereby fulfilling the statement "called to be saints" in I Corinthians 1:2.

"[26] For ye see your calling, brethren, how that not many wise men after the flesh, not many mighty, not many noble, *are called*: [27] But **God hath chosen** the foolish things of the world to confound the wise; and **God hath chosen** the weak things of the world to confound the things which are mighty; [28] And base things of the world, and things which are despised, **hath God chosen**, *yea*, and things which are not, to bring to nought things that are: [29] That no flesh should glory in his presence. [30] But of him are ye in Christ Jesus, who of God is made unto us wisdom, and righteousness, and sanctification, and redemption: [31] That, according as it is written, He that glorieth, let him glory in the Lord" (I Corinthians 1:26-31).

The word "chosen," used twice in I Corinthians 1:27 and again in I Corinthians 1:28, is translated from the Greek word *eklégomai* (ek-leg'-om-ahee). *Eklégomai* is a derivative of the Greek word *eklogē* (ek-log-ay') translated "election" throughout the New Testament. In both cases, the words mean to *select* or *choose* something or someone. As in most all other uses the context establishes this choosing/election "*to be* saints" **vocationally** (not salvationally).

Believers are chosen/elected to be *believer-priests* and are responsible to live sanctified lives before God. Practical sanctification is the primary qualification for God to consecrate the believer to be used by Him in "the work of the ministry."

The importance of the phrase "called *to be* saints" in Romans 1:7 and I Corinthians 1:2 is that God **will not** consecrate the unsanctified and **cannot use** those He has not consecrated for the "work of the ministry." Part of the "work of the ministry" is to "earnestly contend for the faith, which was once delivered unto the saints" (Jude 3).

"[1] I beseech you therefore, **brethre**n, by the mercies of God, **that ye present your bodies a living sacrifice, holy, acceptable unto God**, *which is* your reasonable service. [2] And **be not conformed to this world** {*separated from worldliness*}: but **be ye transformed** {*present, passive, imperative*; *progressively transfigured*} by the **renewing of your mind** {*separated unto godliness and learning/living God's Word by grace enabling*}, that **ye may prove** {*through God's use of your sanctified and consecrated life*} what *is* that good, and acceptable, and perfect, will of God. [3] For I say, through the grace given unto me, to every man that is among you, not to think *of himself* more highly than he ought to think; but to think soberly, according as God hath dealt to every man the measure of faith. [4] For as we have many members in one body, and all members have not the same office: [5] **So we** {*the Church and the priesthood of all believers*}, *being* many, are one body in Christ, and **every one members** {*union in the body of Christ*} one of another" (Romans 12:1-5).

"Mercy, Peace, and Love Multiplied"

The epistle of Jude was written in approximately 66 A.D. All Christians, and particularly Jewish Christians, were being persecuted by the corrupted priesthood of Israel. This epistle is written just before the Roman destruction of the Temple in Jerusalem by Titus in 70 A.D.

However, the Romans did not distinguish between Jews and Jewish Christians in their persecutions. Therefore, the Romans were also persecuting Christians.

Secondly, local churches were being infiltrated with Jews who professed faith in Christ as Messiah but still wanted to function under the Mosaic Covenant thereby corrupting the faith and the "gospel" as Paul addresses in Galatians 1:6-9.

The Romans hated the Jews because the Jews were vehemently monotheistic while the Romans were equally vehemently polytheistic. Both the Jews and the Romans hated the Christians because the Christians believed Jesus was the one true God and that Jesus was Jehovah incarnate.

"[1] Jude, the servant of Jesus Christ, and brother of James, to them that are sanctified by God the Father, and preserved in Jesus Christ, *and* called: [2] **Mercy unto you, and peace, and love, be multiplied**" (Jude 1-2).

The world at the time of the writing of the epistle of Jude was a harsh and dangerous world in which to live as a true Christian. There was an enormous incentive for Christians to compromise the Lordship of Jesus and the doctrines of Jesus ("the faith").

Often compromise equaled physical survival. However, faithful Christians would not confess the emperor of Rome to be Lord to avoid the condemnation of Rome. Faithful Christians would not accept the corrupt distortions of the Gospel by the corrupted priesthood of Israel thereby continuing under the abrogated responsibilities of the Mosaic Covenant. **Therefore, God's "mercy, peace, and love" needed to "be multiplied."** The strength of human flesh could not sustain itself in face of the overwhelming onslaught of opposition.

Few Christians understand their mission in the world or their own hopelessness to fulfill that mission without God's enabling grace. Most Christians see salvation as a fire escape from Hell and not much of anything else. Most Christians have never proactively engaged their neighbors, let alone the world, with the Gospel of Jesus Christ. Most Christians are not proactive in their own discipleship let alone the discipleship of others. This does not just mean that *Christianity* has changed. This means in most part that *Christianity* has ceased to be true Christianity.

To "earnestly contend for the faith which was once delivered unto the saints" (Jude 3) has lost all context for most professing to be *Christians* in the last days of the Church Age. As already said to "earnestly contend for the faith which was once delivered unto the saints" (Jude 3) is what defines faithfulness and therefore *Christianity*. This is the reason Christianity is described in military terminology throughout the epistles.

The reason most Christians have lost their zeal for souls and discipleship is because they lack any understanding of what "the faith" that was "delivered unto them" even is. No one can pass on to another generation what has not already been passed to them with understanding. Christianity is a fight to **gain** "the faith," a fight to **retain** "the faith," and a fight **maintain** "the faith" by passing it on to another generation. Just *being* a Christian is warfare on every front of a believer's existence while at the same time every evil force in the world offers an opportunity for compromise.

Friendship with the world is enmity with God. There is no middle ground of neutrality. This is an either/or issue of faithfulness. As the epistle of James, written "to the twelve tribes which are scattered abroad" (James 1:1) explains, that the nature of our flesh is our own worst enemy. The corrupt and fallen human nature is the greatest weapon against humanity, and we hurt ourselves and everyone around us with it. The point is that our own lusts and carnal affections are destructive to every good quality that God wants to instill in us.

"[1] **From whence *come* wars and fightings among you? *come* they not hence, *even* of your lusts that war in your members?** [2] Ye lust, and have not: ye kill, and desire to have, and cannot obtain: ye fight and war, yet ye have not, because ye ask not. [3] Ye ask, and receive not, because ye ask amiss, **that ye may consume *it* upon your lusts** {*prayer life is consumed with personal and carnal wants rather than with God's will*}. [4] Ye adulterers and adulteresses, **know ye not that the friendship** {*fondness for worldly things*} **of the world is enmity** {*hostility*} **with God?** whosoever therefore will be a friend of the world {*fondness for worldly things*} **is the enemy** {*actively hostile*} of God. [5] Do ye think that the scripture saith in vain, **The spirit that dwelleth in us lusteth to envy?** [6] But he giveth more grace. Wherefore he saith, **God resisteth the proud, but giveth grace unto the humble** {*the 'humble' are those that recognize and acknowledge their innate carnal tendencies before God and the world with a genuine attitude of both remorse and regret*}. [7] **Submit** {*subordinate to God's will*} **yourselves therefore to God** {*for the resolution of the innate problem of worldliness for God enabling grace to overcome it*}. **Resist** {*oppose, stand against*} **the devil** {*who tempts our carnal desires*}, and he will flee from you. [8] **Draw nigh to God, and he will draw nigh to you. Cleanse *your* hands, *ye* sinners; and purify *your* hearts, *ye* double minded.** [9] **Be afflicted, and mourn, and weep** {*the reflection of genuine repentance for the innate carnality of the lusts of the flesh*}: let your laughter be turned to mourning, and *your* joy to heaviness. [10] **Humble yourselves** {*live within the humiliation knowledge of the carnal condition of the corrupt human heart and will for the things of this world*} **in the sight of the Lord ,** and **he shall lift you up** {*exalt you out of this hopeless pit of despair by His enabling grace*}" (James 4:1-10).

The significance of James 4:1-10 regarding the statement "mercy unto you, and peace, and love, be multiplied" (Jude 2) is that the multiplication of "mercy," "peace, and love" can only be done by God's enabling grace. There is nothing within the believing sinner's character or nature that makes it remotely possible to accomplish the things expected of him/her as a believer-priest.

God is expecting some extreme dedication and commitment of His New Covenant believer-priest, for which they have NO spiritual resources for success apart from His indwelling Spirit. This is essentially what James 4:1-10 is about.

"Mercy" is from the Greek word *éleos* (el'-eh-os), which refers to *compassion*. **However, the context of Jude implies a *compassion* that is beyond human *compassion*. Therefore, this "mercy" must be referring to a "fruit" of the Spirit of God although "mercy" is not listed in Galatians 5:22. In other words, this "multiplied" . . . "mercy" is divine mercy released through the yielded believer's life.**

Although sinners may have a degree of human compassion, sympathy, or even empathy towards others, no one possesses the kind of "mercy" that God naturally possesses and wants to supernaturally provide in the believer's life.

Divine "mercy" is essential to spiritual ministry because most faithful Christians will face oppositions that are exceedingly beyond their capabilities. The very people we love the most and want to help through ministry will reject us, hate us, persecute us, badmouth, and blaspheme us, even seek to have us isolated for what we say and believe.

Jesus addressed the world's hatred for Him and His followers in John 15:18-21 after prefacing this text with the essential of abiding in Him as the Vine in John 15:1-8. No one can face the true and faithful Christian and the opposition to that life without learning to "abide in the Vine."

"[18] If the world hate you, ye know that it hated me before *it hated* you {*normal Christianity*}. [19] If ye were of the world, **the world would love his own: but because ye are not of the world, but I have chosen you out of the world, therefore the world hateth you.** [20] Remember the word that I said unto you, The servant is not greater than his lord. **If they have persecuted me, they will also persecute you**; if they have kept my saying, they will keep yours also. [21] But all these things will they do unto you for my name's sake, **because they know not him that sent me**" (John 15:18-21).

"Peace" also must be "multiplied" in the believer's life. "Mercy, peace, and love" must be "multiplied" not merely added to what the believer already has in himself. "Multiplied" is from the Greek word *plēthýnō* (play-thoo'-no) meaning to *increase abundantly* like one seed of corn increases into ears of corn. Obviously, this is beyond human ability without God's partnership and power/resources.

The moment a believer is "born again" of the Spirit of God he has both "peace with God" (Romans 5:1) and the "peace of God" (Philippians 4:7 and Colossians 3:15). **The "peace" of Jude 2 that needs to be "multiplied" is the struggle to "contend for the faith" (Jude 3) when doing what Romans 12:14-18 commands.** Again, this is an impossible set of commands considering the wicked attitudes of the opposition to the things of God. The kind of "peace" of which Jude 2 speaks is beyond human capabilities apart from the indwelling Christ.

"[14] **Bless them which persecute you**: bless, and curse not. [15] Rejoice with them that do rejoice, and weep with them that weep. [16] *Be* of the same mind one toward another. **Mind not high things**, but condescend to men of low estate. Be not wise in your own conceits. [17] **Recompense to no man evil for evil**. Provide things honest in the sight of all men. [18] If it be possible, **as much as lieth in you, live peaceably with all men**" (Romans 12:14-18).

Lastly in Jude 2, "love" must be "multiplied." "Love" here is from the Greek word *agápē* (ag-ah'-pay). *Agápē* is the love of God that was willing die for the redemption of sinners. This kind of love is the willingness to do the best we can for those that hate us. Therefore, the kind of "love" that needs to abound abundantly in the believer's life BEFORE he/she will ever "contend earnestly for the faith" is the kind of sacrificial love Christ *exhibited* on the Cross. Love *exhibited* is the key to understanding the "love" Christ wants "multiplied." Love is not merely an emotion. *Agápē* is ALWAYS willing to make the extreme sacrifice to benefit the needs of others.

"[6] For when we were yet without strength, in due time **Christ died for the ungodly**. [7] For scarcely for a righteous man will one die: yet peradventure for a good man some would even dare to die. [8] But **God commendeth his love toward us, in that, while we were yet sinners, Christ died for us**" (Romans 5:6-8).

Attempts at true ministry is a fool's business apart from the multiplication of divine mercy, peace, and love. Attempts at true ministry is a fool's business without these attributes because the fool never counts the potential costs of true spiritual sacrifice. True Christian ministry is much more than just personally expensive.

True Christian ministry will always cost you everything and every believer that wants to practice true Christian ministry better be prepared to pay that price. This was the substance of the parable of Jesus in Luke chapter fourteen about counting the cost of being His disciples and DOING true ministry.

"[25] And there went great multitudes with him: and **he turned**, and said unto them, [26] If any *man* come to me, and **hate not** {*by comparison to their love for Christ and His ministry*} his father, and mother, and wife, and children, and brethren, and sisters, yea, and his own life also, **he cannot be my disciple**. [27] And **whosoever doth not bear his cross** {*not willing to die for Christ and His ministry*}, and **come after me** {*as a pattern of intent*}, **cannot be my disciple**. [28] For which of you, intending to build a tower, sitteth not down first, and **counteth the cost** {*not talking about building structures, but rather the cost of doing ministry*}, whether he have *sufficient* to finish *it*? [29] Lest haply, after he hath laid the foundation, and is not able to finish *it*, all that behold *it* begin to mock him, [30] Saying, **This man began to build, and was not able to finish**. [31] Or what king, going to make war against another king, sitteth not down first, and consulteth whether he be able with ten thousand to meet him that cometh against him with twenty thousand? [32] Or else, while the other is yet a great way off, he sendeth an ambassage, and desireth conditions of peace. [33] **So <u>likewise</u>, whosoever he be of you that forsaketh not all that he hath, he cannot be my disciple.** [34] Salt *is* good: but if the salt have lost his savour, wherewith shall it be seasoned? [35] **It is neither fit for the land, nor yet for the dunghill** {*the point is such people are useless*}; *but* men cast it out. He that hath ears to hear, let him hear" (Luke 14:25-35).

Jude
Contending for the Faith
Chapter Two
Common Salvation

Early Christianity was constantly being bombarded with all forms of attacks and discouraging problems. Paul said, "our flesh had no rest, but we were troubled on every side; without *were* fightings, within *were* fears" (II Corinthians 7:5).

Satanic corruptions of two doctrines have been historic constants throughout the dispensations of God. With the beginning of every new dispensation, God corrected the corruptions of the doctrine of salvation and the doctrine of sanctification with additional Scriptural revelations.

Under the Mosaic Covenant, God used various prophets to speak to these corruptions and correct them. At the beginning of the New Covenant and the Church Age, God used the epistles of Paul, Peter, James, John, and Jude to address these corruptions and the many streams of these corruptions entering true Christianity.

"[3] Beloved, when I gave all diligence to write unto you of the **common salvation**, it was needful for me to write unto you, and exhort *you* that ye should earnestly contend for the faith which was once delivered unto the saints. [4] For there are certain men crept in unawares, who were before of old ordained to this condemnation, ungodly men, turning the grace of our God into lasciviousness, and denying the only Lord God, and our Lord Jesus Christ" (Jude 3-4).

The Abrahamic Covenant was given to govern believers during the Age of Promise (Genesis 12:1 through Exodus 19:8). The Abrahamic Covenant established that salvation was gift of grace received through faith. Salvation was a gift from God given to those who believed solely in the promise of God portrayed in the Abrahamic Covenant, which Abraham entered by faith.

God confirmed the Abrahamic Covenant and fulfilled all the covenant conditions of the promises to Abraham based solely upon God's promise and what God would do, adding no conditions for

Abraham or his descendants. A sinner entered the Abrahamic Covenant solely by faith and provided solely by God's grace.

God's confirmation of the unconditional Abrahamic Covenant is recorded in Genesis 15:7-21. When reading the text, we must understand that Abraham asks how he would "know" God would keep His promise. God's confirmation involved Abraham bringing specific sacrificial animals, killing those animals, and splitting the carcasses in half laying the pieces beside each other.

Covenants were made when the parties entering the covenant with each other walked between the divided carcasses thereby agreeing that if one of the parties should break the covenant, what happened to the sacrificial animals would happen to them.

"[7] And he said unto him, I *am* the LORD that brought thee out of Ur of the Chaldees, to give thee this land to inherit it. [8] And he said, Lord GOD, **whereby shall I know that I shall inherit it?** [9] And he said unto him, Take me an heifer of three years old, and a she goat of three years old, and a ram of three years old, and a turtledove, and a young pigeon. [10] And he took unto him all these, and **divided them in the midst, and laid each piece one against another**: but the birds divided he not. [11] And when the fowls came down upon the carcases, Abram drove them away. [12] And when the sun was going down, **a deep sleep fell upon Abram**; and, lo, an horror of great darkness fell upon him. [13] And he said unto Abram, **Know of a surety** that thy seed shall be a stranger in a land *that is* not theirs, and shall serve them; and they shall afflict them four hundred years; [14] And also **that nation** {*Egypt*}, whom they shall serve, will I judge: and afterward shall they come out with great substance. [15] And thou shalt go to thy fathers in peace; thou shalt be buried in a good old age. [16] But in the fourth generation they shall come hither again: for the iniquity of the Amorites *is* not yet full. [17] And it came to pass, that, **when the sun went down, and it was dark, behold a smoking furnace, and a burning lamp that passed between those pieces.** [18] In the same day the LORD made a covenant with Abram, saying, Unto thy seed have I given this land, from the river of Egypt unto the great river, the river Euphrates: [19] The Kenites, and the Kenizzites, and the Kadmonites, [20] And the Hittites, and the Perizzites, and the Rephaims, [21] And the

Amorites, and the Canaanites, and the Girgashites, and the Jebusites" (Genesis 15:7-21).

Abraham had absolutely nothing to do in fulfilling the conditions of the Abrahamic Covenant. This covenant was between the Father and the Son of God. The smoking furnace was the ancient oriental furnace called the *Chiminea*, which produced a blast furnace effect from its chimney (from where we get the word chimney). Large furnaces of this type were used to produce enormous heat for blacksmithing, smelting iron, and other metals.

The "burning lamp" most probably means the stream of fire coming out of the chimney like a blow torch. The "burning lamp" is typical of Jesus as the "light of the world," revealing God's gracious provision of the gift of salvation received "through faith."

The "smoking furnace" and "burning lamp" portray the propitiation of God's wrath through the death of the incarnate Son of God on the Cross of Calvary. The sacrificial animals are typical of Jesus Christ. Understanding this type and it fulfilment in Christ is critical to understanding the "common salvation."

The promises of the Abrahamic Covenant were not given to the physical "seed" of Abraham but rather to the faith "seed" of Abraham. In other words, the complete fulfillment of the promises of the Abrahamic Covenant will be ONLY to Jews who are "born again" through faith in the finished redemptive work of Jesus Christ. Paul explained this thoroughly in Galatians 3:6-18. This is another critical text to understand the "common salvation" for which all believers are to "contend."

"[6] **Even as Abraham believed God, and it was accounted to him for righteousness.** [7] Know ye therefore that **they which are of faith, the same are the children of Abraham.** [8] And the scripture, foreseeing that God would justify the heathen through faith, preached before the gospel unto Abraham, *saying,* **In thee shall all nations be blessed.** [9] So then **they which be of faith are blessed with faithful Abraham.** [10] For as many as are of the works of the law are under the curse: for it is written, Cursed *is* every one that continueth not in all things which are written in the book of the law to do them. [11] But that no man is justified by the law in the sight of God, *it is* evident: for, The just shall live by faith. [12] And **the law is not of faith**: but, The man that doeth them shall live in them. [13] Christ hath redeemed us from the curse of the law, being made a curse for us: for it is written, Cursed *is* every one that hangeth on a tree: [14] **That the blessing of Abraham might come on the Gentiles through Jesus Christ; that we might receive the promise of the Spirit through faith.** [15] Brethren, I speak after the manner of men; Though *it be* but a man's covenant, **yet *if it be* confirmed**, no man disannulleth, or addeth thereto. [16] Now to **Abraham and his seed** were the promises made. He saith **not, And to seeds, as of many; but as of one, And to thy seed, which is Christ**. [17] And this I say, *that* the covenant, that was confirmed before of God in Christ, the law, which was four hundred and thirty years after, cannot disannul, that it should make the promise of none effect. [18] For if the inheritance *be* of the law, *it is* no more of promise: but **God gave *it* to Abraham by promise**" (Galatians 3:6-18).

This is the "common salvation" to which Jude refers; "by grace . . . through faith" (Ephesians 2:8). However, then the second problem entered Judaism. Because salvation was a gift received totally "through" the instrumentality of "faith," believers came to think they could live any way they wanted without consequences. This is what Paul is addressing in Ephesians 2:4-10. This explains why the Law (Mosaic Covenant) was "added" to the Abrahamic Covenant (Galatians 3:19-29) for practical sanctificational purposes.

"[4] But God, who is rich in mercy, for his great love wherewith he loved us, [5] Even when we were dead in sins, hath quickened us together with Christ, (by grace ye are saved;) [6] And hath raised *us* up together, and made *us* sit together in heavenly *places* in Christ Jesus: [7] That in the ages to come he might shew the exceeding riches of his grace in *his* kindness toward us through Christ Jesus. [8] For by grace are ye saved through faith; and that not of yourselves: *it is* the gift of God: [9] Not of works, lest any man should boast. [10] **For we are his workmanship, created in Christ Jesus unto good works, which God hath before ordained that we should walk in them**" (Ephesians 2:4-10).

The Jews' corrupt application of the Mosaic Covenant was that a person was **saved by** faith, but that salvation was **kept by** the obeying the Law. This foolish notion is continued in Christianity through various forms of the corruptions of *Replacement Theology* and *Second Blessing Theology*. The Mosaic Covenant was added to the Abrahamic Covenant to define sin and to establish the basis for practical sanctification before God.

Positional sanctification before God (Romans 5:1-2) is the gift of the righteousness of God to the believing sinner (*imputed* to the believer in the Old Covenant and *imparted* to the believer in the New Covenant). Sin never affects positional sanctification because it is a gift received, not an accomplishment achieved. Understanding this fact is also a major part of the "common salvation" for which all believers are to "earnestly contend" (Jude 3).

"[19] **Wherefore then *serveth* the law?** It was added because of transgressions, **till the seed should come** to whom the promise was made; *and it was* ordained by angels in the hand of a mediator. [20] Now a mediator is not *a mediator* of one, **but God is one**. [21] *Is* the law then against the promises of God? God forbid: for **if there had been a law given which could have given life, verily righteousness should have been by the law.** [22] But the scripture hath concluded all under sin, that **the promise by faith of Jesus Christ might be given to them that believe**" (Galatians 3:19-22).

However, this enters the believer into the second arena of opposition and confusion regarding the responsibilities of **being** a "born again" child of God. Every "born again" child of God is responsible to live like God's child by searching the Scriptures for God's will and **being** "doers of the Word, and not hearers only" (James 1:22). Being what God wants us to be is really what defines loving Him. This responsibility was the daily reminder of the proclamation of the *Shema* of Israel. ***Being* is a manifestation of saving faith.**

"[4] Hear, O Israel: The LORD our God *is* one LORD: [5] And **thou shalt love the LORD thy God with all thine heart, and with all thy soul, and with all thy might.** [6] And these words, which I command thee this day, **shall be in thine heart:** [7] And thou shalt teach them diligently unto thy children, and shalt talk of them when thou sittest in thine house, and when thou walkest by the way, and when thou liest down, and when thou risest up" (Deuteronomy 6:4-7).

Herein lies the great ease of corruption of those who profess to be "born again" believers. The trend is to have a kind of faith that has a *head* for Jesus, but not a *heart* for Jesus. The "common salvation" for which all true believers are to "earnestly contend" is the kind of faith that has a heart for Jesus. Yes, there must also be a kind of faith that has a head for Jesus, but faith without a heart for Jesus is vain faith. **Therefore, genuine repentance is integral to real faith.** This was the grand and generational failure of Israel, as many professed faith in God but fornicated in idol worship on the numerous "high places" of paganism.

"The beauty of Israel is slain upon thy high places: how are the mighty fallen" (II Samuel 1:19)! (*The last phrase is not a question, but an exclamation!*)

The doctrine of salvation that defines the "common salvation" extends beyond the salvation of the soul. Salvation is a gift that *positionally* includes the salvation of the soul. Salvation *practically* is the *progressive* salvation of a life (*salvation from a wasted life*) through *practical* sanctification. Salvation *ultimately* is the salvation of the body through glorification. Because of ignorance of these three aspects of the "common salvation" many people are confused when they do not understand Scriptural context addressing these three aspects of the "common salvation."

Contending for the purity of the gift of salvation provided solely by the grace of God and received solely through the decision of faith in the finished redemption of the death, burial, resurrection, and glorification of the Lord Jesus Christ has been an historical constant from the beginning of time.

This is certainly manifested early in the book of Genesis in the tension between Cain with Abel. Abel had no tension with Cain except to confront him about his inappropriate sacrifice of the work of his own hands. **Abel contended for "the faith." Cain compromised "the faith." A person's offerings manifest the substance of that person's**

faith! The expression of a person's worship manifests his understanding and appreciation of grace.

"[1] And Adam knew Eve his wife; and she conceived, and bare Cain, and said, **I have gotten a man from the LORD** {*she believed Cain was God's promised Seed of Genesis 3:15*}. [2] And she again bare his brother Abel. And Abel was a **keeper of sheep**, but Cain was a **tiller of the ground.** [3] And in process of time it came to pass, that Cain **brought of the fruit of the ground an offering unto the LORD.** [4] And Abel, he also **brought of the firstlings of his flock and of the fat thereof.** And the LORD **had respect unto Abel and to his offering:** [5] But unto **Cain and to his offering he had not respect.** And Cain was very wroth, and his countenance fell. [6] And the LORD said unto Cain, Why art thou wroth? and why is thy countenance fallen? [7] If thou doest well, shalt thou not be accepted? and if thou doest not well, **sin lieth at the door.** And unto thee *shall be* his desire, and thou shalt rule over him. [8] And **Cain talked with Abel his brother:** and it came to pass, when they were in the field, that Cain rose up against Abel his brother, and slew him. [9] And the LORD said unto Cain, Where *is* Abel thy brother? And he said, I know not: *Am* I my brother's keeper? [10] And he said, **What hast thou done?** {*God knew what Cain had done. God wanted Cain to confess and repent.*} the voice of thy brother's blood crieth unto me from the ground. [11] And **<u>now</u> *art* thou cursed from the earth** {*Cain was already cursed in the fall. This curse is upon the ground Cain tilled because Cain refused to repent and confess*}, which hath opened her mouth to receive thy brother's blood from thy hand; [12] **When thou tillest the ground**, it shall not henceforth yield unto thee her strength; a fugitive and a vagabond shalt thou be in the earth" (Genesis 4:1-12).

The *Jamieson-Fausset-Brown Commentary* gives us an expanded understanding of the meaning of God respecting Abel's offering, but not respecting Cain's offering. The word "respect" is more significant than a merely different attitude towards the two offerings.

"[T]he Lord had respect unto Abel, not unto Cain, &c.--The words, 'had respect to,' signify in *Hebrew,*--'to look at any thing with a keen earnest glance,' which has been translated, 'kindle into a fire,' so **that the divine approval of Abel's offering was shown in its being consumed by fire** (see **Ge** 15:17; **Jg** 13:20)"[1].

Worship practices must reflect our understanding of the grace of God and the overwhelming aspect of substitutionary death to pay the price of a sinner's redemption from the bondage of sin and death. Therefore, anytime a saved sinner approaches the throne of God in worship or prayerful petition, the basis of that approach must be on the ground of completely undeserved favor (grace) from God. Obviously, this understanding is incredibly important to God.

There was no forgiveness of sin available to either Abel nor Cain based on their offerings. Neither Abel or Cain could add anything to what God offered in the gift of the salvation that is given as a gift of grace and received solely through pure faith in God's Promised One (Genesis 3:15). Abel's offering *reflects an understanding* not evident in Cain's offering. Cain's offering reflects the works of his hands. Abel's offering reflects an understanding of grace and substitutionary atonement.

When God sees Cain's anger at the rejection of his offering, God confronts Cain and lovingly explains to him the simplicity of the appropriate offering necessary to reflect grace; "If thou doest well, shalt thou not be accepted? and if thou doest not well, **sin lieth at the door**" (Genesis 4:7). The word "sin" in this verse means *sin offering.* "Sin" is translated from the Hebrew word *chaṭṭâ'âh* (khat-taw-aw') meaning *sacrifice* or *expiation/propitiation.* Obviously, God was referencing another lamb readily available to Cain, although Cain would probably need to acquire one from shepherd Abel.

There is an apparent pride issue with Cain and some jealousy issues with his brother that kept Cain from accepting God's gift of salvation by grace through faith in the substitute Redeemer promised in Genesis 3:15. Cain was the firstborn and expected the preeminence

---

[1] **Jamieson-Fausset-Brown Commentary,** Module file location: C:\Program Files\SwordSearcher\Modules\JFB.ss5cmty, Module file time: 7/31/2011 7:15:28 PM UTC.

of consideration before God. God is no respecter of positions or prominence.

Cain wanted to be accepted by God based upon his own works, not the works of another. Either Adam and Eve failed to adequately explain this to Cain, or Cain simply rebelled against what he was taught and rejected the grace way for the works way. Or, Cain could have thought he was saved by grace, but kept by works.

We do not know for sure. We do know that Cain's offering was rejected, and Cain was condemned for murdering Abel. The ground Cain tilled was cursed even more than it was in the original curse. Hebrews 11:4 gives us additional insight into the meaning of this.

"By faith Abel offered unto God a more excellent sacrifice than Cain, by which he obtained witness that he was righteous, God testifying of his gifts: and by it he being dead yet speaketh" (Hebrews 11:4).

God's testimony of Abel's "gifts" (offerings) was that Abel was "righteous." This statement by God does not mean that Abel was sinless. This means that Abel was saved by the gift of *Godkind righteous* imputed to him because he believed God's promise and his faith rested in the promised One of Genesis 3:15. The point of the word "gifts" being plural was that Abel consistently offered thanksgiving offerings to God for the gift of his salvation and Godkind righteousness.

Every offering Abel provided declared to God that Abel had not forgotten and never took the gift of his redemption for granted. This is the "common salvation" for which believers are commanded to "contend." This contending is first reflected in our offerings and how we worship before we ever "contend" for the *doctrine of salvation.*

Every aspect of our worship and prayer life should reflect a deep respect and reverence for God. He is a God of grace, and we deserve nothing from Him. Every aspect of our worship and prayer life should reflect separation from worldliness and separation unto holiness in reverential fear of God. Cain's anger with his brother reflects none of these characteristics of salvation or worship.

God contended for "the faith" and the "common salvation" by confronting Cain's contradicting offering, thereby seeking to

correct Cain's false beliefs and lead Cain to repent. Cain refused to repent and murdered Abel instead. Contending requires confronting.

According to Hebrews 11:4, Abel contended for "the faith" and the "common salvation" by consistency in his faith and by his offering aligning with the consistency of his faith in God's promised One of Genesis 3:15. Nothing anyone does can ever merit God's good favor. God provides because He is graciously loving, not because sinners are ever lovely.

Abel's offerings reflected this attitude birthed from this understanding. The word "gifts" reflect that this attitude was maintained throughout his many offerings. The main point of Hebrews 11:4 is that Abel's ongoing "gifts" continue to testify throughout history to God's faithfulness: "by **it** {*Abel's offering*} **he** {*Abel*} **being dead yet speaketh** {*continues the same testimony*}" that God is gracious.

The word "diligence" in Jude 3 in the phrase, "Beloved, when I gave all diligence to write unto you of the common salvation," communicates that doing this was a matter of urgency requiring immediate attention. The word "diligence" is from the Greek word *spoudē* (spoo-day'), which simple means *speedy* or *doing something with haste*.

The moment false teaching arises and is recognized as such, that false teaching must be immediately confronted and corrected calling the person propagating it to repentance. **Give false teaching a *go* and it will *grow*.** Soon the *weeds* will over grow the garden. The word "earnestly" is the Greek word *agōnízomai* (ag-o-nid'-zom-ahee) with the *epi* prefix intensifying the verb. These words together communicate an urgent, intense struggle demanding immediate attention.

Paul communicated a similar urgency to the believers at Philippi in Philippians 1:27-30. The admonition is preceded by the revelation that there were believers that were preaching the Gospel because they wanted Paul's persecution to increase. "[15] Some indeed preach Christ even of envy and strife; and some also of good will: [16] The **one preach Christ of contention, not sincerely, supposing to add affliction to my bonds**: [17] But the other of love, **knowing that I am set for the defense of the gospel**" (Philippians 1:15-17).

Whether the motivation for preaching the Gospel by the Philippian believers was out of jealousy or love, Paul rejoiced that the

Gospel was being preached (Philippians 1:18). Yet, Paul confronts them with the fact that their "conversation" should be graciously in alignment with the "the gospel of Jesus Christ."

"[27] Only **let your conversation be as it becometh the gospel of Christ**: that whether I come and see you, or else be absent, I may hear of your affairs, **that ye stand fast in one spirit, with one mind striving together for the faith of the gospel**; [28] And in nothing terrified by your adversaries: which is to them an evident token of perdition, but to you of salvation, and that of God. [29] For unto you it is given in the behalf of Christ, **not only to believe on him, but also to suffer for his sake**; [30] **Having the same conflict which ye saw in me**, and now hear *to be* in me" (Philippians 1:27-30).

The word "conversation" is translated from the Greek word *politeúomai* (pol-it-yoo'-om-ahee). The word means to live like a citizen of heaven, manifesting the character of a "born again" saint. Of course, this is a rebuke to those preaching Christ out of jealousy. This heavenly citizenship is defined specifically by the words "stand fast in one spirit, with one mind striving together for the faith of the gospel" (Philippians 1:27b).

The word "becometh" is translated from the Greek word *axíōs* (ax-ee'-oce), which means *comparably representative or suitable*. The intent of the verb is that true believers' lifestyles ought to be representatively suitable to the Gospel message, rather than contradictory to the love of God. Attitudes are important to contending. What motivates to faithfulness is important to God and to God's blessings on what we do.

Contending as a Needed Ministry

"[3] Beloved, when I gave all diligence to write unto you of the common salvation, **it was needful for me to write unto you, and exhort *you* that ye should earnestly contend for the faith** which was once delivered unto the saints. [4] For there are certain men crept in unawares, who were before of old ordained to this condemnation, ungodly men, turning the grace of our God into lasciviousness, and denying the only Lord God, and our Lord Jesus Christ" (Jude 3-4).

The difficulties of doctrinal and practical discipleship are diverse and detailed. It is not enough to merely teach right doctrine and how to "rightly divide the word of truth. We must also teach people how to live the truths they know through the enabling grace of the indwelling Christ. This latter aspect is as equally important as knowing "the faith" and correctly teaching "the faith."

The consequence of trying to teach "the faith" without teaching how to live "the faith" is to cancel all practical meaning of the word Christian. Unfortunately, canceling out all practical meaning of the word Christian is exactly what has happened in the majority of Ecumenicism, Pluralism, New Evangelicalism, Gospel Centrism, and the Emergent Church Movement. The *Bridge Builders* of New Evangelicalism have finally finished their bridge to nowhere!

There is no such place as *theological limbo* when believers are called to "earnestly contend for the faith which was once delivered unto the saints." There is only faithfulness and unfaithfulness. Every believer is responsible to "rightly divide the word of truth" and will be held accountable to do so.

Yes, Christ will hold all believers accountable at the Judgment Seat of Christ. However, local churches are also supposed to hold people accountable for being proactive in their own discipleship. Most local churches fail because they do not know this is their responsibility.

Compromising "the faith" in any way to any degree to simply pacify those who do not want to live according to the specificity of the doctrine of Christ is unfaithfulness. There is every degree of compromise imaginable in *apostate Christianity* (an oxymoron since apostasy ceases to be Christian) both doctrinally and practically.

Apostasy means departure from "the faith" and departure to any degree by compromise or laziness is apostasy by that degree. The moto of the Emergent Church is do whatever is necessary to keep the cows coming to the barn to give milk.

There is no doubt about the doctrines and practices for which believers are to "earnestly contend." These are defined in detail in the epistles. The epistle to the Romans contends for the doctrines of condemnation, the propitiation of God's wrath, justification through faith alone, positional, practical, and ultimate sanctification, God's plan for Israel past, present, and future, what defines the Biblical response of saving faith, and what is necessary for a believer to be consecrated by God to ministry service. Romans chapter sixteen is a summary chapter defining how we are to "earnestly contend for the faith."

People who are called to serve the Lord as pastors, missionaries, and evangelists understand the insecurity of ministry. They know that people are often fickle. Pastors understand the volatile nature of local church ministries. Many local churches are like *powder kegs* that could explode at the first spark of a personality clash.

The natural tendency for pastors and missionaries living in such volatile conditions is to live by the simple principle – PROCEED WITH CAUTION! Sadly, in many cases, pastors and evangelists simply avoid any thing that is controversial just to protect the little bit of *job security* that they have.

The central thrust of Romans 16:17-20 is a warning about the subtlety of the failure to deal with the issues of false doctrine that regularly arise within local churches. The thrust of the warning is found in verse 18 – **"For they that are such serve not our Lord Jesus Christ, but their own belly**; and by good words and fair speeches **deceive the hearts of the simple."** The "simple" in the text are those doctrinally ignorant and without discernment. Certainly, the epistle to the Romans is a primer on the things for which all believers are to "earnestly contend."

"[17] Now I beseech you, brethren, **mark them which cause divisions and offences contrary to the doctrine which ye have learned; and avoid them**. [18] For they that are such serve not our Lord Jesus Christ, but their own belly; and by good words and fair speeches deceive the hearts of the simple. [19] For your obedience is come abroad unto all *men*. I am glad therefore on your behalf: but yet **I would have you wise unto that which is good, and simple concerning evil.** [20] And the God of peace shall bruise Satan under your feet shortly. The grace of our Lord Jesus Christ *be* with you. Amen" (Romans 16:17-20).

Compromise is often expressed and spread in small increments of change or questions that seek a pathway around pure obedience. There is a subtle and dangerous *undercurrent* in the temptation to compromise to keep followers.

However, this is foolish because as soon as one compromises doctrine or practice, he ceases to make followers of Christ (disciples). The *undercurrent* has to do with a pastor's inherent desire for self-protection and survival in the ministry. It also affects leaders of ministries like Bible colleges and seminaries.

When a pastor allows such inherent feelings to dominate his thinking, he will soon be led into varying degrees of incremental compromise to maintain his own personal validation in ministry. Pragmatic measurements, particularly in using numbers of people in validating ministry successes, lead many men astray. No one wants to see the numbers of people diminish under their leadership whether it is in a local church, Bible college, or seminary.

Talk to any pastor who has lost large numbers of people and almost always you will find a man who believes he has failed. The fact is, he may have been faithful in preaching the "whole counsel of God" and some people just did not like it. When the solution to losing numbers of people is anything other than revival, there will be the willingness to compromise doctrine or practice somewhere *in the mix.*

Perhaps the main reason Paul was so faithful in his many battles for "the faith" was that he saw himself as a "sheep for the slaughter." He told the Roman believers earlier in his epistle to the Romans that their thinking of themselves as "sheep for the slaughter" ought to be the norm for all true believers.

"As it is written, For thy sake we are killed all the day long; we are accounted as sheep for the slaughter" (Romans 8:36).

Maintaining an attitude of selflessness in our ministries is certainly difficult. To maintain such an attitude, it demands that we do not view our ministry as a *job*, and that we do not give ourselves *self-importance*. Although pastors serve people, people are not their employers. God is their *boss,* and it is to Him they will ultimately answer for our leadership.

All of this is even more difficult when considering the threat to the financial security of their families. In most cases, pastors cannot be *men-pleasers* (I Thessalonians 2:4) if they are going to be God's *ambassadors* (II Corinthians 5:16-21). Although those that genuinely love the Word of God will be pleased when it is preached without consideration of the fear or favor of men, those who do not love the Word of God will wince and retreat when it is proclaimed.

I Corinthians contends against carnality and divisiveness in the local church, rebuking their variations of compromise in fourteen of the sixteen chapters with chapter fifteen being a thorough desertion of the resurrection and the glorified body of the believer. Chapter fourteen of I Corinthians deals with the abuses of *spirituals* (sign gifts).

It is almost a *doctrinal taboo* to preach against sign gifts or restrict them even according to the instructions of I Corinthians chapter fourteen. *Pentecostalism* and the *Charismatic Movement* have become dominant due to this neglect allowing for the entrance of *Contemporary Christian* worldly music into most of professing Christianity (again, an oxymoron).

II Corinthians deals with the battle of allowing variations of the integration of pagan practices into the church. II Corinthians chapter six calls the Corinthians to separation from these integrations and to keep their local congregations pure from these conflagrations. The doctrine of separation is a rapidly eroding doctrine even within so-called *Fundamentalism* these days. There are few doctrines deemed important enough over which to separate in this departure from Biblical teaching on separation.

***Gospel Centrism* is being fleshed out by a form of some type of *New Fundamentalism*. These *New Fundamentalists* hate the kind of Christians that practice separation according to the *old paths*.** Unfortunately, this *New Fundamentalism* looks much like old *New Evangelicalism*.

New Evangelicalism essentially renounced Biblical separation to *build bridges* between Evangelicalism and Liberalism (Theological Modernism). *Gospel Centrism* is a group within *New Fundamentalism* (who really are New Evangelicals), trying to *build bridges* to the ever-drifting New Evangelicals, now rapidly becoming the Emergent Church. Dr. Kent Brandenburg defines the issues in this form of compromise very well in a new book he has recently edited, and in which he has written several chapters:

"Disobedience to the Biblical doctrine of separation follows the spirit of this age, which reflects post-enlightenment human reasoning. The world will get to where man is in charge of everything, but to get to that goal, there will be a series of compromises fitting to a Hegelian dialectic. Dialogue and consensus building are the means. The goal is the 'third way' that we often read about in politics today. The first and Biblical way is separation. The second and man's way is getting along. The third way is the compromise of separation in order to get along more. The result of the compromise is called progress, reaching toward the end of world peace. Churches are now caught up in this cycle.

Compromise is called love, which is really sentimentality. The watering down of doctrine is labeled humility, which is really pride. Humility submits to God. Pride replaces what God said with man's ideas, elevating men. Pride is the new humility, however, in the new political and theological correctness. The new humility emphasizes nuance and repudiates dogmatism. Finally, anything anyone believes is accepted so that everyone can get along with everyone else, except God."[2]

"[17] Now I beseech you, brethren, **mark them which cause divisions and offences contrary to the doctrine which ye have learned; and avoid them**. [18] For they that are such serve not our Lord Jesus Christ, but their own belly; and by good words and fair speeches deceive the hearts of the simple. [19] For your obedience is come abroad unto all *men*. I am glad therefore on your behalf: but yet **I would have you wise unto that which is good, and simple concerning evil**. [20] And the God of peace shall bruise Satan under your feet shortly. The grace of our Lord Jesus Christ *be* with you. Amen" (Romans 16:17-20).

It is exceedingly difficult to understand how knowledgeable men can be so easily led into the *ditch of philosophical compromise*.

---

[2] Brandenburg, Kent, editor. Contributing authors: Custer, Michael; Mallinak, Dave; McCandless, Erich; Mitchell, Bobby; Smith, Thomas; Sutton, David; and Webb, Gary. *A Pure Church: A Biblical Theology of Ecclesiastical Separation*. El Sobrante, CA: Pillar and Ground Publishing, 2012, page 296-297.

It is difficult to understand how knowledgeable men can justify using the *language of Centrism* when they must know it is the language of *cultural manipulation*. I think they must understand their methodology and have adapted certain agreed upon *talking points*.

If they are right (and their argument is that they are right), then everything to the right of them is wrong and everything to the left of them is wrong. Yet, they are willing to label everyone they say is to the *right* of them as *Hyper*, while labeling select individuals to the *left* of them as friends. Then, they separate from those to the right of them (which means all those unwilling to accept their *new center*) and maintain fellowship with those they admittedly understand to be to the left of them.

It does not seem too difficult to discern the direction in which they are moving, even though they claim they have not moved. This obviously tells us something about them. Either they never were where they once professed to be, or they have moved. Either of those two possibilities is unacceptable.

In Romans 16:19, Paul commends the Roman believers for their obedience to "the faith" and then warns them in the next sentence – "For your obedience is come abroad unto all *men*. I am glad therefore on your behalf: **but yet I would have you wise unto that which is good, and simple concerning evil.**"

The word "evil" is from the Greek word *kakos* (kak-os'). The context would imply the meaning to be about *worthless teaching* that is *harmful* or *injurious*. This context is established because the word "simple" is from the Greek word *akeraios* (ak-er'-ah-yos), meaning *unmixed* in the sense of being *unmixed with false teaching*. Therefore, the word "simple" here means *harmless*.

An alternative reading of last part of Romans 16:19 might be, "I would have you wise unto that which is good, and harmless concerning harmful *false doctrine*." The "harmful *false doctrine*" refers to what Paul said earlier when speaking of "good words and fair speeches" intended to "deceive the hearts of the simple."

The Biblical doctrine of separation is nothing with which to trifle. The Biblical doctrine of separation should certainly never be reduced the way the *Gospel Centrists* are attempting to reduce it. **To propose that Christians focus on the *center* while ignoring the *parameters* is ludicrous and bizarre.** Such a proposition is to say the *center* of Biblical truth is more important than the *boundaries* established by Biblical truth.

In Amos chapter three verses 3-7, God asks seven rhetorical questions all demanding a negative reply to God the Questioner. The first question establishes the purpose of the six other questions – Israel's fellowship with God was broken with Him. "Can two walk together, except they be agreed" (Amos 3:3)? The intent of the question is that two people cannot walk together unless they have agreed to go to the same destination. **The destination is the will of God revealed by the Word of God.**

Different beliefs about the will of God will determine different pathways upon which people walk. The *pathway* of God's will is always singular ("the faith") to which God's Word often refers as "the way of the Lord," or just "the way." Obviously, no person can walk on two different pathways at the same time, although many people attempt to do so in their own self-deception. **God only walks on His pathway.**

"[21] Wherefore **lay apart** {*put away or put down; stop planning to do what is wrong*} **all filthiness** {*moral turpitude*} **and superfluity** {*overly abundant*} **of naughtiness** {*depravity*}, and **receive with meekness the engrafted word,** which is able to save your souls. [22] But be ye doers of the word, and not hearers only, **deceiving your own selves**" (James 1:21-22).

To emphasize *unity* at the sacrifice of doctrinal continuity is equally ludicrous and bizarre. This is what the New Evangelicals have done for years and is the practice of those within the varying degrees of Emergent Christianity. We all certainly understand we are not talking about *doctrinal unanimity.* No two people will ever be perfectly unanimous doctrinally.

However, there certainly should be *doctrinal unanimity* on what defines the Church and how it is to be governed. There certainly should be *doctrinal unanimity* on what the Gospel is and how people get saved. There certainly should be *doctrinal unanimity* on what the Bible teaches about the end times and the Christian's part in these future events. There certainly should be *doctrinal unanimity* on whether *sign gifts* have ceased or if they continue throughout the Church Age. These are especially important orthodox issues that radically impact orthopraxy and orthopathy.

To define the "unity of the Spirit" outside of its parameters given in the statement of Ephesians 4:5-6 is equally ludicrous and bizarre – "5 One Lord, one faith, one baptism, 6 One God and Father of all, who *is* above all, and through all, and in you all." This simple statement does not reduce unity down to one commonality as does *Gospel Centrism*. **This simple statement in fact expands the "unity of the Spirit" exponentially by the phrase "one faith."**

There is but one true God and He has given only one inspired Bible. Therefore, there is only one correct interpretation that defines the "one faith." True "unity of the Spirit" will only be found where there is unanimity within all the parameters of the "one faith."

Who then gets to decide what defines *unanimity*? Does a Bible college get to define this? Does a seminary get to define this? No, every individual and every local church must define *unanimity* for themselves. Then they must decide how they are going practice separation within their own definition and agreement. They must do this to ensure no believer will be led astray by identifying with someone, or another local church, that teaches false doctrine or practices separation that appears to endorse false doctrine.

Romans 16:17-20 appears almost as a parenthesis within the context of Paul's salutation to the faithful believers within various local churches at Rome. The text is Paul's final statement defining a true *Opus Dei* (*the universal call to holiness*). Paul pleads with these faithful believers to "mark them which cause divisions and offences contrary to the doctrine **which ye have learned**; and avoid them" (Romans 16:17). Obviously, those to be marked and who are causing "divisions" are professing believers in the Church.

There are two admonitions in the text. These faithful believers were to "mark" these people that causes "divisions and offences contrary to the doctrine" and they were to "avoid them." The word "mark" is from the Greek word *skopeo* (skop-eh'-o), which literally means to *take aim at*. The intent is to put a mark on them like *a point on a target*. The word "avoid" is from the Greek word *ekklino* (ek-klee'-no), which means *to deviate*. The idea is to *walk away* from such a person. Obviously, the intent of the verb is separation.

God only has one will and one pathway of His will: "the faith." *Gospel Centrism's* new pathway is a pathway on which true believers cannot faithfully walk with these compromisers. It is serious enough to require Biblical separation from these men. It is serious enough for spiritual men to separate them from their associations. Thousands over the centuries have adorned the true doctrine of biblical separation with their own blood.

We must understand Paul's instruction to "mark them" and his command to "avoid them" as referring to anything that departs from "the faith" he had just laid out in careful divisions and meticulous detail. These details included the vocational election of national Israel, the details of the Abrahamic Covenant, the Mosaic Covenant, the Palestinian Covenant, the Davidic Covenant, and the place of Church Age believers in the unfolding *already, not yet* **beginning of the New Covenant.**

Paul gives details of Pneumatology in Romans chapters six and twelve regarding the supernatural baptism with the Holy Spirit (6:1-18) and the supernatural enabling of the Holy Spirit in the lives of consecrated believers (12:1-8). Paul gives details of the Church Age priesthood of all believers in Romans chapter eleven and warns them of the consequences of unfaithfulness by disobedience to what they were saved to be - *Ambassadors of Reconciliation.*

In most part, those promoting *Gospel Centrism* **have been New Evangelicals who are also part of the** *Sovereign Grace Movement* **(Calvinism).** These *Gospel Centrists* are part of a *New Reformed movement* intent on unifying Christianity (redefined) by dominating the teaching within local churches with the *Sovereign Grace* doctrines *(T.U.L.I.P).* Anyone accepting the *Sovereign Grace* doctrines are included in their self-proclaimed circle of *orthodoxy,* regardless of numerous other doctrinal inconsistencies. **Oppose their** *Sovereign Grace* **doctrines and those doing so will quickly find themselves ostracized, labeled as ignorant, and ridiculed for divisiveness.**

This paradox is like the person judging another person for being judgmental. **Their hypocrisy is only surpassed by their arrogance.** These are those in the *darkness* cursing the *light* for exposing what goes on in the *darkness.* Heresy is almost always highly organized and unified in its purposes, covertly directing their armies of converts against those contending "for the faith." History bears record to the accuracy of this statement.

Secondly, two practical outcome failures are addressed in the statement "cause divisions and offences contrary to the doctrine" in Romans 16:17.

1. Divisions . . . contrary to the doctrine

2. Offences . . . contrary to the doctrine

Those to be *marked* and *avoided* are those involved in these two corrupt outcomes. The words "the doctrine" are synonymous with the words "the faith" used elsewhere in Paul's epistles. In fact, Paul uses the phrase "the faith" to refer to the complete inscriptuarlized doctrines of the Word of God repeatedly in his epistles.

Paul uses the phrase '"the faith" on twenty different occasions and Peter and Jude each use it once. The phrase "the faith" is what Paul refers to in Acts 20:27 as he addressed the "elders" of the local churches of Ephesus, "For I have not shunned to declare unto you **all the counsel of God**."

The word "divisions" in Romans 16:17 is from the Greek word *dichostasia* (dee-khos-tas-ee'-ah), which means *disunion*. Paul is referring to *doctrinal dissension* resulting in *division* or *sedition*. Therefore, the primary meaning of "divisions" is the dividing of what was previously joined together. **"Divisions" is *doctrinal disunity* as contrasted with *doctrinal unity*.**

Contending Against *Gospel Centrism*

"[17] Now I beseech you, brethren, **mark them which cause divisions and offences contrary to the doctrine which ye have learned; and avoid them**. [18] For they that are such serve not our Lord Jesus Christ, but their own belly; and by good words and fair speeches deceive the hearts of the simple. [19] For your obedience is come abroad unto all *men*. I am glad therefore on your behalf: but yet **I would have you wise unto that which is good, and simple concerning evil.** [20] And the God of peace shall bruise Satan under your feet shortly. The grace of our Lord Jesus Christ *be* with you. Amen" (Romans 16:17-20).

Once a *division* is created and an individual is disjoined from the unity of the "one faith," this creates a *faction* or *new sect* within Christianity. Therefore, this *division* in doctrine leads to *heresy*.

The word *heresy* in the New Testament is from the Greek word *hairesis* (hah'-ee-res-is), which basically means to *choose a party or sect.* The negative aspect of the word *heresy* refers to the removing of an individual from the *mainstream* of Bible believing Christianity to a *division* that wants to represent itself as the *mainstream* or the *norm.*

The Greek word *hairesis* (hah'-ee-res-is) is often translated by the word *sect* rather than by the word *heresy.* There was "the sect {*hairesis*} of the Sadducees" (Acts 5:17). There was "the sect {*hairesis*} of the Pharisees" (Acts 15:5). On two occasions, true Christianity was called *heresy* by the Jews (Acts 24:5 and 14). Paul refers to the divisions within the church at Corinth as *heresy* (I Corinthians 11:17-19).

Paul referred to "heresies" as one of the manifestations of the "works of the flesh" in Galatians 5:19-21. Peter referred to the divisive teaching of the "false teachers'" as "damnable heresies" in II Peter 2:1 that ultimately denies the Lordship of Jesus Christ. The point is that even though individuals who pretend *unity* but hold to some divisive theological position thereby creating a new *faction* or *sect* within Christianity.

These *divisions* are the very essence of what defines the word *heresy.* Therefore, although Paul's use of the word "divisions" in Romans 16:17 is not the Greek word *hairesis,* the outcome of these "divisions" is *heresy* (new *sects*).

"The faith" is fundamentally Biblical. The Bible is the revelation of God and God's will to be known only through *faith* by believing the Bible to be the inspired Words of God. Any form of *Christianity* that is not Biblical ceases to be Christianity. "Rightly dividing the Word of truth" is what defines Biblical fundamentalism. If some adds to what the Bible teaches, their Christianity ceases to be fundamentally Biblical.

If someone subtracts or reduces what the Bible teaches, their Christianity ceases to be fundamentally Biblical. In either case, Biblical Christianity (*Fundamentalism*) ceases and becomes something else. Adding to what the Bible teaches is **Hyper-fundamentalism** (*more than*). Subtracting, reducing importance, or minimizing the doctrines that the Bible teaches is **Hypo-fundamentalism** (*less than*). Both can be equally troublesome and divisive.

"[1] Now therefore hearken, O Israel, **unto the statutes** {*all of God's directives regarding sanctity and worship details*} and **unto the judgments** {*all of God's directives regarding civil* *affairs}*, which I teach you, **for to do** *them*, that ye may live, and go in and possess the land which the LORD God of your fathers giveth you. [2] **Ye shall not add unto the word which I command you, neither shall ye diminish** *ought* **from it**, that ye may keep the commandments of the LORD your God which I command you" (Deuteronomy 4:1-2).

Nine Characteristics of *Hypo-Fundamentalism*

The prefix *hypo* is derived from a Greek word meaning *under*, *defective*, or *inadequate*.

1. Hypo-fundamentalism abdicates Biblical dogmatism and promotes an ever-growing inclusivism in theological issues. Although Hypo-fundamentalism may not accept false doctrines as true, they are tolerant and accepting of those holding various degrees of false doctrine. Therefore, they seek to redefine *Biblical Separatism*. This was the sin of Peter and Barnabas at Galatia (Acts 15:1-6 and Galatians 2:11-12).

2. Hypo-fundamentalism has a corrupted view of Ecclesiology. Failing to make distinctions regarding dispensational transitions, they adopt the *Kingdom Age* view of the Church and adapt that view into the Church Age. This corrupts such texts as Ephesians 4:1-16 from a *local view of the Church* (Ecclesiology) to a *universal* or *mystical view* of Ecclesiology within all the ambiguity of what defines modern day Christianity. Hypo-fundamentalism increasingly accepts varying degrees of Reformed Theology often beginning with Calvin's Soteriology and the willingness to accept, or tolerate, Reformed views of Eschatology and Ecclesiology.

3. Hypo-fundamentalism rejects the preservation of God's inspired Words and accepts and adopts Eclectic Textual Criticism as their model of Eclectic Reconstructionism of the Bible. Although they claim to believe in the verbal, plenary inspiration of the Scriptures in the *autographs* (originals), they do not believe they have the preservation of those inspired Words in any apograph or group of *apographs* (copies of the originals). Although they usually reject *Dynamic Inspiration* of the Originals, in their view of preservation, they then practically can only accept Dynamic Preservation because they can never be confident their *reconstructed texts* have the exact preserved words from the originals.

4. Hypo-fundamentalism rejects militant opposition against doctrinal heretics and promotes an ongoing dialogue with them as opposed to separation from them - *apposition* **rather than** *opposition.* In *apposition* there are varying degrees of allowed "fellowship" (ambiguously defined) so as to allow for ongoing *discussion* rather than obeying the Biblical mandate: "A man that is an heretick after the first and second admonition reject" (Titus 3:10).

5. Hypo-fundamentalism accepts ever-increasing degrees of *Soteriological Inclusivism* **and** *Soteriological Reductionism.* These varying degrees extend into Lordship Salvation, Monergism, Predestinationism, or Predeterminism, Easy Believism, Only Believism, even into the Crossless Gospel extremes. Although there is ongoing discussion regarding these variations, they continue in varying degrees of cooperative ministry within the dialogue.

6. Hypo-fundamentalism seeks cultural relevancy above personal sanctity. This exists on numerous levels. However, on whatever level it exists, it is sacrificing God's supernatural and enabling grace for the world's *friendship* (acceptance). This is another level of *apposition* – the belief that ministry to a culture is done as part of that culture rather than separation from that culture by establishing a local church counterculture within the culture. Hypo-fundamentalists seek to obfuscate the line of demarcation that separates the believer from being "in the world" (John 17:11), rather than "of the world" (John 15:18-19 and 17:14).

7. Hypo-fundamentalism seeks to avoid being viewed as *religious fanatics* **at almost any sacrifice to true Biblicism.** This is manifested in the extreme by introducing contemporary *Christian rock music* into worship services and the toleration of practices such as Contemplative Prayer, tongues speaking, social drinking, pre-marital sex, and general worldliness in dress and entertainment. Many hypo-fundamental churches no longer require abstinence from the use of alcohol and refuse to make social drinking a test of fellowship. Sin is spoken of in generalities rather than specifics. Their common word expressing distaste for these tests of fellowship is the word *Legalism* as defined by them contrary to Biblical norms.

8. Hypo-fundamentalism adopts the *Right* **and** *Left* **terminology of** *Centrism* **while always viewing themselves as being the center.**

Their word for this is *balanced,* which means only their own defined deviations from their center are allowed. All to the right of them are dogmatic *hypers* and therefore rejected as unmovable. Everyone to the left of them are potential friends. True Biblicists see no right or left when referring to Biblical truth. True Biblicists see only right and wrong.

9. Hypo-fundamentalism favors varying degrees of multiplicity of elder rule that leans more towards Presbyterian Polity in Board administrated churches rather than Congregation Polity administrated under the leadership of a godly Pastor/Elder/Bishop. In many cases, this is theological reaction against the apparent abuses of ungodly Pastors/Elders/Bishops, who "lord over" God's people. Abuses give no mandate to abandon established Biblical precedents. Rather, true *Congregational Polity* should Biblically correct these abuses through confrontation and reproof. **Hypo-fundamentalists think they have a better way than God's way.**

Gospel Centrism and its Neo-orthodox Foundations

Gospel Centrism has been around for many years. In most part, it has been in the *Neo-evangelical* and *Neo-orthodox* camps of theology. Within these camps *Gospel Centrism* has always been part of varying degrees of false views regarding the doctrine of the Church. Both *Neo-evangelical* and *Neo-orthodox* proponents view the Church as some large *mystical entity* of all the "elect" (the regenerated and yet to be regenerated).

This view of the Church has been rapidly spreading through independent, fundamental Baptist churches as they become converted to Reformed Theology in varying degrees. Because of this errant view of the Church, their view of biblical unity is proportionately distorted as well. Depending upon what *camp* to which someone aligns theologically, there is a proportionate reduction of necessary of agreement (theological unity) on other doctrines before fellowship can be established.

In I Corinthians chapter three, the Apostle Paul harshly corrected the Corinthian believers for their carnal divisions in the church. His rebuke was not because they had refused to separate from those teaching false doctrine. He rebuked them because they

had created divisions between themselves regarding who it was that baptized them and of who they considered the higher authority for what was being taught.

Divisions in the church were developing that would lead to *sectarianism* like the *Rabbinical Schools* existing within Judaism. **Sectarianism was not to be part of Christianity.** Unfortunately, this is not what has come to pass. We have men who are more loyal to their *alma mater* or some *teacher/professor* than they are to Christ. Such is the problem caused by the movement that has come to be known as *Gospel Centrism.* Bible Colleges and Seminaries are the new *Rabbinical Schools* and Bible Professors are the *new Rabbis.*

Gospel Centrism fines its origins in Karl Barth's *Dialectic Theology* that came to be known as *Neo-orthodoxy. Neo-orthodoxy* was nothing *new* and it was not *orthodox.* Charles Ryrie addressed Barth's unorthodox *Gospel Centrism* by addressing Barth's radical view of his Neo-orthodox and existential view of Biblical inspiration. Ryrie said:

> "Karl Barth (1886-1968), though one of the most influential theologians in recent history, held a defective and dangerous view of inspiration, a view many continue to propagate. Barthians generally align themselves with the liberal school of biblical criticism. Yet they often preach like evangelicals. This makes Barthianism more dangerous than blatant liberalism."[3]

Granted, most of the (*so called*) *fundamental Gospel Centrists* would not go so far as Barth in his very weak view of inspiration. However, like Barth, they do tend to *categorize doctrines* according to some highly subjective criteria of importance. Can we find any such pattern in their discussions for such *subjective categorizing of doctrine* according to *importance* so they might have some form of ambiguous unity? Yes, many Fundamentalists categorize doctrine by *categories of importance* to them.

Again, there is a consensus of agreement that defining the Gospel must be the first *doorway* anyone must cross before any kind of unity might be had. However, that discussion has never taken place in any public forum coming from the *Gospel Centrists.*

---

[3] Ryrie, Charles C. *Basic Theology.* Wheaton, IL: Victor Books 1994, page 75.

To make the Gospel the *only* significant *doorway* to some basic agreement to unity is naive and an extreme form of theological reductionism. Before there can be real *Biblical fellowship* with other believers and other local churches, there MUST BE LIKE PRECIOUS BIBLICAL FAITH!

The list of departures from "the faith" is never ending and expands with every generation. Satan is the great inventor of human deceptions and doctrinal corruption. Like an insane spiritual psychopath he can blend and merge false doctrines with unbelief to make them appeal to sinners. There is no end to his imaginations and those corruptions always increase and never diminish.

When one generation is warned of a particular deception, he simply alters it a little and blends it with new cultural nuances to corrupt the next generation, where there is no one with enough patience to continue warning. Contending is a never-ending cycle with a history of more failures than successes because most people want less restrictions upon their carnal natures.

The point here is that the list of false doctrines will be constantly evolving entities like human genealogy. The *parent* false doctrines will remain, and a new blend of numerous *children* false doctrines generated by mergers with other false doctrines will be constantly developing.

Undoubtedly, the Bible is Christocentric. No one should argue with that statement. This fact is a reality from Genesis 3:15 through Revelation 22:20. Therefore, no one should really argue against the fact that the Bible is *Gospel centered.*

The Bible certainly is *Gospel centered.* Neither should anyone argue that the Gospel is the primary defining factor for the *arena of agreement* necessary to *Biblical fellowship* (meaning *cooperative ministry*) with another professing believer or with other local churches. Paul clearly established the priority of a pure Gospel as a necessity for fellowship with other professing believers or other local churches in his epistle to the Galatian churches. **However, the *great departure* (apostasy) is not what defines the Gospel, but what one must do in response to the Gospel to be "born again."**

"⁶ I marvel that ye are so **soon removed** {*to change sides*} **from him** that called you into the grace of Christ unto another gospel:
⁷ Which is not another; but there be some that trouble you, and

would pervert the gospel of Christ. [8] But though we, or an angel from heaven, preach any other gospel unto you than that which we have preached unto you, let him be accursed. [9] As we said before, so say I now again, If any *man* preach any other gospel unto you than that ye have received, let him be accursed" (Galatians 1:6-9).

Certainly, we understand that the perversion Paul addressed in Galatians was *adding* "the works of the law" to the Gospel as a necessity for salvation. "The works of the Law" included making any type of Moralism or Ritualism necessary to someone's salvation. We would also agree that many other perversions of the Gospel have developed over the centuries that carry the same *anathema* of Paul's statement in Galatians 1:9.

In fact, Paul's *anathema* on the false Gospel has more to do with **unbiblical responses** to the death, burial, and resurrection of Christ than it does with the **objective facts of the Gospel**. It is not that the Judaizers disagreed with the objective facts of Christ's accomplished redemption. They disagreed about the necessary response to the Gospel to be saved.

The Judaizers saw justification as a *process* rather than an *event*. Men like Luther and Calvin also viewed justification as a *process*. In fact, Calvin's *perseverance of the saints* is really a view of justification as a *process*. In Calvin's *Institutes of Religion*, he has dedicated the whole fourteenth chapter to the discussion of *progressive justification*, which is just an extension of his false doctrine of Monergism.

If one reads through all of Calvin's convoluted nonsense, a person will soon discover that Calvin believed that justification "by grace through faith" is not an *event*, but rather a *progressive process*. **Calvin and Luther both believed in an extreme form of the false doctrine of Monergism (regeneration by God apart from the human will), confusing or comingling justification with progressive sanctification.** This is a common problem within traditional Calvinism and New Calvinism. Calvin said:

"On the contrary, though we may be redeemed by Christ, still, **until we are ingrafted into union with him by the calling of the Father, we are darkness**, the heirs of death, and the enemies of God. For Paul declares that we are not purged and washed from our impurities by the blood of Christ **until the Spirit accomplishes that cleansing in us** (1 Cor. 6:11). Peter, intending to say the same thing, declares that the sanctification of the Spirit avails "unto obedience and sprinkling of the blood of Jesus Christ," (1 Pet. 1:2). If the sprinkling of the blood of Christ by the Spirit gives us purification, let us not think that, previous to this sprinkling, we are anything but sinners without Christ. Let us, therefore, hold it as certain, that the beginning of our salvation is as it were a resurrection from death unto life, because, when it is **given us on behalf of Christ to believe on him** (Phil. 1:29), then only do we **begin to pass from death unto life**." [4] (Bolding added.)

Calvin's convolution into *progressive justification* is also expressed in his commentary on I John 1:9:

"This passage is remarkable; and from it we first learn, that the expiation of Christ, effected by his death, does then properly belong to us, **when we, in uprightness of heart, do what is right and just for Christ is no redeemer except to those who turn from iniquity, and lead a new life.** If, then, we desire to have God propitious to us, so as to forgive our sins, we ought not to forgive ourselves. In short, remission of sins cannot be separated from repentance, nor can the peace of God be in those hearts, where the fear of God does not prevail.

Secondly, this passage shews that the gratuitous pardon of sins is given us not only once, but that it is a **benefit perpetually residing in the Church**, and **daily offered to the faithful**. For the Apostle here addresses the faithful; as doubtless no man has ever been, nor ever will be, who can otherwise please God, since all are guilty before him; for however strong a desire there may be in us of acting rightly, we always go haltingly to God. Yet what is half done obtains no approval with God. In the meantime, by new sins we continually separate ourselves, as far as we can, from the grace of God. Thus it is, that **all the saints have need of the daily forgiveness of sins; for this alone keeps us in the family of God**."

---

[4] Calvin, John. *Institutes of the Christian Religion.* Public Domain PDF: http://www.ccel.org/ccel/calvin/institutes.html, Third Book, Chapter Fourteen, page 483.

"**9** *If we confess* He again promises to the faithful that God will be propitious to them, provided they acknowledge themselves *to be sinners*. It is of great moment to be fully persuaded, that when we have sinned, there is a reconciliation with God ready and prepared for us: we shall otherwise carry always a hell within us. Few, indeed, consider how miserable and wretched is a doubting conscience; but the truth is, that hell reigns where there is no peace with God. The more, then, **it becomes us to receive with the whole heart this promise which offers free pardon to all who confess their sins**. Moreover, this is founded even on the justice of God, because God who promises is true and just. For they who think that he is called *just*, because he justifies us freely, reason, as I think, with too much refinement, because **justice or righteousness here depends on fidelity, and both are annexed to the promise.** For God might have been just, were he to deal with us with all the rigor of justice; but as he has bound himself to us by his word, he would not have himself deemed just, except he forgives."[5] (Bolding added.)

The obvious error here is that Calvin confuses regeneration with salvation. Salvation is an *event* that begins the *process of regeneration* that culminates in the believer's glorification. The so-called *Golden Chain* of Romans 8:29-30 is in fact the *order of "the regeneration,"* not the *order of salvation.* Although regeneration and salvation are connected, they are two separate doctrines. They are *synchronous*, but not *synonymous*.

However, there is never any doubt about the ultimate outcome in that every believer is "complete in Him" upon the moment of their salvation decision. Paul, in dealing with the heresy of Gnosticism, warns against the "philosophy" of progressive justification in Colossians chapter two and makes some very definitive statements condemning such an idea.

"[8] Beware lest any man spoil you through philosophy and vain deceit, after the tradition of men, after the rudiments of the world,

---

[5] Calvin, John. *Commentaries on the Catholic Epistles*. Grand Rapids, MI: Christian Classics Ethereal Library, http://www.ccel.org/ccel/calvin/calcom45.pdf, page 143.

and not after Christ. [9] For in him dwelleth all the fulness of the Godhead bodily. [10] And **ye are complete** {*perfect, passive*} in him, which is the head of all principality and power: [11] In whom also **ye are circumcised** {*aorist, passive*} with the circumcision **made without hands**, in putting off the body of the sins of the flesh by the circumcision of Christ: [12] **Buried** {*aorist, passive*} **with him in baptism** {*with the Spirit*}, wherein also **ye are risen** {*aorist, passive*} **with *him*** through the faith of **the operation of God** {*reason for passive voice*}, who hath raised him from the dead" (Colossians 2:8-12).

The great fallacy of the philosophical ideology of *essential/non-essential doctrines* is that some so-called *religious authority* is establishing what is important to God and what is not important to God. **This foolishness is the epitome of theological arrogance.**

The categorizing of doctrines according to some goal of ambiguous nondefinable *unity* is ridiculous. Such foolishness is a consensus of compromise and not Biblical unity at all. However, this nonsense is not theocentric (God-centered). This nonsense is anthropocentric (man-centered).

This nonsense takes away the grand responsibility of preaching and teaching "all the counsel of God" to every believer to ensure there is always a new generation of believers perfected to do the same for the next generation. It can be said with full assurance of the facts that this failure to pass on the understanding of "all the counsel of God" to the next generation defines the ongoing failure of every generation of believers. This failure causes Christianity to progressively morph into various sects of *theological monsters* and aberrations that are in disconnected from Biblical Christianity.

"[26] Wherefore I take you to record this day, that I *am* pure from the blood of all *men*. [27] For **I have not shunned to declare unto you all the counsel of God**. [28] Take heed therefore unto yourselves, and to all the flock, **over the which the Holy Ghost hath made you overseers, to feed the church of God**, which he hath purchased with his own blood. [29] For I know this, that after my departing shall grievous wolves enter in among you, not sparing the flock. [30] Also of your own selves shall men arise, speaking perverse things, **to draw away disciples after them**. [31]

Therefore watch, and remember, that by the space of three years I ceased not to warn every one night and day with tears" (Acts 27:26-31).

It is foolish to say that agreement alone on the Gospel should be the only thing that determines what belongs in the *arena of agreement* for any cooperative ministry to be blessed of God. After all, should not the determining factor for fellowship be about what is necessary for God's blessings on cooperative ministry?

Granted, there are some nuances of doctrine over which one should not separate. However, in the propagation of *Gospel Centrism*, we find its proponents radically silent on even general areas of doctrinal agreement. Instead, they make wide, sweeping arguments for *unity* without any Biblical exegesis for the basis of that *pseudo-unity*. Have *unity* and *fellowship* somehow become two separate and disconnected entities? Can Christians unite for fellowship without any definitive theological foundations for that unity?

Many are throwing around theological terms while trying to purposefully make the meaning of those terms ambiguous. **The job of theologians is to provide answers, not raise doubts and questions that essentially abrogate dogmatism.**

Apparently, the *Gospel Centrists* are striving for the kind of *unity* had by the leaders of the Reformation. We would be foolish to think that there was close agreement between most of the players within the Reformation. On a few occasions, they tried to have one another killed. The leaders of the Reformation were united in what they *opposed*.

The leaders of the Reformation opposed Roman Catholicism and Papalism, but never opposed Rome's radically corrupted Theonomic views of Ecclesiology or Eschatology. The leaders of the Reformation opposed all who refused to baptize infants, even persecuting, and killing those with opposing views. Are *Gospel Centrists* seeking a softer, gentler *New Reformation*?

Apparently, the Gospel Centrists are really trying to cultivate a twenty-first century *New Reformation*. **Gospel Centrists are proposing a *New Reformation* that is not based upon doctrinal agreement, but upon denigrating those they oppose or who oppose them.** Many of the *Gospel Centrists* are trying to accomplish this *New*

Reformation within their own ambiguous confession of faith known as *Fundamentalism* and *Conservative Evangelicalism.*

If you understand the formation of the *movement* known as *Fundamentalism,* you understand that their unity was in what they opposed rather than the few things upon which they agreed. This is not Biblical unity! Biblical unity has a trinity of agreementy:

1. Right doctrine (orthodoxy)
2. Right practice (orthopraxy)
3. Right purpose (orthopathy)

Careful exegesis of Ephesians chapter four will provide ample foundations for this *trinity of unity.* Of course, there will be small nuances of disagreement within each of these three areas of agreement. We are not looking for *unanimity.* However, there should be a very broad and definitive arena for agreement. If not, the Scriptures have not given enough weight of evidence for dogmatism.

There surely is enough weight of evidence to be dogmatic about every general category of doctrine. In these general categories of doctrine there must be agreement before unity can be achieved.

In Ephesians chapter four, the emphasis is to seek unity with the Godhead. The simple truth of the chapter is that all those in unity with the Godhead will be in unity with one another.

The unity the Godhead enjoys is a tri-unity both in their Persons and in the three areas of orthodoxy, orthopraxy, and orthopathy. We need to put a stop to all the theological ambiguity of *Gospel Centrism* and mark it for its reductionist's goals of a pseudo unity lacking any theological parameters.

Instead of continuing a discussion engulfed in theological ambiguity defining the *center*, perhaps the wiser of those in the discussion should be more involved in a discussion of what defines the broader parameters of agreement for unity.

Gospel Centrists refuse this part of the discussion because they know their movement will immediately disintegrate into a thousand factions if they do. Their answer to those wanting them to define these parameters is – WE WON'T GO THERE! They know that true separatism, when practiced Biblically, will dissolve their pseudo unity like sugar in water.

Talking about *Gospel centered ministry* sounds wonderful. Who would not agree that every ministry should be *Gospel centered*? However, the terminology is purposefully deceptive, because the *gospel* of *Gospel Centrism* is Calvin's Sovereign Grace *gospel* of Monergism. *Gospel Centrism* is an attempt at a *New Reformation.* This *New Reformation* joins together all those holding to various positions of Reformed Theology together by Calvin's Sovereign Grace *gospel* centered in Monergism.

To achieve this *New Reformation* that focuses on this new radical center, most other categories of doctrine must be minimalized and marginalize to achieve the goal of *Sovereign Grace Gospel Centered Unity* (This would at least be an honest name for the movement.). The naiveties within Fundamentalism are being *suckered* into this deception. If you do not believe this is true, *connect the dots* to those promoting *Gospel Centrism.*

If nothing else, this *New Reformation* is the outcome of the *Gospel Centrism.* This *New Reformation is* propagated by a book entitled *The Gospel as Center* edited by D.A. Carson, and Timothy Keller, with contributing articles by thirteen other men, all New Evangelicals.

Another book, written with a similar premise, is *Reclaiming the Center: Confronting Evangelical Accommodation in Postmodern Times.* This book was edited by Millard J. Erickson, Paul Kjoss Helseth, and Justin Taylor with thirteen other contributing authors; **all New Evangelicals calling themselves Contemporary Evangelicals.**

Most Biblical Baptists and Biblical Fundamentalists do not read these kinds of books. They probably should read these books just to stay informed on the terminology and on the source of these terms. Although these men may have some good things to say, there is a compromising spirit engrafted in their universal view of the Church.

The common denominator among all these men is their connections to Reformed Theology. Propagation of their *New Reformation* has come through conferences such as Gospel Coalition, Together for the Gospel (T4G), the Ligonier Conference of the Reformed theologian R.C. Sproul, and the Acts 29 Convention. Gospel Centrism is a *Sovereign Grace* movement to capture evangelical Christianity and much of Fundamentalism with Calvinism. There is no doubt about it! The only difference is that the reformed fundamental

Baptists are trying to achieve the same goal while hiding behind ambiguous terminology.

Unless these Gospel Centrists are uprooted from our Baptist Bible colleges and Baptist sSeminaries, they will turn many Baptist churches into Reformed Baptists in their doctrine. Before recommending any student to a Bible college or seminary, ask those institutions who on their staff holds to any degree of Reformed Theology. Do not let them get by with their deceptions. Bring them out of the shadows by shining the light upon their hidden goals.

"[7] Go from the presence of a foolish man, when thou perceivest not *in him* the lips of knowledge. [8] The wisdom of the prudent *is* to understand his way: but the folly of fools *is* deceit" (Proverbs 14:7-8).

Unfortunately, even when theological errors are exposed, seldom to people return to *Sola Scriptura* for solutions to their errors. In most cases, they simply try to reform the areas they see as failures. In most cases, they simply see things as shortcomings that can be easily *adjusted* rather than failure needing *radical repentance* and complete abandonment.

Historically, Christians (especially Baptists) have been willing to die very gruesome and horrible deaths rather than deny the true faith in the true Gospel refusing to accept infant baptism (Paedo-baptism), baptismal regeneration, transubstantiation or consubstantiation, and other such nonsense.

Many pages of Baptist history have been written with the blood of faithful martyrs who were tortured and murdered simply because they refused to believe in anything else but salvation as a gift of God's grace received through faith in the finished work of Christ, totally apart from any good works by the individual and totally apart from any religious ceremony or ritual.

Apart from the preservation of the Word of God, it has been God's grace manifested through the lives and testimonies of the faith of such remarkable individuals that the truth of the purity of the Gospel has been preserved for all these centuries.

The Militancy of Contending for "the Faith"

The questions we must ask ourselves are simple. Do we have the kind of militancy that is willing to die rather than

compromise God's message of salvation (the Gospel)? Would we be willing to be tortured and murdered rather than accept a man-made way of salvation?

The test of our militancy is the price we are willing to pay to maintain a pure testimony of salvation by grace alone through faith alone in Christ alone. If we are not willing to die to maintain that testimony, we have abandoned the apostolic faith. "The faith" must become important enough for us to die to maintain it.

The fact that people believe Jesus is the Messiah is not sufficient evidence to the reality of their salvation. Here is the central dividing line of truth between true Christianity and apostate Christianity. This dividing line is that apostate Christianity believes that Jesus was the Messiah of God; they believe He died on the Cross, but they do not understand what He accomplished on the Cross for them. They believe in Jesus but reject the Gospel of grace.

Acts 15:5 says this "sect of the Pharisees. . . believed." This means they believed Jesus was their historical and promised Messiah, but the facts of the rest of Acts 15:5 reveal to us they did not understand the Gospel and therefore continued to rely upon their religious ceremonies and rituals to be saved.

This is equally true of most Reformers and Reformed churches. They continued to believe that religious rituals (such as circumcision) were necessary to salvation. This is clear evidence they did not understand the Gospel and therefore could not rest by faith in the truths of the Gospel. If we allow ANYTHING to be added to what Christ has done to save us, we have allowed the corruption of the Gospel.

"And certain men which came down from Judaea taught the brethren, *and said*, Except ye be circumcised after the manner of Moses, ye cannot be saved" (Acts 15:1).

It is amazing that those who seek tolerance of their false doctrines are the most intolerant of those unwilling to compromise truth for false unity. It was these "false brethren" who were intolerant. They were willing to accept anyone into their circle of compromise, but they have historically sought to annihilate anyone who was not willing to compromise to accept them.

The whole of the issue to be resolved in Acts chapter fifteen was the issue of the Judaisers in Galatia demanding that Gentiles be circumcised to complete their salvation. Peter and Barnabas tolerated this nonsense rather than contend against it.

This tolerance created a tremendous compromise that threatened every one of the local churches at Galatia. Paul saw the need to confront it and contend against it to gain a consensus regarding what defined "the faith."

"[3] But neither Titus, who was with me, being a Greek, was compelled to be circumcised: [4] And that because of false brethren unawares brought in, who came in privily to spy out our liberty which we have in Christ Jesus, that they might bring us into bondage: [5] To whom we gave place by subjection, no, not for an hour; that the truth of the gospel might continue with you" (Galatians 2:3-5).

Before God can revive His Church and bless the way He wants to bless, the members of a local church must determine they will die rather than compromise the Gospel, die rather than become tolerant of false doctrine, and die rather than join hands in partnership ("fellowship") with those preaching salvation by *ritual purgation* or *sacramental cleansing of sin*. This is the challenge of the Apostle Paul in Galatians 5:1-9.

"[1] **Stand fast** {*hold your ground*} therefore in the liberty wherewith Christ hath made us free, and **be not entangled again with the yoke of bondage**. [2] Behold, I Paul say unto you, that **if ye be circumcised** {*for salvation*}, **Christ shall profit you nothing**. [3] For I testify again to every man that is circumcised {*for salvation*}, that he is a debtor to do the whole law. [4] **Christ is become of no effect unto you, whosoever of you are justified by the law**; ye are fallen from grace. [5] For we through the Spirit wait for the hope of righteousness by faith. [6] For **in Jesus Christ neither circumcision availeth any thing, nor uncircumcision**; but faith which worketh by love. [7] Ye did run well; who did hinder you that ye should not obey the truth? [8] This persuasion *cometh* not of him that calleth you. [9] **A little leaven leaveneth the whole lump**" (Galatians 5:1-9).

"Stand fast" in Galatians 5:1 is from the Greek word *steko* (stay'-ko) meaning *to persist*. The idea is *to be uncompromising*. "Persuasion" in Galatians 5:8 is from the Greek word *peismone* (pice-mon-ay'), which can mean *a treacherous or deceptive persuasion*.

The "little leaven" of Galatians 5:9 refers to allowing any *ritual purgation* to compromise the purity of the Gospel of grace regardless of how insignificant it may seem. Allow any amount to be part of your faith, you leaven the whole of your faith with false doctrine making your profession of faith false and unprofitable (Galatians 5:2).

Militancy is an Integral Aspect of "the Faith"

This world is steeping in a brew of evil growing ever stronger each moment it continues to steep. We have seen the kind of evil of which humanity is capable of heaping upon one another already written on the pages of historical infamy. Humanity would be as evil as Satan himself if we were left to our own devices unrestrained by a working conscience because that conscience is restrained by the knowledge of God through faith in God's Word. Without that "the faith" the human conscience does not work.

We are rapidly approaching another historical epoch like Genesis 6:5 where God said, "And GOD saw that the wickedness of man *was* great in the earth, and *that* every imagination of the thoughts of his heart *was* only evil continually."

In Genesis 6:3, God said, "My spirit shall not always strive with man." The Great Flood is historical testimony that God's longsuffering eventually comes to an end. Satan has historically done everything in his power to mock, eradicate, and eclipse the testimony of God's judgment in the Great Flood. Christians must fight to keep these testimonies alive.

"[6] But godliness with contentment is great gain. [7] For we brought nothing into *this* world, *and it is* certain we can carry nothing out. [8] And having food and raiment let us be therewith content. [9] But they that will be rich fall into temptation and a snare, and *into* many foolish and hurtful lusts, which drown men in destruction and perdition. [10] For the love of money is the root of all evil: which while some coveted after, they have erred from the faith, and pierced themselves through with many sorrows. [11] But thou, O man of God, **flee these things; and follow after**

righteousness, godliness, faith, love, patience, meekness. [12] fight the good fight of faith, lay hold on eternal life, whereunto thou art also called, and hast professed a good profession before many witnesses" (I Timothy 6:6-12).

The Word of God is redundant with *militant terms*. These *militant terms* are used to describe the struggle of the Christian life - terms like "war a good warfare" (I Timothy 1:18), "fight the good fight" (I Timothy 6:12), "so fight I" (I Corinthians 9:26).

In Ephesians 6:11, believers are commanded: "Put on the whole armour of God, that ye may be able to stand against the wiles of the devil." Understanding the Bible's teaching on a life of faith is to understand that believers will be at war against evil and its influences until the creation of the new Heaven/Earth.

"Contending for the faith" involves every believer in a spiritual war that began with the insurrection of an angel of God called Lucifer, who rebelled against God's sovereignty and usurped His authority by the deception of Eve.

In this war, casualties are more severe than in other wars in that these casualties involve the loss of souls, lost for all eternity, and the loss of lives wasted in the pursuit of sinful pleasures that lead men and women to live their lives in ways unimaginable.

For the Christian, "contending for the faith" is about *recovering dominion*. Although the Christian's soul has been redeemed and eternally secured by the Cross-work of Jesus Christ "by grace through faith," every Christian must *fight the fight of faith* in the recovery of this temporal life from the dominion of sin through his own practical sanctification.

This is a life-long battle with no intermissions or rest periods. Like swimming upstream in a strong current, stop the struggle for one moment and you are carried downstream. It will be a constant struggle to maintain every inch of spiritual ground that is gained.

In II Corinthians 10:3-5, Paul talks about not warring "after the flesh," "the weapons of our warfare" not being "carnal" weapons, and about the enemies against which we fight; "casting down imaginations, and every high thing that exalteth itself against the knowledge of God, and bringing into captivity every thought to the obedience of Christ."

The battleground involves temptations from *without*, perverse desires from *within*. This is a battle with humanity's corrupted, un-

Biblical, extra-Biblical, and perverted knowledge of God. Simply because believers still possess a sin nature does not mean their sinful natures must possess them. All believers can be enabled to live righteously by the enabling power of the indwelling Holy Spirit.

"[20] O Timothy, **keep** {*isolate truth from contamination*} that which is committed to thy trust, avoiding profane *and* vain babblings, and oppositions of science falsely so called: [21] Which some professing have erred concerning **the faith**. Grace {*enabling of the Holy Spirit*} *be* with thee. Amen" (I Timothy 6:20-21).

In Ephesians 6:10-18, Paul talks about the warfare "against principalities, against powers, against the rulers of the darkness of this world, against spiritual wickedness in high *places*." He goes on to talk about the believer's spiritual armament, commanding believers to "take unto you the whole armour of God, that ye may be able to withstand in the evil day, and having done all, to stand." Of course, *standing* in these verses refers to *standing in battle* against the influences of evil as opposed to retreating in defeat. He uses a similar analogy to describe the struggle of the faith in I Thessalonians 5:8-9.

"[8] But let us, who are of the day, **be sober**, **putting on** {*both*} the **breastplate of faith** and **love**; and for an helmet, the hope of salvation. [9] For **God hath not appointed us to wrath, but to obtain** {*to acquire the end of*} **salvation** {*used here in the sense of the final victory over the flesh in the believer's glorification and reign with Christ in the Kingdom Age*} by our Lord Jesus Christ" (I Thessalonians 5:8-9).

In I Thessalonians 5-8, the emphasis of the battle against the forces of evil is the guaranteed victory "by our Lord Jesus Christ" at His second coming. The emphasis of the warfare of the believer is simply to be faithful in the battle, which is already won. Why then fight if the victory is already won?

As we battle *by faith for the faith*, those fighting against us who are under the influences of evil, are won to Christ and are joined with us through their faith in Christ in the guaranteed victory. Evangelism in sanctification is part of the battle. **We fight "for the faith" but also for lost souls.**

In II Timothy 2:1-4, Paul uses similar military terminology to describe the spiritual struggles of men in the pastorate.

"[1] Thou therefore, my son, be strong in the grace {*the enabling of the indwelling Spirit*} that is in Christ Jesus. [2] And the things that thou hast heard of me among many witnesses, the same commit thou to faithful men, who shall be able to teach others also. [3] Thou therefore **endure hardness, as a good soldier of Jesus Christ. [4] No man that warreth entangleth himself with the affairs of *this* life**; that he may please **him** {*Jesus*} who hath chosen him to be a soldier" (II Timothy 2:1-4).

All the days that we live in this body of flesh, the Christian life will be an unending warfare "contending for the faith." There can be no allowance for compromise in any form, for the enemy takes no prisoners. The enemy is described as the "deceiver" and the "destroyer." He is described as a "lion" that devours his prey bite by bite. He destroys lives by getting people addicted to self-destructive, sinful practices, and perversions of theology.

Satan's tactics are ancient, perfected in their use, and well developed in their application. These tactics are always aimed at our faith in that they almost always question God's wisdom or what God has said, seeking to pervert understanding of both faith and truth.

The history of those of faith throughout the Bible is a history of failures with those failures escalating in the generations that followed because of the duplicity of the parent generation in living their faith. The history of those of faith throughout the Bible is a history of trying to minister to the people that witnessed the duplicity of the parent generation and decided their parents' faith was counterfeit and therefore unworthy of duplication.

The fact is that every single believer will fail in living for the Lord and at some point in his/her life will require forgiveness and a chance to start again. In most cases, this will happen many times throughout a lifetime.

Contending for the Truth while Contending for the Sinner

The need for compassionate forgiveness and the repeated need to give people opportunities to start again is so that doing this

becomes the practical aspect of "the faith" exemplified through a believer's life. The failure to give compassionate forgiveness and the chance to start again (and again if necessary) is really the heart of Jesus's "Judge not, that ye be not judged" command (Matthew 7:1).

The "Judge not, that ye be not judged" command was about the hypocrisy of judging others **without** the reciprocity of judging one's own life by the same standard of righteousness. This was one aspect of *Phariseeism* that reflected a counterfeit of practice of the "the faith."

Such a contradiction to the practice of "the faith" was not to be condoned and not condoning it was contending "for the faith" (Jude 3). This is what Jesus addressed in Matthew chapter twenty-three, declaring such practices as hypocrisy and those doing this to be *hypocrites*.

All that can be produced by such hypocrisy is whitewashed "sepulchres, which indeed appear beautiful outward, but are within full of dead *men's* bones, and of all uncleanness" (Matthew 23:27). **This nonsense changes the outside appearance never touching the heart.**

"[1] {*part one*} **Judge not, that ye be not judged.** [2] For with **what judgment ye judge, ye shall be judged:** and with what measure ye mete, it shall be measured to you again. [3] And why beholdest thou **the mote that is in thy brother's eye**, but considerest not the beam that is in thine own eye? [4] Or how wilt thou say to thy brother, Let me pull out the mote out of thine eye; and, behold, a beam *is* in thine own eye? [5] **Thou hypocrite**, first cast out the beam out of thine own eye; **and then** shalt thou see clearly to cast out the mote out of thy brother's eye. [6] {*part two*} **Give not that which is holy** {*sacred*} **unto the dogs** {*those who hate truth and who are hostile to righteousness*}**, neither cast ye your pearls before swine** {*unable to truly the treasures of God's truths*}**, lest they trample them under their feet** {*these truths mean nothing to these types of people who view them as worthless*}**, and turn again and rend you** {*in the hatred and rejection of God's convicting Words, such people will turn on you as their enemies*}" (Matthew 7:1-6).

Part two of this admonition in Matthew 7:6 is what Jesus reveals about the nature of the unbeliever in the dynamic of the hardened heart. When a believer attempts to *force* the truth upon the unbeliever, the believer's lack of compassion generates contempt for that truth in the heart of the unbeliever.

Second, when the believer tries to **force** the unbeliever into subjection to God's Holy Words this creates hatred in the unbeliever towards the believer and ends any possibility of the unbeliever heeding the truth, now or in the future. Then the human will, now in contempt, hardens his heart to anyone trying to reach him in the future, thereby often sealing the destiny of the unbeliever in hardened unbelief.

Christ's pattern was to **appeal** to rebels and unbelievers by exposing them to the consequences of their unbelief. **Contending "for the faith" must take these issues into careful consideration lest we do more damage than good.** Contenders must maintain the perspective that while contending "for the faith" they are also contending for the soul of the unbeliever.

"24 And the servant of the Lord **must not strive** {*fight or argue*}; but **be gentle** {*friendly, good natured, congenial*} unto all *men*, **apt to teach** {*instructive*}, **patient** {*enduring and willing to wait*}, 25 **In meekness** {*gentle humility; not proud or overbearing*} instructing those **that oppose themselves**; if **God peradventure will give them repentance** to the acknowledging of the truth; 26 And *that* **they may recover themselves** out of the snare of the devil, who are taken captive by him at his will" (II Timothy 2:24-26).

Therefore, if we claim we are contending "for the faith" while maintaining the reality of contending for the souls of sinners, we should be able to pass the test of II Timothy 2:24-26. If we fail at one point in our evaluation of our contending, we have failed to contend in the manner Scripture instructs us.

1. Did we argue or persuade in the spirit of compassion? The answer must come from the person for which we contend. How did they perceive what we said?
2. Were we friendly, considerate, sweet spirited, and congenial listening, hearing, and carefully considering the things the person for which we contend is saying. How would this person(s) evaluate us in this area?

3. Was our conversation instructive, asking questions about Scripture and what the person for which we contend understands from that Scripture?

4. Did the person with whom we spoke consider us to be spiritually proud and overbearing or humble and gentle with them?

5. Are we trying to *force* or *bully* a person into subjection to our view or are we following the Biblical pattern of God, allowing people *individual soul liberty* to make the *free will choices* given them by God and explaining that they will bear the consequences of choices right or wrong?

"Now the serpent was more subtil than any beast of the field which the LORD God had made. And he said unto the woman, Yea, **hath God said**, Ye shall not eat of every tree of the garden (Genesis 3:1, ***The question mark is important <u>for it</u> is the seed of all corruption.***)?

  The militant struggle contending for the purity of "the faith" (right doctrine and right practice from God's Word) involves every Christian in a spiritual war fought on two fronts. Every Christian must involve himself in the fight **by faith** and the fight **"for the faith."** Although these two fronts are not the same, they are dynamically connected.

  Our knowledge of the Word of God, our living the Word of God, and our use of the Word of God to bring the lost to saving faith in Christ is what it means to fight **by faith**. The battle against the corruption of Bible doctrine by the never-ending sedition of the worldly influences of various levels of evil is what it means to contend **"for the faith."**

"¹⁷ For therein is the righteousness of God revealed from {*saving*} faith to {*living*} faith: as it is written, **The just shall live by faith** {*knowing, understanding, and living God's Word*}. ¹⁸ **For** {*because*} the wrath of God is revealed from heaven against all ungodliness and unrighteousness of men, who **hold** {*withhold or suppress*} **the truth** {*the idea is to withhold truths for self-protection or self-promotion*} **in unrighteousness** {*wicked injustice*}" (Romans 1:17-18).

The fight of faith involves the believer with three enemies of a living faith. These three enemies are the trinity of the fall: sin, self, and Satan. Satan is the tempter, the liar, and the deceiver. He tempts with sin. Sin is anything that defiles the believer's sanctification before God and breaks "fellowship" with God. Sin is anything that the believer is forbidden to do. Sin is also a failure in doing anything God commands to be done.

The paradox is that, in the fall of mankind, all of us received a *sin nature (selfish, prideful ambitions and lusts)* that wants to sin and is filled with pride. The Bible words for *self* (the *sin nature*) are words like the "old man," the "flesh," or simply "sin."

The point is that all men and women, believers, and unbelievers alike, have a serious *wanter* problem when it comes to sin. We all have an insatiable appetite for sin. The Bible word for this is "lust." Therefore, the believer in his fight **by faith for the faith** fights even against his own evil influences upon the world.

There are three main avenues for sin in our lives. The wise believer understands that he must keep vigilant guard upon these three doorways for sin. He must build reinforced gates against them with the understanding that his own desires will want to leave them wide open and unrestrained. These three main avenues for sin are defined for us in Satan's deception of Eve in the Garden of Eden and they are described by the Apostle John.

"And when **the woman saw** that the tree *was* good for food, and that it *was* **pleasant to the eyes**, and a tree to **be desired to make** *one* **wise**, she took of the fruit thereof, and did eat, and gave also unto her husband with her; and he did eat" (Genesis 3:6).

"For all that *is* in the world, the **lust of the flesh**, and the **lust of the eyes**, and the **pride of life**, is not of the Father, but is of the world" (I John 2:16).

Every believer must learn to meticulously guard these three *doorways* of sin. Just as it took only one sin to bring God's curse upon all of humanity, one sin is all it will take to defile the believer before God, making that believer "unclean." Once this happens, restoration to "fellowship" with God must be restored through repentance, confession, and cleansing (I John 1:7-9) before God can bless the believer's works or answer his prayers.

The central purpose of the forgiveness of sins is not the removal of guilt from the believer's heart, but it is about the restoration of "fellowship" with God so that a God-blessed working relationship can once again take place.

The struggle of a militant faith is about living the truth in unbroken "fellowship" with God. This is a critical truth to the Christian life. This is the heart and soul of the doctrine of grace in the New Covenant.

This word "fellowship" is so often misunderstood and misapplied. It is often only defined as *relationship* without the emphasis upon *the purpose of that relationship.* **The purpose of "fellowship" is a *working partnership* with God in the fight by faith for the faith in bringing lost souls to receive the gift of salvation and to be "born again."**

The word "fellowship" in the Bible is usually translated from the Greek word *koinonia* (koy-nohn-ee'-ah). Its usual meaning is *a communion of joint participation in something.* In other words, it is a word describing a *working relationship* of two or more people joining their energies and resources to achieve a common goal or purpose.

Therefore, "fellowship" with God involves the believer in, and with, supernatural forces and resources. In this "fellowship," the power of the Divine is united with the yielded and believing human. Therefore, a critical aspect of "fellowship" with God and *the fight of faith* is about this "unity" with God in living the truth. Paul talks about this "unity" in Ephesians chapter four.

Notice the emphasis on two areas in the fight **by** faith and the fight **for** the faith as these two arenas of struggle are discussed under the doctrine of grace (God's divine enabling through His Holy Spirit).

"[1] I therefore, the prisoner of the Lord, beseech you that ye walk worthy of the vocation *{the priesthood of all believers}* wherewith ye are called, [2] With all lowliness and meekness, with longsuffering, forbearing one another in love; [3] **Endeavouring to keep the unity of the Spirit** in the bond of peace. [4] There *is* one body, and one Spirit, even as ye are called in one hope of your calling; [5] One Lord, one faith, one baptism, [6] One God and Father of all, who *is* above all, and through all, and in you all. [7] But unto **every one of us** *{believer priests}* **is**

given grace {*God's enabling*} according to the measure of the gift of Christ. [8] Wherefore he saith, When he ascended up on high, he led captivity captive, and gave gifts {*listed in verse eleven*} unto men. [9] (Now that he ascended, what is it but that he also descended first into the lower parts of the earth? [10] He that descended is the same also that ascended up far above all heavens, that he might fill all things.) [11] And he gave some, apostles; and some, prophets; and some, evangelists; and some, pastors and teachers; [12] **For the perfecting** {*equipping, maturing, think basic training for warfare*} **of the saints, for the work of the ministry** {*spiritual warfare to engage the world with the Gospel of Jesus Christ and make disciples of Jesus Christ*}, for the edifying {*building up and strengthening of the structure of the Church*} of the body of Christ: [13] Till we all come in the **unity of the faith**, and of the knowledge of the Son of God, unto a perfect man, unto the measure of the stature of the fulness of Christ" (Ephesians 4:1-13).

The critical part of a *living faith* is that "fellowship" with God cannot exist apart from a life separated from sin (holiness) and separated unto God (sanctification). These two arenas of Christian responsibility are the arenas in which the fight **of** faith and the fight **for** the faith are fought. This is what Christian *growth* is about and how it is measured (progressive sanctification).

The purpose of the "perfecting of the saints" is for "fellowship" with God to be achieved so that the "work of the ministry" can be supernaturally actuated. The "work of the ministry" is *spiritual work* demanding supernatural forces and resources. Christ refers to the critical spiritual dynamic of this "fellowship" in John chapter fifteen in His use of the words "abide in him" involving the requirement of being "clean."

"[1] I am the true vine, and my Father is the husbandman. [2] Every branch in me that beareth not fruit he taketh away: and every *branch* that beareth fruit, he purgeth it, that it may bring forth more fruit. [3] Now ye are clean through the word which I have spoken unto you. [4] **Abide in me, and I in you**. As the branch cannot bear fruit of itself, except it abide in the vine; no more can ye, except ye abide in me. [5] I am the vine, ye *are* the branches: **He that abideth in me, and I in**

him, the same bringeth forth much fruit: for without me ye can do nothing. [6] If a man abide not in me, he is cast forth as a branch, and is withered; and men gather them, and cast *them* into the fire, and they are burned. [7] If ye **abide in me, and my words abide in you**, ye shall ask what ye will, and it shall be done unto you. [8] Herein is my Father glorified, that ye bear much fruit; **so shall ye be my disciples**" (John 15:1-8).

Being a disciple of Jesus involves a believer in *following* Jesus in His warfare against the forces of evil. Disciples understand their own frailties when it comes to battling against powers far greater than we can imagine. The believer's abiding in Christ and Christ's abiding in the believer is the only possible way the believer can win occasional victories in warring for the salvation of lost souls and their discipleship after their salvation.

Therefore, do not miss the connection of the warfare **by** faith **for** the faith – winning lost souls to Christ and making disciples. **You are the connecting link!** Your saved soul and sanctified life are the means through which Christ wages His war for lost souls. Your personal compromises regarding any issue of sin or false doctrine keeps Christ from being able to do what you have been saved for Him to do *through* you.

When this spiritual warfare vision of reality is a part of a person's everyday life, fighting the fight of faith will become a priority. Without this vision of reality, there really is no reality of personal faith and therefore the battles **by** faith **for** the faith are never fought.

Without abiding in Christ and Christ's abiding in the believer, these battles certainly cannot be won. It is in this arena that a missional vision must find its foundation, for, apart from this spiritual dynamic of holiness (separation from the world) and sanctification (separation unto God), missions (the "work of the ministry") is nothing but an operation in futility.

When we think in the reality of the spiritual and eternal, we are immediately transported into another real existence where miracles are commonplace, where there is no such thing as the impossible, and where the grace of God overwhelms any problem or difficulty that Satan might throw at us to get us off track.

When we think spiritually and eternally, we move into a real realm of existence where the Creator of Heaven and earth lives and reigns; a Kingdom of light and life; a place where power is unlimited, and dreams always become realities. Even though we must continue to live in this present, wicked, temporal world, we must work to keep our thinking and desires fixed on the spiritual and eternal.

Therefore, contending for the faith by living the faith has three objectives.

The first objective is to reveal the character and nature of God (glorify God) through rightly dividing the Word of truth and rightly living the Word of truth through the supernatural enabling of the indwelling Spirit of Christ (living by grace).

If the Word of God and its commands are corrupted or compromised to any degree, the believer will misrepresent the character and nature of God and enters, by the degree of corruption, into the realm of the blasphemy of God. Blasphemy is born out of an attitude of carelessness leading to disrespect of the character and nature of God.

The believer must take the failure in taking the responsibility of seriously and soberly rightly dividing the Word of Truth. This responsibility must be carefully and respectfully considered to ensure the righteous understanding and communicating of the character and nature of God. This failure is where compromise begins.

"[1] I therefore, the prisoner of the Lord, beseech you that ye walk worthy of the vocation wherewith ye are called, [2] With all lowliness and meekness, with longsuffering, forbearing one another in love; [3] **Endeavouring to keep the unity of the Spirit in the bond of peace.** [4] *There is* one body, and one Spirit, **even as ye are called** {*vocationally*} in one hope of your calling; [5] One Lord {*singular*}, one faith {*singular*}, one baptism {*singular*}, [6] One God {*singular*} and Father of all, who *is* above all, and through all, and in you all. [7] But unto **every one of us is given grace** {*supernatural enabling through the indwelling Spirit of Christ*} according to the measure of the gift of Christ. [8] Wherefore he saith, When he ascended up on high, he led captivity captive, and gave gifts unto men. [9] (Now that he ascended, what is it but that he also descended first into the lower parts of the earth? [10] He that descended is the same also that ascended up far above all heavens, that he might fill all things.)" (Ephesians 4:1-10).

The second objective of contending for the faith by living the faith is to be empowered by the indwelling Christ through the filling of His Spirit. We should be very careful not to disconnect the practical responsibilities of Ephesians 4:1-10 from the practical responsibilities of Ephesians 4:11-16.

"The faith" for which all believers are commanded to contend has the objective of "perfecting of the saints {*individually and corporately*}, for the work of the ministry." This objective is to be pursued vigorously and preeminently until "we all come in the unity of the faith." How can believer-priests contend for the faith if they have not been perfected (equipped or matured) in knowing and living the faith?

"[11] And he gave some, apostles; and some, prophets; and some, evangelists; and some, pastors and teachers; [12] For the perfecting of the saints, for the work of the ministry, for the edifying of the body of Christ: [13] Till we all come in the unity of the faith, and of the knowledge of the Son of God, unto a perfect man, unto the measure of the stature of the fulness of Christ: [14] That we *henceforth* be no more children, tossed to and fro, and carried about with every wind of doctrine, by the sleight of men, *and* cunning craftiness, whereby they lie in wait to deceive; [15] But **speaking the truth in love**, may grow up into him in all things, which is the head, *even* Christ: [16] **From whom** the whole body fitly joined together and compacted by that which every joint supplieth, according to the effectual working in the measure of every part, maketh increase of the body unto the edifying of itself in love" (Ephesians 4:11-16).

The third objective of contending for the faith by living the faith is found in Ephesians 4:14-16; "But speaking the truth in love, may grow up into him in all things, which is the head, *even* Christ."

The purpose for the existence and creation of every local church cannot be established or maintained if every believer-priest of which that local church is comprised is not perfected for the work of the ministry. Then, this "perfecting" involves that person in contending for the faith. Without this spiritual maturity, every local church is condemned to its own suicide.

Therefore, the *continuity* and *perpetuity* of any local church must be focused upon perfecting EVERY saint for the work of the ministry, which then involves those perfected believers in contending for the faith by living the faith. Knowing this without doing this is the most subtle of all self-deceptions and the most common of failures. The value the believer-priest puts upon the ruling "elder" is measured by the effort and enthusiasm investing in learning the "word and doctrine" being taught by God's gifted man to the local church.

"Let **the elders** {*term used to describe the office of an Israelite Sanhedrist*} **that rule well** {*preside or maintain*} be counted worthy of **double honour** {*remuneration*}, especially they who labour in the word and doctrine" (I Timothy 5:17).

The opposite of I Timothy 5:17 has become the norm. The compromising Church does not want to hear the whole counsel of God. The compromisers demand license and *easy listening* sermons that make no demands and bring no guilt.

The compromisers are soft and weak because they demand preachers who are soft and weak. These watered down, lukewarm compromisers will never contend for anything because they believe nothing with all their hearts, souls, and might. The justification for their hypocrisy is a false unity that has no qualifying criteria for unity.

"[1] I charge *thee* therefore before God, and the Lord Jesus Christ, **who shall judge the quick and the dead at his appearing and his kingdom;** [2] Preach the word; be instant in season, out of season; reprove, rebuke, exhort with all longsuffering and doctrine. [3] **For the time will come when they will not endure sound doctrine; but after their own lusts shall they heap to themselves teachers, having itching ears;** [4] And they shall turn away *their* ears from the truth, and shall be turned unto fables. [5] But watch thou in all things, endure afflictions, do the work of an evangelist, make full proof of thy ministry" (II Timothy 4:1-5).

The Oxymoron of *Compassionate Indifference*

The grand travesty against spiritual maturity is that most Christians live within one of two forms of *compassionate indifference.* In other words, most Christians fail to gain a practical balance between "speaking the truth in love" (Ephesians 4:15) and contending "for the faith."

Some have *compassion* for contending "for the faith" and *indifference* for those unwilling to believe. Thereby, through that failure, they are willing to throw away people and try to bully them into believing. Some have *compassion* for people and indifference for contending "for the faith."

Thereby, they compromise the truth at the destruction of the very people they seek to disciple. Both failures are equally perverse and ridiculous regardless of which side the focus of *compassion* and *indifference* falls. The outcome is equally devastating to the faithful longevity of local church.

Jude
Contending for the Faith
Chapter Three
"Crept in Unawares"

The objective of Jude's epistle is found in verse four in the words "For there are certain men crept in unawares." Of course, the place into which they have "crept" is local churches. There is an ever-increasing populace of those deceived. The natural course of things within the curse and the fall of humanity possessing a fallen and sinful nature is departure from "the faith" and towards selfish worldliness. **The deceived become deceivers because all men become evangelists to their own mindsets, no matter how wrong those mindsets become.** Although not all these corrupted evangelists are vocal in their man-centered philosophies, they certain corrupt by influence, example, and seduction by succumbing to their sinful lusts.

The evangelists of carnal seductions are certainly diligent in their efforts to corrupt. However, they require little effort or few enticements to their corruption because fallen sinners are already bent in the direction of those carnal enticements. Giving "diligence" to the proclamation of the need to be "born again" through faith in "the common salvation" requires a discerning and committed mindset willing to "contend for the faith."

Contending "for the faith" is the purpose for which "the faith which was once delivered unto the saints." To fail to be diligent in this purpose is unfaithfulness to this *responsibility* "once delivered unto the saints." Cultural corruption grows when there are more *sowers of weeds than mowers of weeds.* Theological and philosophical *weeds* grow fast and spread quickly where there are more people sowing them than those contending against them. The grand difficulty in mowing the weeds of theological and philosophical corruptions is taking care to convert the sowers of those weeds while still killing the weeds. **Weeds produce seeds.**

"³ Beloved, when I gave all diligence to write unto you of the common salvation, it was needful for me to write unto you, and exhort *you* that ye should earnestly contend for the faith which was once delivered unto the saints. ⁴ **For there are certain men crept**

in unawares, who were before of old ordained to this condemnation, ungodly men, turning the grace of our God into lasciviousness, and denying the only Lord God, and our Lord Jesus Christ" (Jude 3-4).

Theological and philosophical corruptions are like viruses that evolve and mutate. Just as soon as an immunity or vaccine is created to combat a virus, it evolves and mutates into something else needing a different vaccine or the development of a new immunity. Evolution and mutation describe the difficulty of the "diligence" necessary in combating the spread of false doctrines. Discernment in defining the evolution and mutation requires knowing the truth. The faithful will not discern degrees of darkness if not living in the light. Those overwhelmed with the beauty of the sunset will never differentiate between them and the sunrise. The former is a fading of the light. The latter increases the light. There is a difference. If one loves the darkness, he will long for the sunsets. If one loves the light, he will long for the "day star" rising in his heart (II Peter 1:19).

"Crept in Unawares"

How could this possibly happen in a local church that is grounded in the Word of God and involved in contending "for the faith"? This happens when congregational polity of the "body of Christ" fails to do the job ordained by her "Head" to do. Almost everyone understands that inviting guests into your home is not the same as making them residents. The membership of every local assembly is composed of people who became repentant sinners "born again" of the Spirit of Christ and began to become faithful disciples of Jesus Christ as testified to by water baptism. These three decisions are the first prerequisites to becoming members of the local assembly rather than guests.

1. Genuine and manifested repentance
2. Genuine and manifested conversion of the heart in the New Birth
3. Genuine and manifested proactive commitment to learning and living God's Word

Imagine a school yard full of little children and a man is seen sneaking around hiding behind the bushes near where they play. How would responsible adults respond to this rather precarious situation? This man has "crept in unawares" when no one responds with an appropriate response to the potential threat to the children. The man's presence might be innocent. "Crept in unawares" means the man's character and nature are UNKNOWN. Therefore, any threats are *unknown* ("unawares"). However, the adults present should be more concerned with the safety of those under their guardianship than with the possibility of offending the one who has "crept in unawares." **The point is that being "unawares" is gross negligence to the wards under their guardianship.**

The responsibility of guardianship in local church congregational polity is to be aware and become aware of the character and nature of every person attending the assembly. We should not assume they are horrible perverts, but neither should we assume they are moral giants without character flaws. There is a grand difference between being *concerned skeptics* and *cynical skeptics*. Being skeptical simply means we do not know the person's character and move forward with caution. However, within that skepticism, it is the goal of the mature saint to honestly evaluate and minister to the guest at whatever place that person is found to be.

Congregational polity understands that ministry to a guest in the assembly is allowing that person to influence and interact with other children on the playground in the process of their own discipleship. Therefore, doctrinal statements and understanding the structure of local church organization become essential. Formal membership to a local assembly of believers enrolls a person into the discipleship purpose and structure of how the process of discipleship is designed by God to work.

Formal membership is an agreement/covenant to work within the God designed structure in the process of one's own discipleship. Post-modern Christianity wants to remove most of the structure and accountability to merely increase the size of the crowd by allowing all the creeps in "unawares." This nonsense is completely irresponsible to God's designed stewardship ordained in local church membership.

False teachers do not begin as false teachers. False teachers begin as false converts, who then begin to teach false doctrines and corrupted philosophies by which they then live. The time to start contending "for the faith" is before the simple become converts to the false doctrines and corrupted philosophies of false teachers. Seldom do false teachers ever repent. They will oppose the truth until their death and eternal judgment. False teachers have occasionally repented but doing that is far from the norm. If a false teacher changes at all, he will merely reform his false doctrine and mutate into other "damnable heresies" (II Peter 2:1). Then they do their corrupting teaching surreptitiously ("privily" or secretively) and "unawares."

False teachers are Satan's *pied pipers*. Immature children will follow their enticing music with innocent disregard to where they are being led. Satan's *pied pipers* will lead the undiscerning to a destiny prepared for Satan and his other fallen angels. This is the ultimate destiny of false doctrine. Yet, they will create enormous destruction on their way to that destiny.

False doctrines lead people *astray* but *astray* is a long and painful journey. Those trafficking in false doctrines are Satan's human traffickers of souls to keep them within the prisons of death. The warning of Scripture about these people is quite graphic and purposefully so. The destiny of the damned is seldom considered, while enjoying "the pleasures of sin for a season" (Hebrews 10:25). Only those knowing the truth will know and heed the danger of the destiny of deception.

"[1] But there were false prophets **also** among the people, even as **there shall be false teachers** among you, **who privily shall bring in damnable heresies**, even denying the Lord that bought them, and **bring upon themselves swift destruction**. [2] And **many shall follow their pernicious ways**; by reason of whom the way of truth shall be evil spoken of. [3] And **through** {*in; covetousness is the medium of motivation in which they function*} **covetousness shall they with feigned** {*plastic, artificial and carefully manipulative molded*} **words make merchandise** {*buy and sell; people become the merchandise in which these deceivers trade*} **of you**: whose judgment now of a long time lingereth not, and **their damnation slumbereth not** {*they will eventually get what they have coming to them, but will do enormous damage to people on the way to their destiny*}" (II Peter 2:1-3).

False teachers must be confronted and then removed from the assembly BEFORE they make converts with their "damnable heresies." Their confrontation is calling them to immediately and publicly repent of their "damnable heresies" before they make a convert. This confrontation must be a firm and unified effort by all the formal members of the assembly. This must be done because after a convert has been made the *seed of the weed* has been sown and it will produce other *weed seeds*.

Weed seed **is all the** *weeds* **can produce.** These *weeds* are destined for the fire because they are good for nothing else. One cannot rescue *weeds*. *Weeds* must be confronted and converted to become something else by the grace of God. Contending "for the faith" is contending against *weeds* being able to produce more *weed seeds*. Contending "for the faith" happens by trying to convert *weeds* into being "born again" Ambassadors for Christ doing the "ministry of reconciliation (II Corinthians 5:17-21). **If they will not repent, they must be removed.**

Jude addresses this need to take action upon those that had "crept in unawares" in verses Jude 12-13. It is obvious from these few verses of Scripture that the emphasis is that these people are not what they appear to be.

"**¹² These are spots** {*rocks*} **in your feasts** {*rocks in food pose their own painful dangers*} of charity, when they feast with you {*they are in the assembly*}, feeding themselves without fear: **clouds** {*another simile*} *they are* without water, carried about of winds; **trees** {*another simile*} whose fruit withereth, without fruit, twice dead, plucked up by the roots; ¹³ **Raging waves of the sea** {*another simile*}, foaming out their own shame; **wandering stars** {*another simile*}, to whom is reserved the blackness of darkness for ever" (Jude 12-13).

What exactly was the problem with these creeps who had "crept in unawares. Jude tells us that these creeps were "ungodly men." They "were before of old ordained to this condemnation, **ungodly men,** turning the grace of our God into lasciviousness, and denying the only Lord God, and our Lord Jesus Christ" (Jude 4). Because they were "ungodly men" they turned grace enablement into grace permissiveness ("lasciviousness"). Thereby they denied Jesus

His Lordship or their lives by refusing to be subjects of His revealed will revealed in "the faith."

There is a foreordained judgment prescribed for this corruption. Although these particular men will receive this foreordained (*written beforehand*) judgment, the judgment is universally applicable to every similar failure to know the truth and live the truth.

The reason these men began to lead others astray is because they were reckless in the care of their own doctrines and practices. They cannot be rescued from the predestined judgment upon their offences until they repent and turn from those offenses.

However, the only hope they have of repenting and turning is listening to the very people they oppose with their false doctrines. The compassionate faithful must be able to communicate their compassion for the deceivers to bring them to repentance. They must do this without being pulled into the fires of judgment by being persuaded in some degree of compromise with the unfaithful. This is the warning of some of the last verses of Jude.

"²¹ Keep yourselves in the love of God, looking for the mercy of our Lord Jesus Christ unto eternal life. ²² And **of some** {*not all*} **have compassion**, making a difference: ²³ And **others** {again, *not all*} **save with fear, pulling *them* out of the fire**; hating even the garment spotted by the flesh" (Jude 21-23).

To persuade the student of his error is to rescue one. To persuade the false teacher of his error is to rescue multitudes. However, the struggle between wanting to see souls saved and discipled and keeping the local church pure of false doctrines and false believers, who tend to creep "in unawares," is constant, tedious, and never-ending. Everyone wants a garden, but no one wants to pull the weeds.

"Before of Old Ordained to This Condemnation"

"For there are certain men crept in unawares, who were before of old ordained to this condemnation, ungodly men, turning the grace of our God into lasciviousness, and denying the only Lord God, and our Lord Jesus Christ" (Jude 4).

God's prophetic revelation of those departing from the faith and corrupting others in that departure is an historical constant throughout Scriptural history. All sin and all false teachers will be judged. This judgment is foreordained by God as well as fore proclaimed by God. Every person, especially those that read the Scriptures, should understand that God hates "every false way" (Psalm 119:104 and 128). The word "condemnation" in Jude 4 is from the Greek word *kríma* (kree'-mah), which describes *a judicial decision in a court of law adjudicating a crime against God often translated judgment, which is the sentence assigned for a crime.*

Most people divide sins into levels of severity according to some highly subjective criteria. Murder and sexual offenses usually are at the top of their list with assault and thievery following. Seldom is teaching false doctrine ever even considered as one of the *cardinal sins*, which are lust, gluttony, greed, sloth, wrath, envy, and pride. These seven sins are often called *the seven deadly sins.*

Of course, there is no such list given in the Bible even though most of them are mentioned in one way or another. However, teaching false doctrine or leading people astray is not on the list or is ever considered a major sin by most people. The three prejudged sins listed in Jude 4 do not make anyone's list of *capital sins.*

Teaching false doctrine and leading people astray from godliness makes God's list. These failures are gross failures because they destroy whole generations of people and can keep people from genuine repentance and even from being "born again" through "the faith" correctly understood and applied. These failures are indiscriminately genocidal in nature. Their crime is compounded when we consider the place where the crime takes place - IN THE CHURCH. Secondly, the crime is compounded because it is committed secretly.

We might equate this gross corruption of godliness by "ungodly men" to putting poison in the treats provided at a daycare center. The words "crept in unawares" are translated from *pareisdýnō* (par-ice-doo'-no). The word is a composite of *pará* (par-ah') meaning *to come alongside, eis* (ice) meaning *to* or *purpose/direction,* and *dýnō* (doo'-no) meaning *to sink* or *take down.* The meaning therefore is to come alongside someone with purpose of *taking them down* or destruction.

This is what happens when "the faith" is destroyed or corrupted and why there must be an intensity in contending for "the faith." The failure is singular but with two outcomes that are equally heinous.

1. "Turning the grace of our God into lasciviousness"
2. Thereby "denying the only Lord God"
3. Thereby "denying . . . our Lord Jesus Christ"

The very nature of the word "turning" is heinous. "Turning" is translated from *metatíthēmi* (met-at-ith'-ay-mee). This too is a composite word of *metá* (met-ah'), meaning *accompaniment*, and *títhēmi* (tith'-ay-mee), meaning *to place* or *neutralize*. We might equate this to a rider on a horse joining a herd of cattle to turn them in another direction.

However, the destiny of that other direction is over a cliff to their death. The point is that the *metatíthēmi* (met-at-ith'-ay-mee) carries sinister connotations in the context. When the heart of the teacher is "ungodly" the destination will always be "ungodliness."

The target of this "turning" is focused upon "grace of our God." The new destiny is no longer *godliness* (*living like God wants us to live*) but is "into lasciviousness." The words "the grace of our God" are profoundly deep in there meaning. Therefore, they are profoundly complex. These types of truths are the easiest to corrupt because most new Christians do not understand complex terms totally outside of their normal life experience.

The words "the grace of our God" introduce the "born again" believer into a new supernatural spiritual dynamic of life providing to that believer the supernatural enabling of the indwelling Holy Spirit of Christ to live the life defined by the teachings of Jesus. Although when Jesus ascended into the light of God's eternal glory leaving believers in the darkness, He did not leave us alone in the darkness. He then sent His Spirit to the indwell every believer and to empower every believer who is willing to fully surrender their wills to the will of the indwelling, empowering Spirit of Christ. This is what the words "the grace of our God" means.

The words "the grace of our God" communicate the most intimate of personal relationships ever created or ever possible. These words define a permanent union with the Person of God whereby the very Life of God, His Spirit, now exists within the body of every "born again" person. The word "licentiousness" means shameless, promiscuous, and unbridled debauchery. This is living one's life without the responsibilities of staying within defined moral boundaries. This is permissiveness that constantly increases to the place where nothing is condemned, or nothing is condemning.

This "turning," or *change of direction*, from a heartfelt pursuit after godliness is gradual beginning with a change in heart/attitude about sin (unrepentance by degrees). This change of direction ("turning") is after salvation and aimed at the priority of the heart in its expression of love towards God.

***Godliness* is the all-consuming desire of the truly repentant.** Those involved in "turning" try to redefine *godliness*. *Godliness* is defined with specificity by "the faith." Therefore, contending "for the faith" is contending for what defines *godliness.*

"**¹⁵ If ye love me, keep my commandments.** ¹⁶ And I will pray the Father, and he shall give you another Comforter, that **he may abide with you for ever**; ¹⁷ *Even* the Spirit of truth; whom the world cannot receive, because it seeth him not, neither knoweth him: but ye know him; for **he dwelleth with you, and shall be in you**" (John 14:15-17).

"Ungodly men" are always trying to redefine *godliness* to justify their lowering the Biblical standards of holiness. Contextually, it is apparent that these "ungodly men" had "crept in unawares" into the local churches were taking some type of unauthorized positions of authority to which they were not ordained by the congregations of those local churches.

Therefore, Jude addresses the destiny of the ordination of their corruptions - "condemnation." These "ungodly men" were targeting the undiscipled simpletons in the local churches who were undiscerning about the complexities of living by the grace of God's indwelling enabling.

Obviously, living the Christ-life is impossible without the grace of God's enabling (John 15:5). This fact gives an open door to "ungodly men" to turn the heart of simpletons to permissiveness. This is what Paul addressed to believers in the opening verses of Romans chapter six.

"[1] **What shall we say then? Shall we continue in sin, that grace may abound?** [2] God forbid. How shall we, that are dead to sin, live any longer therein? [3] Know ye not, that so many of us as were {*Spirit*} baptized into Jesus Christ were {*Spirit*} baptized into his death? [4] Therefore we are buried with him by {*Spirit*} baptism into death: that **like as** {*exactly like*} Christ was raised up from the dead by the glory of the Father, **even so we also should walk in newness of life**" (Romans 6:1-4).

Since the gift of God's righteousness is solely gratuitous (gift of grace), there is no moral or ritual acts ("works") required from the believing sinner to be justified and "born again."

Therefore, the question then arises. Can the "born again" sinner continue living in slavery to his sin nature so that God's abounding graciousness may then superabound. The question exposes a complete misunderstanding of God's grace in saving the sinner. Saving grace becomes enabling grace within the "born again" believer's life through yielding to the indwelling Spirit of Christ.

The point here is that there is no excuse for living under slavery to one's fallen "old man" when that "old man" was "crucified with Christ" (Romans 6:6). "The faith" for which all believers are commanded to contend MUST include teaching the doctrine of God's enabling grace as believers pursue with their whole hearts unto godliness.

Every contact of God with the fallen human race is an act of His wondrous, abounding grace. The question of Romans 6:1 refers to the *infected* realm of the fall into sin. "Shall we continue {*living our lives*} in {*the realm of*} sin, that grace may abound?"

Or should we move our new lives into the realm of the *new creation* "in Christ" where "we have access by faith into this *new realm of* grace in which we stand" (Romans 5:2)? Just as we are saved by grace through faith, we must practically *move* our new lives "in Christ" into the realm of Grace "by faith" ("the just*ified* shall live by faith," Romans 1:17) to produce God-kind righteousness through our new lives "in Christ."

It is not enough to involve our physical bodies in an external form of obedience. There MUST BE a complete involvement of our beings spiritually, emotionally, and physically in this obedience. This is what *whole-heartedness* means. This answers the questions of Romans 6:1-3.

The essence of these questions is this, since the salvation of our souls from eternal separation from God is not dependent in any way on how we live, does that mean God does not care how we live? Are we free to live any way we want to live? The answer is simply, "God forbid." Peter addresses this in the first chapter of his second epistle as Peter foresees and addresses the pending departure from the faith.

"[1] Simon Peter, a servant and an apostle of Jesus Christ, to them that have obtained like precious faith with us through the righteousness of God and our Saviour Jesus Christ: [2] **Grace and peace be multiplied** unto you through the knowledge *{epignosis; intimate relational knowledge}* of God, and of Jesus our Lord, [3] According **as his divine power hath given unto us all things that** *pertain* **unto life and godliness**, through the knowledge of him that hath called us to glory and virtue: [4] Whereby are given unto us exceeding great and precious promises: that **by these ye <u>might be</u> partakers** *{sharers or associate}*, **of the divine nature**, having escaped the corruption that is in the world through lust" (II Peter 1:1-4).

Peter defines these deceivers in the second chapter of his second epistle, which description is very similar to what Jude describes.

"[1] But there were false prophets also among the people, even as **there shall be false teachers among you**, who **privily shall bring in damnable heresies**, even **denying the Lord that bought them**, and **bring upon themselves swift destruction**. [2] And many shall follow their pernicious ways; by reason of whom the way of truth shall be evil spoken of. [3] And through covetousness shall they with feigned words make merchandise of you: whose judgment now of a long time lingereth not, and their damnation slumbereth not" (II Peter 2:1-3).

"Denying the Only Lord God, and Our Lord Jesus Christ"

Grandville Sharp's Rule applies here. The words "only Lord God and our Lord Jesus Christ" all refer to Jesus as One. When there are two nouns, which are not proper names, which are describing a person, and the two nouns are connected by the word "and," and the first noun has the article ("the") while the second does not, both nouns are referring to the same person. The first noun refers to Jehovah and the second equates Jesus as Jehovah with the sovereign authority of Jehovah.

Therefore, to deny "our Lord Jesus Christ" is to deny His divine authority to define what is involved in *godliness*. Secondly, this redefining and denying of His authority denies that people will be judged by Him when they live outside of these parameters of *godliness*.

This removes fear of His judgment or fear of unfaithfulness. Ungodliness immediately moves a person outside of the boundaries of godliness and outside of the potential for grace-enabling and blessing. "Denying" is a contradiction of the divine and sovereign authority of Jesus to judge. "Denying" the Lordship of Jesus is to abnegate, reject, and/or refuse that authority. This is what the "ungodly men" (the *judge-not* crowd) do when they say *Jesus won't judge you for many of the things the legalists say are sinful.*

Paul addresses the issue of questionable practices in Romans chapter fourteen. Many people want *a list of do and don't things* to make it easy for them. The list would never end and may be completely wrong. The conclusion of Romans chapter fourteen gives one simple criterion for establishing permission when it comes to questionable practices (a statement often ignored by those teaching liberty or permissiveness).

"¹⁹ Let us therefore follow after the things which make for peace, and things wherewith one may edify another. ²⁰ **For meat destroy not the work of God**. All things indeed *are* pure; but *it is* evil for that man who eateth with offence. ²¹ *It is* good neither to eat flesh, nor to drink wine, nor *any thing* whereby thy brother stumbleth, or is offended, or is made weak. ²² Hast thou faith? have *it* to thyself before God. Happy *is* he that condemneth not himself in that thing which he alloweth. ²³ And **he that doubteth is damned if he eat**, because *he eateth* not of faith: for **whatsoever *is* not of faith is sin**" (Romans 14:19-23).

The point of Romans 14:23 "for whatsoever is not of faith is sin" is the clincher on the subject. If a person does not have clear Scriptural instruction, or a *mandate of permission* from God, then the practice "*is* not of faith" and "is sin." The "ungodly men" of Jude 4 want to take Romans chapter fourteen to give permission for anything God does not specifically forbid. **The opposite is the intent of the text.**

Jude
Contending for the Faith
Chapter Four
Warning Saints "in Remembrance"

Apostates had "crept in unawares" into the churches and were occupying the pulpits. However, apathetic believers were also occupying the pews. Certainly, both failures are deadly to any local church. The point of Jude verse five is that it was the saints in the pew who were being called to action in remembering the consequences of apostasy. God will not tolerate apostasy and departure from "the faith" to any degree.

It is clear from Jude verse five that the saints had forgotten that there are consequences when people lose their grip on "the faith." In Jude 5-7 God reminds the saints when He brought extreme and severe judgment upon apostasy when people and angels departed from what God commanded. **It is obvious that the reason these facts must be put into their memories is that they were being apathic and passive regarding their responsibility to "contend for the faith" that had been delivered into their guardianship.**

The reason these believers needed this warning is that the failure to "contend for the faith" was another form of departure from the faith. Most believers do not see their being passive about contending as unfaithfulness. The point being that God's inspired truths cannot be compromised to any degree. Compromising God's truth will bring judgment by an equal degree upon the compromisers.

"*5* **I will therefore put you in remembrance** {*to put these facts into the mind*}, though **ye once knew this**, how that the Lord, having saved the people out of the land of Egypt, **afterward destroyed them that believed not.** 6 And the angels which kept not their first estate, but left their own habitation, **he hath reserved in everlasting chains under darkness unto the judgment of the great day.** 7 Even as Sodom and Gomorrha, and the cities about them in like manner, giving themselves over to fornication, and going after strange flesh, **are set forth for an example, suffering the vengeance of eternal fire**" (Jude 5-7).

Believers are Put in Remembrance

God judges apostasy in time and apostates in eternity. We should not confuse these two types of judgment. There are degrees of chastisement upon believers and there are degrees of consequences upon the rejection of God's divine authority in unbelief. In Jude 5-7, we have both categories addressed.

The first reminder is the "mixed multitude" that were delivered out of Egypt by God's miraculous plagues. These people came out of Egypt professing to be believers because they saw the works of Jehovah in the plagues and in the parting of the Red Sea. They saw God produce water from the rock and tasted the manna from heaven. Yet, in spite of all these miracles, they could not believe that God could deliver the Promised Land to them when the spies brought back a report that essentially said *the enemy is greater than Jehovah.* For that departure from "the faith," all those over the age of twenty were condemned to die in the wilderness.

As is often the case, what God addresses in one epistle He expands upon in another. The epistle to the Hebrews expands upon what is addressed in Jude 5, which was the failure of the children of Israel at Kadesh-Barnea beginning in Hebrews chapter three and continuing through Hebrews chapter six.

The context of the epistle to the Hebrews is addressed to early Jews who has professed faith in Christ. The epistle to the Hebrews was written about A.D. 64 just before the destruction of the Temple in Jerusalem by Titus in A.D. 70.

This context addresses the issue of *departing* **from faith in the finished work of Christ and from the local church of the New Covenant to return to the practices of the Mosaic Covenant and the Temple order of the Levitical priesthood.** This hypothetical *departure* from the New Covenant to return to the Mosaic Covenant is hypothetically addressed as being equal to the "unbelief" (Hebrews 4:11) of the Jews in the wilderness at Kadesh-Barnea as recorded in Numbers 32:1-15. **This is equated to deserting Christ.**

"[12] Take heed, brethren, **lest there be in any of you an evil heart of unbelief, in departing from the living God.** [13] But exhort one another daily, while it is called To day; lest any of you be hardened through the deceitfulness of sin. [14] For we are made partakers of Christ, if we hold the beginning of our confidence stedfast unto the end; [15] While it is said, To day if ye will hear his voice, **harden not your hearts, as in the provocation.** [16] For some, when they had heard**, did provoke**: howbeit not all that came out of Egypt by Moses. [17] But with whom was he grieved forty years? *was it* **not with them that had sinned, whose carcases fell in the wilderness?** [18] And to whom sware he that they should not enter into his rest, but **to them that believed not?** [19] So we see that they could not enter in because of unbelief" (Hebrews 3:12-19).

There are six warnings given in the epistle to the Hebrews about departing from "the faith." Every Christian would be wise to become familiar with these six warning.

The first warning is found in Hebrews 2:3.

"How shall we escape**, if we neglect so great salvation**; which at the first began to be spoken by the Lord, and was confirmed unto us by them that heard *him* . . . ?"

This warning is both simple and clear. The answer is simple. In short, the unbeliever **will not** escape the judgment of God because he will die in his sins.

"See that ye refuse not him that speaketh. For if they escaped not who refused him that spake on earth, much more *shall not* we *escape*, **if we turn away** {*return to the Mosaic Covenant incompleteness to to abandon New Covenant completeness in Christ, Colossians 2:10*} from him that *speaketh* from heaven" (Hebrews 12:25).

Hebrews 2:3 warns the hypothetical individual who intellectually *believes* in Jesus Christ but has never had a *conversion in his heart.* He has **never been** spiritually reborn.

"And said, Verily I say unto you, **Except ye be converted**, and become as little children, ye shall not enter into the kingdom of heaven" (Matthew 18:3).

"[15] That whosoever believeth in him should not perish, but have eternal life. [16] For God so loved the world, that he gave his only begotten Son, that whosoever believeth in him should not perish, but have everlasting life. [17] For God sent not his Son into the world to condemn the world; but that the world through him might be saved. [18] **He that believeth on him is not condemned: but he that believeth not is condemned already**, because he hath not believed in the name of the only begotten Son of God" (John 3:15-18).

"[8] But what saith it? The word is nigh thee, *even* in thy mouth, and in thy heart: that is, the word of faith, which we preach; [9] That if thou shalt confess with thy mouth the Lord Jesus, and **shalt believe in thine heart** that God hath raised him from the dead, thou shalt be saved. [10] For **with the heart** man believeth unto righteousness; and **with the mouth** confession is made unto salvation. [11] For the scripture saith, Whosoever believeth on him **shall not be ashamed**. [12] For there is no difference between the Jew and the Greek: for the same Lord over all is rich unto all that call upon him. [13] For **whosoever shall call upon the name of the Lord shall be saved**" (Romans 10:8-13).

The second warning is found in Hebrews 3:6.

"But Christ as a son over his own house; whose house are we, **if we hold fast the confidence and the rejoicing of the hope firm unto the end**."

This verse is not a warning about losing our salvation. It is telling us that only those truly "born again" of the Spirit and only those who are in Jesus Christ, and He in them, will be able to "hold fast." The "house" that the Son is over (ruler of) is the *body of Christ,* the Church. Eternally securing the believer is the work of God. If a person is saved, he is eternally secure in that position and preserved by God. **The warning relates to the professing Christian whose religious practices contradict a professed faith in a finished work of redemption.**

"[27] My sheep hear my voice, and I know them, and they follow me: [28] And I give unto them eternal life; and **they shall never perish, neither shall any *man* pluck them out of my hand.** [29] My Father, which gave *them* me, is greater than all; and **no *man* is able to pluck *them* out of my Father's hand.** [30] I and *my* Father are one" (John 10:27-30).

The truly "born again" believer has *assurance* that he has been saved by the evidence of a changed life.

"[21] He that hath my commandments, **and keepeth them**, he it is that loveth me: and he that loveth me shall be loved of my Father, and I will love him, and will manifest myself to him. [22] Judas saith unto him, not Iscariot, Lord, how is it that thou wilt manifest thyself unto us, and not unto the world? [23] Jesus answered and said unto him, **If a man love me, he will keep my words: and my Father will love him, and we will come unto him, and make our abode with him.** [24] He that **loveth me not keepeth not my sayings**: and the word which ye hear is not mine, but the Father's which sent me" (John 14:21-24).

"[14] We know that we have **passed from death unto life, because we love the brethren.** He that loveth not *his* brother abideth in death. [15] Whosoever hateth his brother is a murderer: and ye know that no murderer hath eternal life abiding in him. [16] Hereby perceive we the love *of God*, because he laid down his life for us: and **we ought to lay down *our* lives for the brethren.** [17] But whoso hath this world's good, and seeth his brother have need, and shutteth up his bowels *of compassion* from him, how dwelleth the love of God in him? [18] My little children, **let us not love in word, neither in tongue; but in deed and in truth.** [19] And **hereby we know** that we are of the truth, and shall assure our hearts before him" (I John 3:14-19).

There is a great deal of self-deception when it comes to *orthodoxy* that is absent of *orthopraxy* and *orthopathy*. This self-deception is what I John 3:14-19 addresses and is an equally heinous form of departure from "the faith." To claim orthodoxy without *orthopraxy* and *orthopathy* is serious self-deception that is a contradiction against "the faith."

"Therefore **if any man** *be* **in Christ**, *he is* a new creature: old things are passed away; behold, all things are become new" (II Corinthians 5:17).

The third warning is in Hebrews 3:14.

"For we are made partakers of Christ, **if we hold the beginning of our confidcncc stedfast unto the end.**"

Again, this does not refer to losing, keeping, or earning one's salvation. **Steadfastness in New Covenant doctrine is proof that salvation is real.** Only those truly *in* Jesus Christ, as manifested by New Covenant practices, are those who will be "steadfast unto the end."

One cannot revert to the practices of apostate Judaism in their trust in religious rituals and keeping the Law and still profess to steadfastly believe in salvation by grace alone through faith alone in Christ alone. Neither can a person continue any religious practice, even if it comes under a banner of *Christianity*, which denies a finished work of redemption.

The context of looking at the warnings in the epistle to the Hebrews is addressing the "common salvation" and "the faith" for which every believer/priest is commanded to contended in Jude 3. Again, to reiterate, "the faith" is not a multiple-choice issue. As Ephesians 4:5 says, there is "one faith."

The epistle to the Hebrews addresses the issue that a true believer cannot be both a Mosaic Covenant practitioner and a New Covenant practitioner. To return to the Mosaic Covent practices after professing faith in Christ and the New Covenant is a denial of both the "finished" sacrifice of Christ and the priesthood of all believers in the New Covenant. The fourth warning is found in Hebrews 6:4-6.

The fourth warning is in Hebrews 6:4-6.

"⁴ For *it is* impossible for those who were once enlightened, and have tasted of the heavenly gift, and were made partakers of the

Holy Ghost, [5] And have tasted the good word of God, and the powers of the world to come, [6] **If they shall fall away** {*context is to return to Mosaic Covenant practices*}, to renew them again unto repentance; seeing they crucify to themselves the Son of God afresh, and put *him* to an open shame."

These verses are written to the person who has professed to trust Christ and whose *religious practices contradict* New Covenant doctrine regarding His finished work and a complete salvation. Hebrews 6:4 says they were "once enlightened." It does not say that they believed. **The epistle to the Hebrews hypothetically addresses those considering returning to the Mosaic Covenant as hypothetically lost.** Wuest's *Word Studies in the Greek New Testament* makes these interesting remarks on this portion of Scripture:

"In connection with this solemn warning, the writer reminds these Hebrews of all that a loving God had done for them. They were once enlightened. The word translated 'once' is literally 'once for all,' and is used of that which is so done as to be of perpetual validity, and never needs repetition. That means that as these Hebrews listened to the message of the New Testament, the Holy Spirit enlightened their minds and hearts to clearly understand it. **The work of the Spirit with reference to their understanding of New Testament truth had been so thorough that it needed never to be repeated for the purpose of making the truth clear to them. These Hebrews had understood these issues perfectly.** The type was set aside for the reality, the First Testament for the New. They were enlightened as every sinner is enlightened who comes under the hearing of God's Word. But as the unsaved in an evangelistic meeting today clearly understand the message of salvation but sometimes refuse the light and turn back into the darkness of sin and continued unbelief, **so these Hebrews were in danger of doing a like thing.**

They had tasted of the heavenly gift, and in such a way as to give them a distinct impression of its character and quality, for the words 'once for all' qualify this word also. **These Hebrews were like the spies at Kadesh-Barnea who saw the land and had the very fruit in their hands, and yet turned back (4:1-**

13). One of **the pre-salvation ministries of the Spirit** is to enable the unsaved who come under the hearing of the gospel, to have a certain appreciation of the blessedness of salvation. He equips them with a spiritual sense of taste with reference to the things of God. Many a sinner has been buoyed up by the message of the evangelist, has had stirrings in his bosom, has had a pleasant reaction towards the truth, and **yet when the decision time came has said, 'The world is too much with us' and has turned back into sin."**[6]

Instead of receiving the finished work of Christ once and for all, this hypothetical *professor* of Christ wants to re-crucify the Lamb each time he sins. Understanding the meaning of this warning is essential to understanding the central purpose of this epistle to the Hebrews.

The fifth warning is found in Hebrews 10:24-27.

"[24] And let us consider one another to provoke unto love and to good works: [25] **Not forsaking the assembling of ourselves together** {*not forsaking the church assembly for the Temple*}, as the manner of some *is*; but exhorting *one another*: and so much the more, as ye see the day approaching. [26] For if we sin wilfully after that we have received the knowledge of the truth, there remaineth no more sacrifice for sins, [27] But a certain fearful looking for of judgment and fiery indignation, which shall devour the adversaries."

This warning is to the professing Christian who has "received the knowledge of the truth" (he has not received Christ, only the *knowledge*), but when he sins, he thinks he must return to abrogated Temple sacrifices and religious rituals to be forgiven. **In fact, what he is doing is denying New Covenant doctrine regarding the finished work of Christ.** Instead of finding expected forgiveness in offering an animal as a sacrifice for his sins, he will find God's "judgment" and not mercy for there is "no more offering for sin" (Hebrews 10:18) other than the finished sacrifice of Christ. To trust in anything other than

---

[6] **Wuest's Word Studies in the Greek New Testament**, vol. 2 pages 114-116.

what Christ has already done is to deny the sufficiency of Christ's sacrifice.

The sixth warning is found in Hebrews 12:25-26.

"^{25} See that ye refuse not him that speaketh. For if they escaped not who refused him that spake on earth, much more *shall not* we *escape*, **if we turn away from him that** *speaketh* **from heaven**: ^{26} Whose voice then shook the earth: but now he hath promised, saying, Yet once more I shake not the earth only, but also heaven."

Here we have the final warning and the answer to the question of Hebrews 2:3. The answer is "they escape not." Again, context demands that we understand the *turning* away warning to be returning to the abrogated Mosaic Covenant thereby departing from the New Covenant. To refuse to receive Christ and confess him before men is to bring judgment upon oneself. These people resultantly will not escape. Even those that may appear religious, God looks on the inner man and the false theology behind their religious practices that deny the finished work of Jesus Christ. The judgment is sure, and the judgment is just.

"^{1} **Stand fast** therefore in the liberty wherewith Christ hath made us free, and be not entangled again with **the yoke of bondage**. ^{2} Behold, I Paul say unto you, that if ye be circumcised, **Christ shall profit you nothing**. ^{3} For I testify again to every man that is circumcised, that he is a debtor to do the whole law. ^{4} **Christ is become of no effect unto you, whosoever of you are justified by the law; ye are fallen from grace.** ^{5} For we through the Spirit wait for the hope of righteousness by faith. ^{6} For in Jesus Christ neither circumcision availeth any thing, nor uncircumcision; but faith which worketh by love. ^{7} Ye did run well; who did hinder you that ye should not obey the truth? ^{8} This persuasion *cometh* not of him that calleth you. ^{9} **A little leaven leaveneth the whole lump**" (Galatians 5:1-9).

It is critically important to always maintain the differences between *spiritual unity* and a *spirit of unity*. *Spiritual unity* cannot be had apart from "unity of the Spirit" in right doctrine. The *spirit of unity* demands no such criterion. However, care must be taken in dealing with these differences lest the local church is destroyed by the differences.

These differences must be addressed, but they must be done as skillfully and carefully as a surgeon with his scalpel. **We must always be consciously aware that someone's eternal soul may be in our care as we deal with corruptions of "the faith" and the "common salvation."**

We will not help anyone by bulldozing them over the cliff by responding to hardheartedness by being hardhearted. When dealing with people confused by legalism and false doctrines about salvation, always treat them with the gentleness given to a lost person. There is no room for trying bully someone into getting saved. Be gentle!

"But if ye bite and devour one another, take heed that ye be not consumed one of another" (Galatians 5:15).

Since those still trusting in the religious rituals of the Law had come in and divided the Church, Paul provides an analysis of character as a means of defining individuals who are genuinely born again, and walking yielded to the control of the Holy Spirit (Galatians 5:16-26). Obviously from the context of the Galatians' epistle, there were many people in these churches who were being led astray by this false teaching.

In Galatians chapter six, Paul instructs true believers to seek to restore those who are "overtaken in a fault" (6:1). He also taught them their responsibility in taking care of the physical needs of their pastor (vs. 6). He teaches the responsibilities of the brotherhood of believers using the metaphor of sowing and reaping. **If we sow discord, we reap discord.** If we sow "good" in the lives of one another, we will reap the same.

"[6] Let him that is taught in the word communicate unto him that teacheth in all good things. [7] Be not deceived; God is not mocked: **for whatsoever a man soweth, that shall he also reap.** [8] For he that soweth to his flesh shall of the flesh reap corruption; but he that soweth to the Spirit shall of the Spirit reap life everlasting. [9] And let us not be weary in well doing: for in due season we shall reap, if we faint not. [10] As we have therefore opportunity, **let us do good unto all men, especially unto them who are of the household of faith**" (Galatians 6:6-10).

In Galatians 6:11-13, Paul warns about those teachers whose goal in life is to make *trophies* out of those who will follow their false teaching. "That they may glory in your flesh" (Galatians 6:13) is getting people to *follow them* in the practice of religious rituals. The only thing worth glorying in is a *new creature* (Galatians 6:15) of the life of a believer saved "by grace through faith."

Uniquely, he qualifies his salutation blessing only to those who "walk according to this rule" of dividing between Law and Grace while seeking God's mercy upon the Judaizers.

"[15] For in Christ Jesus neither circumcision availeth **any thing**, nor uncircumcision, but **a new creature**. [16] And **as many as walk according to this rule**, peace be on them, and mercy, and upon the Israel of God" (Galatians 6:15-16).

How do we know that the things addressed in the epistles to the Galatians and Hebrews are some of things for which all believers are to "earnestly contend" (Jude 3-4)? Because these two epistles address the corruptions for which Paul contended and of which were the common departure from the "common salvation."

It is to this departure into unbelief that Jude addresses in the warning "having saved the people out of the land of Egypt, afterward destroyed them that believed not" (Jude 5). This warning addresses the issue of false faith, which really is unbelief.

Subjective faith says God accepts all types of faith without any doctrinal specificity. The is the so-called faith propagated by Ecumenicism and her harlot sister Pluralism. Objective faith says God only accepts faith that is according to His specifications and according to understanding God's Word rightly divided. Every person gets to "divide" the Scriptures for himself, but **God grades the papers.**

God gives two more exemplary warnings in Jude beyond those Jews and the "mixed multitude" that came out of Egypt, but who died in the wilderness because of unbelief (Hebrews 4:6).

What was intended to be a *victory march* into the Promised Land became a thirty-eight year long funeral processional where every person over the age of twenty died in the wilderness. Fallen angels and city-states that rejected His moral laws regarding human sexuality are also warned.

"Angels which kept not their first estate" *{order or rank of precedence}* **Jude 6**

God is consistent in judging both humans and angels. One-third of the angelic host rejected God's sovereign appointment to their being His servants to humanity. Being humanity's servants was "their first estate." Angels rebelled against God's sovereign will and against God's assigned ranking in His dominion over His creation. The first warning in Jude 5 is about the consequences of **unbelief**. This second warning in Jude 6 is about **rebellion**. This warning ensures that even spiritual beings do not escape God's justice when they rebel against His divine order.

"For if God spared not the angels that sinned, but cast *them* down to hell, and delivered *them* into chains of darkness, **to be reserved** unto judgment;" (II Peter 2:4).

The point of the warning is that the angels that rebelled against the *rank* or *order* assigned to them by God as subservient to humanity lost even the rank to which God had assigned them. These angels fell from God's grace into God's condemnation to be eternally separated from Him in a place called "hell." Of course, the warning then extends to the heretics that had "crept in unawares" and the faithful believers' responsibility to warn the heretics of both their unbelief from the first warning and their rebellion against God's sovereignty in the second warning.

No one should be allowed to use this text to support the idea that someone could lose salvation by rebellion. Just like Adam and Eve in their fall, the fallen angels never lost salvation because they never had salvation. Secondly, fallen angels cannot be redeemed even if they believe and trust in Jesus and His finished redemption. This is the point of the statement in II Peter 2:4; "to be reserved unto judgment."

There is no hope for their condemnation to ever be corrected. Hell was created for them and is a place reserved for their eternal separation from God for they are eternal and unrepentant rebels. Their rebellion believes God was unjust in assigning them rank inferior to humans and their sin was rebellion against God by deceiving Eve and tempting Adam to disobey using Adam's love for Eve against him.

Paul extends the warning of maintaining God's order of assigned rank in I Timothy 2:11-14. This warning is to women. Although **there is no extension of eternal condemnation for failure,** there is the warning of the eternal consequences that have **already resulted** in the failure and the fall of all humanity into sin and the seminal inheritance of a sin nature from Adam upon all his descendants.

"[11] Let the woman learn in silence with all subjection. [12] But I suffer not a woman to teach, nor to usurp authority over the man, but to be in silence. [13] For Adam was first formed, then Eve. [14] And Adam was not deceived, but the woman being deceived was in the transgression" (I Timothy 2:11-14).

"[8] But God commendeth his love toward us, in that, while we were yet sinners, Christ died for us. [9] **Much more then, being now justified by his blood**, we shall be saved from wrath through him. [10] For if, when we were enemies, we were reconciled to God by the death of his Son, much more, being reconciled, we shall be saved by his life. [11] And not only *so*, but we also joy in God through our Lord Jesus Christ, by whom we have now received the atonement. [12] Wherefore, as by one man sin entered into the world, and death by sin; and so death passed upon all men, for that all have sinned:" (Romans 5:8-12).

God has no such propensity for the salvation of fallen angels as described in Romans 5:8. Angels have already been "delivered *them* into chains of darkness, **to be reserved** unto judgment;" (II Peter 2:4). Angels cannot be redeemed. This is the warning to the apostates. There is a time when God gives sinners over to a reprobate mind and where His operations of grace in their lives cease and their rebellious choices seal their eternal destinies.

Reprobates are like fallen angels. People refusing to repent reach a point when God gives them over to their reprobate thinking

whereby, they try to justify their own rebellion. There is a progressive digression of hardening against faith in God and against God's conviction upon their hearts found in Romans chapter one.

"28 And even as they did not like to retain God in *their* knowledge, God gave them over to a reprobate mind, to do those things which are not convenient; 29 Being filled with all unrighteousness, fornication, wickedness, covetousness, maliciousness; full of envy, murder, debate, deceit, malignity; whisperers, 30 Backbiters, haters of God, despiteful, proud, boasters, inventors of evil things, disobedient to parents, 31 Without understanding, covenantbreakers, without natural affection, implacable, unmerciful: 32 Who **knowing the judgment of God**, that they which commit such things are worthy of death, not only do the same, but have pleasure in them that do them" (Romans 1:28-32).

God's Three Responses to Lost Mankind's Denial of His Existence (Romans 1:24-32)

1. Given up to uncleanness (1:24)
2. Given up to vile affections (1:26)
3. Given over to a reprobate mind (1:28)

Egypt's Sun *god* Ra was believed to be the *Father* of all *gods*. Ra was Egypt's primary *god*. In God's plagues upon Egypt, He used darkness to show Pharaoh the reality of his unbelief in the true God. Even though Pharaoh believed in Ra and sacrificed to Ra, that false belief was still considered unbelief by God.

The Egyptians, like most pagan nations of ancient times, believed in *Henotheism*. This simply means that some *gods* were considered more powerful than other *gods*. If a nation was victorious over another nation in war, the victorious nation's *god* was superior to the other nation's *god*. The victorious nation would than add the weaker *god* to their pantheon of *gods*. In doing so, the more nations they conquered, the more *gods* they collected and the more powerful they became. Each of the ten plagues was against one of the false *gods* of Egypt. The ninth plague was against the Sun *god* Ra.

Spiritually blind people are almost completely ignorant of Who God is or what He is like. Spiritually blind people do not know they live in the darkness of their own ignorance. They have never known anything but that darkness. In fact, they think living in that darkness is normal. To turn them from the darkness, God must bring a depth of spiritual darkness upon them so severe it can be felt.

"And the LORD said unto Moses, Stretch out thine hand toward heaven, that there may be darkness over the land of Egypt, even darkness *which* may be felt" (Exodus 10:21).

"**[10] Such as sit in darkness and in the shadow of death, *being* bound in affliction and iron**; [11] **Because** they rebelled against the words of God, and contemned the counsel of the most High: [12] Therefore he brought down their heart with labour; they fell down, and *there was* none to help. [13] Then they cried unto the LORD in their trouble, *and* he saved them out of their distresses. [14] He brought them out of darkness and the shadow of death, and brake their bands in sunder. [15] Oh that *men* would praise the LORD *for* his goodness, and *for* his wonderful works to the children of men! [16] For he hath broken the gates of brass, and cut the bars of iron in sunder" (Psalm 107:10-16).

Romans 1:28-32 is the last area in this digression towards reprobation. God wants to turn those who reject His truths and His existence from their chosen pathway of sin. In this last digression, this person's life is filled with the consequences of living their lives in selfish and carnal pursuits for self-fulfillment.

God loves all men too much to allow them to continue such a pathway without doing what is necessary to help them see the hopelessness of it all. The only way to do that is to allow the misery of their choices to become the reality of their existence. Therefore, He foretells what will "come to pass" from these choices of the free will "before they spring forth."

"[5] Thus saith God the LORD, he that created the heavens, and stretched them out; he that spread forth the earth, and that which cometh out of it; he that giveth breath unto the people upon it, and spirit to them that walk therein: [6] I the LORD have called thee in righteousness, and will hold thine hand, and will keep thee, and give thee for a covenant of the people, for a light of the

Gentiles; [7] To open the blind eyes, to bring out the prisoners from the prison, *and* them that sit in darkness out of the prison house. [8] I *am* the LORD: that *is* my name: and my glory will I not give to another, neither my praise to graven images. [9] **Behold, the former things are come to pass,** and new things do I declare: before they spring forth I tell you of them" (Isaiah 42:5-9).

The Paradox of *Blender Theology*

The lack of discernment and unwillingness to "mark" someone as heretical has created a kind of *pseudo-Christianity* that accepts everything and believes very little, if anything, for which it is willing to contend. **We must remember that Luther and Calvin were strong separatists.** The difference between Biblical Christians and men like Luther and Calvin is that the Biblical Christians do not want those that disagree with them killed. There is a vast difference between marking heretics and killing them.

There is a vast difference between *Systematic Theology* and *Systemic Theology*. *Systematic Theology* is the outcome of inductive study of the Bible. *Systemic theology* comes from studying a *system* of theology like Augustinianism, Lutheranism, Calvinism, Methodism, etc. *Systemic Theology* is by its very nature *eisegetical* and *deductive* rather *exegetical* and *inductive*.

Any person having been told what the Bible says before reading the Bible tends to read into the text what he already believes it says. This is presuppositionalism and is what defines *Systemic Theology*. *Systemic Theology* reads the presuppositions of the *system* into the Bible.

Having friends that disagree with what the Bible teaches (*heretics*) is where friendship is really measured. Friends are patient with one another, but that does not mean they avoid any conversation about the things with which they disagree just to maintain a false kind of unity and peace with one another.

Having a discussion and conversation about areas of the Bible with people must begin with an agreement that those in the conversation will actually listen to one another and consider what the other person is saying. Hearing and listening are as much a part of a learning/teaching conversation as is the speaking part.

Finding out exactly what others in the conversation believe and why they believe that (from where they got their beliefs) is integral to the conversation. However, having these conversations is not for theological novices or undiscipled *babes in Christ*. This is lack of listening and understanding was the reason the Hebrew believers addressed in the epistle to the Hebrews were so easily being drawn back to the Mosaic Covenant.

"[10] {*Jesus*} Called of God an high priest after the order of Melchisedec. [11] Of whom we have many things to say, and **hard to be uttered, seeing ye are dull of hearing**. [12] For **when for the time ye ought to be teachers**, ye have need that one teach you again which *be* **the first principles of the oracles of God**; and are become such as have need of milk, and not of strong meat. [13] For **every one that useth milk** *is* **unskilful in the word of righteousness**: for he is a babe. [14] But strong meat belongeth to them that are of **full age** {*téleios; fully matured, i.e., discipled*}, *even* those who by reason of use **have their senses** {*judgment or conscience*} exercised **to discern** {*to be able to separate or judge*} both good and evil" (Hebrews 5:10-14).

Eventually every person must do as the Apostle Paul commands in Romans 16:17, "Now I beseech you, brethren, mark them which cause divisions and offences **contrary to the doctrine** which ye have learned; and avoid them." **The unwillingness to publicly "mark" heretics reveals a false loyalty to them AND a false loyalty to Christ and "the faith."**

This is *exercised discernment* as Hebrews 5:14 says. A main characteristic of New Evangelicals is that they want to be kind without ever marking heretics. This practice is foolish, and it exists nowhere in the epistles or in Church history until the 1800's. In fact, the opposite is true.

John Ashbrook once said, "You cannot preserve a position without crusading for it."[7] The fallacy of Ecumenicalism and its major propagator in New Evangelicalism is this abomination of *theological neutralism*, the *abdication of theological dogmatism*, and the *unwillingness to "mark" heretics* thereby contending "for the faith which was once delivered unto the saints" (Jude 4).

---

[7] Ashbrook, John. **New Neutralism: Exposing the Grey of Compromise**, 1992.

The false dynamic of *theological conversation* without *critical delineation* has declined into a *Blender Theology* that is absent of true debate and a kind of *dialogue* that is absent of *dogmatism*.

Many Christians, especially Evangelicals and New Evangelicals, think that if most Christians really, really want revival that God will turn the hearts of the rebels back to Him. God does not override the human freewill.

Yes, revival always begins with true Christians, but it does not spread into hearts of rebels and unbelievers through social media statements. These intermittent conversations that never unequivocally present the Gospel of Jesus Christ nor demand a correct Biblical response (Romans 10:1-13). A Biblical response begins with repentance of sin and "dead works" resulting in sinners being "born again" whereby their spiritual transformation begins.

It is legitimate to question the genuineness of the salvation profession of most Evangelicals, New Evangelicals, and Emergents with their watered down *Easy Believism*, *Only Believism*, and Ecumenical compromises of the doctrine of salvation.

Then there are others in the so-called *Fundamentalism camp* that propose a salvation decision without repentance or *Quick Prayerism*. These are all rebels against God's declared responses to the Gospel of Jesus Christ. They, just like rebel angels, will argue for and justify their false positions until the day they discover themselves in the torments of the fires of hell.

Can anyone honestly think that God will bring revival to the United States of America or to the nations of the world without their repentance of their indorsement of the millions of murders of innocent babies in their mother's wombs. Do we honestly think God will revive nations that openly shake their rebellious fists in the face of a holy God because He will not compromise His will regarding purity of human sexuality?

The corruptions of the purity of human sexuality begin with heterosexual transgression into fornication and adultery long before they transgress into the sins of homosexuality, lesbianism, sexual child trafficking, and bestiality. Can we really convince ourselves that God will revive nations without those nations turning from these abominations?

These corruptions and deviations from God's commands have

progressed beyond individual transgressions to national transgressions being accepted and even endorsed by the masses. This is mantra of the child that was birthed into the rebellious 1960's culture of *sex, drugs, and rock and roll,* now grown into rebellious adulthood of unbelief and *postmodern thinking* (accept nothing; question everything). This *rebellious spirit* defines this *New Enlightenment* era in which we live.

The exemplary warning of the rebel angels who refused to repent of their rebellion against God's assigned "first estate" (Jude 6) is about the surety of their judgement because of their refusal to repent of what they whole heartedly consider to be a correct decision. This is the same spirit of the *abortion rights activists* and the *homosexual rights activists*. II Chronicles 7:14 does not apply to these people because they are not God's people in the first place.

II Chronicles 7:14 is a promise to the nation of Israel and the faithful of that nation. However, according to this text, God would not bring revival even to His own chosen nation without their genuine repentance and turning. The United States of America is not any form of the falsehood called *British Israelism* and Washington D.C. is not the *New Jerusalem.*

"If **my people, which are called by my name**, shall humble themselves, and pray, and seek my face, and turn from their wicked ways; then will I hear from heaven, and will forgive their sin, and will heal their land" (II Chronicles 7:14).

It would be much wiser to apply the warnings of Romans 1:28-32 to the world's ever-growing atrocities against the moral character of a holy God. This warning applies to those with the dominant characteristic of unbelief and its outcomes. Those who deny God's existence are given over to a reprobate mind.

This refers to the person who has gotten so far away from truth and his conscience that he tries to mentally erase the very idea of God from his *psyche*. Apart from knowledge of the rightly divided "word of truth," the human conscience cannot work as God designed it. Therefore, both ignorance and heresy corrupt the human conscience.

"Reprobate" is from the Greek word *adokimos* (ad-ok'-ee-mos) meaning that which *does not prove itself for its intended purposes*. I think the best English word reflecting the idea behind "reprobate" from the context of Romans 1:28 is the word *unconscionable.*

Unconscionable means not guided or restrained by conscience, therefore excessive or immoderate in practices. This borders on *psychopathy* usually move quickly into *anarchy.*

The word "mind" is translated from the Greek word *nous* (nooce) referring to the mind and its ability to perceive and understand so it can be enabled to make the correct judgments. All five gates of his body (sight, touch, hearing, taste, and smell) are perverted in their ability to make right judgments.

All five gates of his soul (*psyche*: imagination, reason, memory, conscience, and affections) are perverted in their ability to make the right judgments. When the will (the mind) acts upon the everyday judgment calls necessary for an ordered life, the person with a "reprobate mind" will almost always make a choice that takes him deeper and deeper into the darkness of this world. Once God gives him over to this reprobation of his mind, his judgments in everyday life will result in the things listed in Romans 1:29-31.

When God says, "they did not like to retain God in their knowledge," He is referring to that realm of education the secular world calls *knowledge*. Not wanting God in 'knowledge" means they want Him out of *education*.

The word "retain" is from the Greek word *echo* (ekh'-o) meaning here *to hold as a possession of the mind*. In other words, **they totally reject the truth of God's existence and wipe even the possibility of His existence from their minds.** As a result, they totally reject any truth which is proposed to originate with God.

The Pathology of Reprobation

Since imprinting the absolutes of God's truth on the *psyche* is the only way a functioning conscience can make correct judgments, this person is "given over" to a life without a conscience. This depraved reasoning ("reprobate mind") will lead this person "to do those things which are not convenient" (Romans 1:28). The word "convenient" is from the Greek word *katheko* (kath-ay'-ko) referring to practices which are unfitting and inappropriate.

"[28] And even as they did not like to retain God in *their* knowledge, God gave them over to a reprobate mind, to do those things which are not convenient; [29] **Being filled with** all unrighteousness, fornication, wickedness, covetousness, maliciousness; full of envy, murder, debate, deceit, malignity; whisperers, [30] Backbiters, haters of God, despiteful, proud, boasters, inventors of evil things, disobedient to parents, [31] Without understanding, covenantbreakers, without natural affection, implacable, unmerciful: [32] Who knowing the judgment of God, that they which commit such things are worthy of death, not only do the same, but have pleasure in them that do them" (Romans 1:28-32).

According to Romans 1:29, this person's life will become "filled with" unfitting and inappropriate practices. "Being filled with" is from the Greek word *pleroo* (play-ro'-o) meaning a life so full of itself it will be full of these things listed as the consequence.

"All" can be inserted in front of each to express the extreme influence of a "reprobate mind" upon a life. God gives us **twenty-two characteristics** of this last degree of unbelief in an individual's life and in a society predominantly filled with unbelievers. Therefore, Romans 1:29-23 gives a pathology of reprobation. **Pathology is the science of *cause and effect.***

> - **"Unrighteousness"** is from the Greek word *adikia* (ad-ee-kee'-ah) referring to *the violation of justice divinely* ordered or commanded by God. Keeping orders maintains order in a society.
> - **"Fornication"** is from the Greek word *porneia* (por-ni'-ah) referring to any form illicit sexual practices outside of the sanctity of marriage between one man and one woman.
> - **"Wickedness"** is from the Greek word *poneria* (pon-ay-ree'-ah) referring to a depravity in purposes and desires. This describes what *drives* this person's psyche.
> - **"Covetousness"** is from the Greek word *pleonexia* (pleh-on-ex-ee'-ah) referring to a growing, greedy, insatiable desire to have more and more.
> - **"Maliciousness"** is from the Greek word *kakia* (kak-ee'-ah) referring to a desire to injure someone or defame. This is a wickedness that is not ashamed to break laws, malign another's character, or destroy another person.
> - **"Envy"** is from the Greek word *phthonos* (fthon'-os) meaning

life actions always prompted by envy. "Envy" is often a motivator for "maliciousness" and "wickedness." "Envy" is sourced in pride.

- ➤ **"Murder"** is from the Greek word *phonos* (fon'-os) meaning a life full of slaughter. "Murder" is the ultimate digressive byproduct of pride, wickedness, covetousness, malice, and envy. There can be a spirit/desire to murder someone without actually murdering.

- ➤ **"Debate"** is from the Greek word *eris* (er'-is) meaning a life filled with strife and contention. "Debate" refers to a quarrelsome, snarling, mean spirited person always looking for an argument or something about which this person can verbally attack someone.

- ➤ **"Deceit"** is from the Greek word *dolos* (dol'-os) referring to deceptive, crafty manipulation. This person will use lies, half-truths, gossip, inuendoes, or anything at his/her disposal to harm another person or to promote himself/herself.

- ➤ **"Malignity"** is from the Greek word *kakoetheia* (kak-o-ay'-thi-ah) referring to bad character and bad morals. "Malignity" is the fountainhead from which springs destruction upon anything or anyone this character flaw intends to harm.

- ➤ **"Whisperers"** is from the Greek word *psithuristes* (psith-oo-ris-tace') referring to *a secret slanderer*. This is the tool of the assassinator of characters whose malignity is given a secret voice whispered in the shallows and hidden just around the corner. It is the *secret listener* who gives the whisperer power to do his dirty work.

- ➤ **"Backbiters"** is from the Greek word *katalalos* (kat-al'-al-os) meaning a person who secretly defames another or speaks evil of them through *whispers*.

- ➤ **"Haters of God"** is from the Greek word *theostuges* (theh-os-too-gace') referring to a person who is exceptionally impious and wicked. This describes the Atheist, who not only rejects the existence of God, but who vehemently, aggressively, and wholeheartedly attacks the character and nature of God to create unbelief and hatred for the very idea of God's existence.

- ➤ **"Despiteful"** is from the Greek word *hubristes* (hoo-bris-tace') referring to a person who is insolent and who either heaps insulting language upon others or does them some shameful act of wrong. This person respects no one who disagrees with him.

➢ **"Proud"** is from the Greek word *huperephanos* (hoop-er-ay'-fan-os) refers to thinking of oneself as superior to others. This often expresses itself in prejudices by despising others or even treating them with contempt (disrespect). Pride holds no one higher in opinion than oneself.

➢ **"Boasters"** is from the Greek word *alazon* (al-ad-zone') referring to a vain and pretentious person. Such a person must promote himself and often does so by belittling the accomplishments of others. The boaster puffs himself up to make himself bigger than he is.

➢ **"Inventors of evil things"** is from two Greek words, *epheuretes* (ef-yoo-ret'-ace) and *kakos* (kak-os') referring to a person who schemes in his thinking and imagination inventing ways to undermine or harm another person.

➢ **"Disobedient to parents"** is from two Greek words *apeithes* (ap-i-thace') and *goneus* (gon-yooce') referring to a person who obstinately resists the authority of his parents. The idea extends into insubordination against all who have authority over him.

➢ **"Without understanding"** is from the Greek word *asunetos* (as-oon'-ay-tos). It goes far beyond ignorance, referring to a person who lacks any real understanding of the realities of life (including spiritual realities) and therefore makes decisions without any consciousness to the outcomes of those realities.

➢ **"Covenantbreakers"** is from the Greek word *asunthetos* (as-oon'-thet-os) referring to a person who cannot be trusted to keep promises. This person is untrustworthy in anything he does or plans to do.

➢ **"Without natural affection"** is from the Greek word *astorgos* (as'-tor-gos) referring to a person who is incapable of loving anyone but himself. This person is unwilling to sacrifice for the benefit of another without the possibility of gaining an advantage or an I.O U.

➢ **"Implacable"** is from the Greek word *aspondos* (as'-pon-dos) referring to a person incapable of making commitments (let alone keep one). This connects to the pathology of a "covenant breaker" who is "without natural affection." Do not expect any kind of a faithful relationship with such a person.

➢ **"Unmerciful"** is from the Greek word *aneleemon* (an-eleh-ay'-

mone) referring to a person unwilling to help the needy or a person without any compassion for others regardless of the severity of their predicament. These types of people have no compassion on anyone outside of their own circles of life. Disagree with them on any of their hobbyhorse beliefs and that person will immediately become a target for their wrath intent upon merciless destruction.

The closing statement of Romans 1:32 informs us that the Holy Spirit has fully convinced this person of God's pending judgment on his/her life. "Knowing" is from the Greek word *epiginosko* (ep-ig-in-oce'-ko) meaning this person has a thorough perception of what will happen to him once he dies, yet he has no fear of God about it because he continues to deny the inner witness of his conscience to God's truths and existence.

"Judgment" in Romans 1:32 is from the Greek word *dikaioma* (dik-ah'-yo-mah) referring to a sentence by a judge for a crime committed. The intent here is that this person is fully convinced in his conscience about the eternal death sentence upon him (Romans 6:23). Yet, he lives in denial of that cloud of doom over his life. Because of this denial, he not only continues on this pathway to destruction, but he also forms a partnership with others involved in the same practices which reinforces both his sinful practices and theirs.

"Even as Sodom and Gomorrha"

"**Even as** Sodom and Gomorrha, and the cities about them in like manner, **giving themselves over to fornication**, and going after strange flesh, are set forth for an example, suffering the vengeance of eternal fire" (Jude 7).

Obviously, "Even as Sodom and Gomorrha" were two adjacent cities that shared a common culture described as "giving themselves over to fornication and going after strange flesh." The Greek word from which the phrase "giving themselves over to fornication" is translated is *ekporeúomai* (ek-por-yoo'-om-ahee). The word means extraordinary departure from God's restrictions upon human sexuality.

These people pursued "fornication" without restraint. This describes the practices of paganism and idolatry, which in most part were mainly licentious fertility cults corrupting human sexuality in the most extreme ways of which the corrupted human imagination was capable. These corruptions as part of pagan worship practices were not just private and secret but paganism made these practices public and open to public view.

The words "going after strange flesh" means pursuing corrupt sexuality that is unnatural to human reproduction and a husband/wife relationship. This extended into homosexuality, lesbianism, incest, and even bestiality.

Therefore, the words "giving themselves over to fornication" take on an extremely heightened sense of corruption of human sexuality, eradicating every moral boundary imaginable. This is the sexuality described by the acronym LGBTQIA+ (Lesbian, Gay, Bisexual, Transgender, Queer or Questioning, Intersexual, Asexual or Ally, with + meaning anything else or anything goes). This certainly defines the meaning of the Greek word *ekporeúomai* (ek-por-yoo'-om-ahee), translated "giving themselves over to fornication."

The intent of this departure is that ultimately these are practices without compunction. **Without compunction means not feeling any guilt or having any moral scruple that prevents a person from following a departure from what is normal and natural and from doing something evil.** Therefore, there is no restraint upon the human conscience. The culture of this type of society completely accepts and condones all forms of sexuality without any restraints.

The warning of Jude 7 is "<u>as</u> Sodom and Gomorrha, and the cities about them" is that this describes a culture without compunction and total disregard for God's commands regarding human sexuality. The Word of God then reminds people that these cities forming this culture of fornication "are set forth for an example, suffering the vengeance of eternal fire."

The warning is that all such cultures are destined for severe judgment. A major part of contending "for the faith once delivered unto the saints" is making people aware of pending judgment upon cultural acceptance of similar practices. Of course, the intent is a call to repent, turn, and be "born again" even when such a message is being totally rejected by the culture.

The local church is supposed to be a *counterculture*, bringing the voice of conscience upon the subject and offering the only acceptable solution - REPENT and TURN. The exemplary failure is that of Lot and his family as they lived within this corrupt culture. They had become absorbed into the culture and were not the voice of God to the culture.

This does not mean they were involved in these sexual aberrations, but they certainly were no longer shocked by them or feared God's judgment upon the culture that practiced them. Lot's response to the men of Sodom who inquired about the men (angels) that had come to warn Lot reveals that Lot understood that the desires of these men of Sodom were perverse and wicked.

"¹ And **there came two angels to Sodom at even**; and Lot sat in the gate of Sodom: and Lot seeing *them* rose up to meet them; and he bowed himself with his face toward the ground; ² And he said, Behold now, my lords, turn in, I pray you, into **your servant's house**, and tarry all night, and wash your feet, and ye shall rise up early, and go on your ways. And they said, Nay; but we will abide in the street all night. ³ And **he pressed upon them greatly**; and they turned in unto him, and entered into his house; and he made them a feast, and did bake unleavened bread, and they did eat. ⁴ **But before they lay down**, the men of the city, *even* the men of Sodom, compassed the house round, both old and young, all the people from every quarter: ⁵ And they called unto Lot, and said unto him, **Where *are* the men which came in to thee this night? bring them out unto us, that we may know them**. ⁶ And Lot went out at the door unto them, and shut the door after him, ⁷ And said, I pray you, brethren, **do not so wickedly**" (Genesis 19:1-6).

Although Lot was positionally a "righteous" man, meaning righteousness had been imputed to him in the gift of salvation, Lot's practical righteousness had been corrupted by the culture in which he chose to live. However, the corruption was not the blame of the culture, but Lot's choices. This is obvious by his chosen solution to the threat posed by the men of Sodom in their demand for the two men in Lot's house. Lot was willing to offer his two virgin daughters as sacrifices to satisfy the lust of these Sodomites.

"Behold now, I have two daughters which have not known man; let me, I pray you, bring them out unto you, and do ye to them as *is* good in your eyes: only unto these men do nothing; for therefore came they under the shadow of my roof" (Genesis 19:8).

It is difficult to understand why Lot thought the two angels in his household somehow needed his protection. We can only surmise that Lot was not concerned about protecting the two angels but rather protecting the Sodomites from them. If these two angels brought the judgment of God on this culture, everything Lot had acquired would be destroyed as well. Was Lot just protecting his assets and was he really willing to sacrifice his two virgin daughters to the lusts of these pagans to accomplish that?

Although Lot's choice of living in Sodom began with a compromise of Biblical values, compromise never ends where it begins. When anyone is willing to compromise the values that God puts before us to choose volitionally, those values will be constantly eroded into nonexistence by additional compromises made necessary by the culture by which we want acceptance.

When we desire the acceptance of culture, we will always lean in the direction of compromise and will by that degree fail. We will fail because we will all seek the validation our culture if God's will does not already hold the position of primacy. It is the primary responsibility of every believer to keep the primacy of God's will at the forefront of every decision in life. No one can "serve two masters." Lot's decisions simply revealed the idol of his heart rather than worship of the God of Heaven and Earth. Lot decisions revealed what his heart treasured.

"[19] Lay not up for yourselves treasures upon earth, where moth and rust doth corrupt, and where thieves break through and steal: [20] But lay up for yourselves treasures in heaven, where neither moth nor rust doth corrupt, and where thieves do not break through nor steal: [21] **For where your treasure is, there will your heart be also.** [22] The light of the body is the eye: if therefore thine eye be single, thy whole body shall be full of light. [23] **But if thine eye be evil, thy whole body shall be full of darkness.** If therefore the light that is in thee be darkness, how great *is* that darkness! [24] **No man can serve two masters** {*lords; the intent of the simile is the concluding statement of this verse*}: for either he will hate the one, and love the other; or else he will hold to the one, and despise the other. **Ye cannot serve God and mammon**" (Matthew 6:19-24).

Therefore, the warning of Jude verse seven is twofold. There is the warning to those who are "giving themselves over to fornication and going after strange flesh" and there is the warning to the believers within this culture not to become absorbed into this culture and become silent in opposing it morally. Lot receives his final warning from the two angels in Genesis 19:12-14. Lot is instructed to separate from the culture that will be judged and destroyed. Lot is also instructed to get his family out of danger. However, Lot's sons-in-law were part of the culture of which Lot was told to escape. They refused to believe him because they could not take his words seriously. They could not due to Lot's life compromises within the wicked culture in which he chose to raise his family.

"[12] And the men said unto Lot, **Hast thou here any besides?** son in law, and thy sons, and thy daughters, and whatsoever thou hast in the city, bring *them* out of this place: [13] For we will destroy this place, because the cry of them is waxen great before the face of the LORD; and **the LORD hath sent us to destroy it.** [14] And Lot went out, and spake unto his sons in law, which married his daughters, and said, Up, get you out of this place; for the LORD will destroy this city. **But he seemed as one that mocked unto his sons in law**" (Genesis 19:12-14).

When believers compromise the inspired commands of God and the things God holds precious, they also compromise the believability of their testimony to the world. Those who need our testimony will find no credibility in the validity of that testimony. When your life is no different than the culture in which you live, do not expect that culture to give much credibility to the words you speak about God. This is the reality with which Lot was confronted the moment he took the warning from the angels to his "sons in law." They thought he was joking. It was evident that Lot's life had never really taken the things of God seriously before, why should his sons in law take him seriously now?

All the assets Lot had left with which to escape was his wife and two daughters. However, although Lot was able to get them out of Sodom, he was not able to get Sodom out of them. Lot's wife followed him out of Sodom, but her heart remained there. The reason Lot's wife *looked back* was because the treasure of her heart was still in Sodom.

"²⁴ Then the LORD rained upon Sodom and upon Gomorrah brimstone and fire from the LORD out of heaven; ²⁵ And he overthrew those cities, and all the plain, and all the inhabitants of the cities, and that which grew upon the ground. ²⁶ But **his wife looked back from behind him, and she became a pillar of salt**"(Genesis 19:24-26).

The Judas Warning: When Your Heart Betrays Your Profession

"²⁸ **Likewise** also as it was in the days of Lot; they did eat, they drank, they bought, they sold, they planted, they builded; ²⁹ But **the same day** that Lot went out of Sodom it rained fire and brimstone from heaven, and destroyed *them* all. ³⁰ **Even thus shall it be in the day when the Son of man is revealed.** ³¹ In that day, he which shall be upon the housetop, and his stuff in the house, let him not come down to take it away: and he that is in the field, let him likewise not return back. ³² **Remember Lot's wife.** ³³ Whosoever shall seek to save his life shall lose it; and whosoever shall lose his life shall preserve it" (Luke 17:28-33).

"Remember Lot's wife" is a short little verse of Scripture. In fact, it is one of the shortest verses in the Bible. We have this verse on the back wall of the church auditorium (right under the large wall clock). It is a verse of just three little words, spoken by God, which reach out of the annals of ancient history confronting the hearts of all professing believers questioning the reality of their faith in God. We would all be wise to take careful consideration of the warning. It is not a warning to the multitudes. It is a warning for inner circle professing to be disciples of Jesus Christ. It is the *Judas warning*.

"Remember Lot's wife" are **words that tell us that our hearts will either betray or confirm our testimony. The mouth speaks words that may be lies, the heart speaks the truth of our loyalties. What the heart loves is revealed by what makes the eyes twinkle.**

"A good man out of the **good treasure of his heart** bringeth forth that which is good; and an evil man out of the **evil treasure of his heart** bringeth forth that which is evil: for **of the abundance of the heart his mouth speaketh**" (Luke 6:45).

The message of Luke 17:28-33 was not spoken to the multitudes that followed Jesus. Nor was it spoken to most of the professing disciples who lived on the periphery of commitment to Him. **It was inner circle teaching to the twelve (Luke 17:22). The teaching of Luke 17:28-33 centers upon the time of the second coming of Christ at Armageddon (not the rapture).** The focus of the teaching is a warning to those living during the tribulation time regarding the enormous persecution that will come upon them at the hands of the Antichrist and his cohorts of the *New Babylon*.

It seems puzzling why Jesus would single out these twelve disciples to teach this. After all, none of them would be living on Earth at the time of His second coming. How could this warning possibly apply to them? The warning is about a broad principle that applies to all Christians throughout the Church Age. "Remember Lot's wife" is a warning about worldliness and the self-deception of worldliness. There was but one of the twelve to which this warning applied. However, the primary target of the warning was a man named Judas whose heart would betray his profession. Make sure you are not of this type!

Why then does Christ communicate this warning to His inner circle disciples that are the most committed to living for Him? He does so because He knows they will be faithful in communicating this warning to the lost and to those professing disciples living on the periphery of total commitment. This issue of worldliness raises serious doubt about the sincerity of a person's salvation. That is a consistent message communicated throughout the Scriptures.

Worldliness is a contradiction against genuine repentance. "Remember Lot's wife" should be words commonly spoken between believers. Scriptures repeatedly give similar warnings. **Lot's wife needed someone to remind her to guard her heart against loving the world and the things of this world (I John 2:15). The evident reality was Lot's wife was lost!**

"[15] Love not the world, neither the things *that are* in the world. If any man love the world, the love of the Father is not in him. [16] For all that *is* in the world, the lust of the flesh, and the lust of the eyes, and the pride of life, is not of the Father, but is of the world. [17] And the world passeth away, and the lust thereof: but he that doeth the will of God abideth for ever" (I John 2:15-17).

Literally, I John 2:15 says, "If any man loves the world, he does not love the Father." Of course, our salvation is not based on loving the Father. Loving the Father is defined as keeping His commandments and we know that has nothing to do with being saved (Ephesians 2:8-9). However, our "works" should bear testimony to our *New Creation* (Ephesians 2:19). If your soul longs for the things of this world, your treasures are in this world and that is what you love. If your soul longs to be in the presence of God and the wonders of His glory, your treasures are in Heaven. One verse simplifies this issue.

"If ye love me, keep my commandments" (John 14:15).

Why does Jesus give this "remember Lot's wife" warning and make such a serious issue about worldliness? The answer is simple. Worldliness (or the lack thereof) is a spiritual barometer of a genuinely transformed life. The worldlier a person is, the more he should question the reality of his regeneration and transformation. **Satan seeks to make worldliness *fashionable*.** In fact, there is a popular magazine with a title that is another word for worldliness: *Cosmopolitan*.

Regeneration and transformation are two separate issues; however, they are connected. Where there is life, there is growth. Where there is no growth, there is no life. There ought to be visible evidence of spiritual growth and eternal life in the life of every genuine believer whose heart longs to please the Savior.

"[21] For as the Father raiseth up the dead, and quickeneth *them*; even so the Son quickeneth whom he will. [22] For the Father judgeth no man, but hath committed all judgment unto the Son: [23] **That all *men* should honour the Son, even as they honour the Father.** He that honoureth not the Son honoureth not the Father which hath sent him. [24] Verily, verily, I say unto you, He that heareth my word, and believeth on him that sent me, hath everlasting life, and shall not come into condemnation; but is passed from death unto life" (John 5:21-24).

"[11] And this is the record, that God hath given to us eternal life, and this life is in his Son. [12] **He that hath the Son hath life** {*the Christ-life dwelling within*}; *and* he that hath not the Son of God hath not life. [13] These things have I written unto you that believe on the name of the Son of God; that ye may know that ye have eternal life, and that ye may believe on the name of the Son of God" (I John 5:11-13).

"We know that whosoever is born of God sinneth not; but **he that is begotten of God keepeth himself**, and that wicked one toucheth him not" (I John 5:18).

Spiritual growth is measured on a very simple scale. It is measured by the degree we separate ourselves from worldliness and the degree we are dedicated, committed followers of Jesus Christ. The issue here is not about **results** as much as it is about the **direction of our efforts** and the **motivation** behind those efforts. The questions we must learn to ask ourselves are the same questions we will ultimately have to answer at the Judgment Seat of Christ.

Is my life preoccupied with a struggle for righteousness (separation from selfish and carnal pursuits and being separated unto doing God's will)? Secondly, what motivates me to that preoccupation? Am I motivated to separate myself from worldliness for the purposes of self-promotion or self-aggrandizing? Or am I motivated to separate myself from worldly pleasures and pursuits because I genuinely love the Lord and want to be used to His glory?

The fact of the matter is that many people are concerned about moral issues because they are concerned about impressing their peers or out of fear of being ostracized by their peers. The reality of this person's faith relationship with God will be simply measured by what he does when he knows his peer group will have no knowledge of what he does in secret. This kind of motivation is really a manifestation of unbelief in God.

Another shortfall motivation for practical righteousness is fear of chastisement or loss of spiritual benefits ("blessings") from God.

Yes, "The fear of the Lord is the beginning of knowledge" (Proverbs 1:7a), but *fear motivation* is an infantile form of righteousness motivation. Little children obey because they fear being disciplined when they disobey. Mature believers are motivated to right living and faithfulness because of a genuine faith and a real love for God.

We can say with assurance that the person who lives with a secret sin life does not have a real faith relationship with God because if he did, he would know that God knows and sees all that he thinks or does (even in secret). Yet, that person does not live within the realm of that reality; because he lives like God does not exist.

"[1] The transgression of the wicked saith within **my** heart, *that there is* no fear of God before his eyes. [2] For he flattereth himself in his own eyes, until his iniquity be found to be hateful. [3] The words of his mouth *are* iniquity and deceit: he hath left off to be wise, *and* to do good. [4] He deviseth mischief upon his bed; he setteth himself in a way *that is* not good; **he abhorreth not evil**" (Psalm 36:1-4).

God expects His children to learn to hate evil. God expects His children to learn to completely abandon worldliness in every avenue and aspect of their lives. **The person who continues in worldliness and worldly pursuits manifests a "double minded" person (James 1:8 and 4:8).** To be "double minded" is the same as being "carnally minded" (Romans 8:6). This refers to the direction in which our soul is moving or reaching (or seeking to move, i.e., grow).

This is like a plant that grows in the direction of the sun because the sun is its source for photosynthesis. We stretch ourselves towards what we think will fulfill us. If we think that we will be fulfilled by pleasure or things, we stretch ourselves towards the world and its resources and become preoccupied with those resources. If we think that we will be fulfilled by spiritual things and a relationship with our Creator, we will stretch ourselves in His direction and become preoccupied with Him. What we stretch ourselves toward is what we really believe will give us fulfillment, and that is the measurement of the reality of our faith.

God emphatically informs us that "death" will be the ultimate result of a pursuit after worldliness. We may find "the pleasures of sin for a season" (Hebrews 11:25), but there will be no lasting satisfaction or fulfillment. The reality is that "the end thereof are the ways of death" (Proverbs 14:12).

"⁵ For they that are after the flesh do mind the things of the flesh; but they that are after the Spirit the things of the Spirit. ⁶ For to be carnally minded *is* death; but to be spiritually minded *is* life and peace" (Romans 8:5-6).

It is to this issue of worldliness that Christ teaches His disciples and gives this warning summarized in the words, "Remember Lot's wife." Why did Lot's wife turn to look back at Sodom and Gomorrah? She looked back at Sodom because that was where her heart was. She looked back because she loved the things of this world and was preoccupied with them. She looked back because she was more concerned with the things of this world than she was about being obedient to God. She looked back and God's judgment fell upon her hypocrisy. She looked back, and it ended in her death.

Christ gave this warning to the inner circle of His most committed disciples because He knew that there is the danger of self-deception in even the most dedicated people. We deceive ourselves about the reality of our faith relationship when we refuse to confront this issue of worldliness and our tendency towards it.

We hide behind our self-constructed façade of spirituality because we are not willing to confront our own hypocrisy. We willingly deceive ourselves about the reality of our faith in God, and we hope we deceive our peers, but the only person that really matters is not going to be deceived.

"Examine yourselves, whether ye be in the faith; prove your own selves. Know ye not your own selves, how that Jesus Christ is in you, except ye be reprobates" (*adokimos*; not standing the test, not approved, II Corinthians 13:5)?

Are we going to be like Lot's wife who never dealt with the issue of the reality of her faith relationship with God until the day she was confronted with the judgment of God? Are we just going to continue to rationalize about our double mindedness and continue to deceive ourselves that we have something we really don't have? Think about the risk involved!

"But be ye doers of the word, and not hearers only, deceiving your own selves" (James 1:22).

"Remember Lot's wife." We think our secret, but habitual sin life is inconsequential. We have our sepulcher whitewashed and we deceive ourselves into thinking all is right with God. Yet, Christ reminds all of us that it is the sin of the heart that leads us astray. It was the sin of the heart that caused Lot's wife to take that casual glance over her shoulder that cost her her life. That is where our worldliness must be confronted and dealt with: in our hearts.

It is in our hearts that we set up the idols of a secret fantasy life and those secret sins that we keep hidden from our peers. We hide it from our peers without even considering that our heart is the living room of God. It is in this filth and degradation of the carnal lusts of our hearts that we force God to live.

It is in our hearts that sin must be confronted and dealt with in the harshest way. We must learn to abhor it. We must learn that sin in any form grieves the Spirit of God within us. We must learn to weep and be broken about the state of our soul and the spiritual condition of the Temple of God (our bodies).

Holiness can never exist on the outside of our lives until it exists in the inner sanctum of our hearts. That is the central problem of an externalistic Christianity. We become more concerned with the external *spit and polish* than with genuine issues of the heart. What do we love? What we love is *the tell* of our soul.

"[13] If thou prepare thine heart, and stretch out thine hands toward him; [14] If iniquity *be* in thine hand, put it far away, and let not wickedness dwell in thy tabernacles. [15] For then shalt thou lift up thy face without spot; yea, thou shalt be stedfast, and shalt not fear: [16] Because thou shalt forget *thy* misery, *and* remember *it* as waters *that* pass away: [17] And *thine* age shall be clearer than the noonday; thou shalt shine forth, thou shalt be as the morning" (Job 11:13-17).

"Remember Lot's wife," who in one small and seemingly insignificant moment of her life looked over her shoulder for one last fleeting glimpse of the treasures of her heart. In that one fleeting moment, she revealed the idol of her heart, and God built a monument to that moment in a pillar of salt with her at its center. Death is a fatal time to find out that our faith has been a façade all of our lives. Worldliness and "idols of the heart" are what the Biblical story of Lot is all about. Worldliness is the most deceptive kind of idolatry. Worldliness is about putting anything before God in our lives.

"[1] Then came certain of the elders of Israel unto me, and sat before me. [2] And the word of the LORD came unto me, saying, [3] Son of man, these men have set up their idols in their heart, and put the stumblingblock of their iniquity before their face: should I be enquired of at all by them? [4] Therefore speak unto them, and say unto them, Thus saith the Lord GOD; Every man of the house of Israel that setteth up his idols in his heart, and putteth the stumblingblock of his iniquity before his face, and cometh to the prophet; I the LORD will answer him that cometh according to the multitude of his idols; [5] That I may take the house of Israel in their own heart, because they are all estranged from me through their idols. [6] Therefore say unto the house of Israel, Thus saith the Lord GOD; Repent, and turn *yourselves* from your idols; and turn away your faces from all your abominations. [7] For every one of the house of Israel, or of the stranger that sojourneth in Israel, which separateth himself from me, and setteth up his idols in his heart, and putteth the stumblingblock of his iniquity before his face, and cometh to a prophet to enquire of him concerning me; I the LORD will answer him by myself: [8] And I will set my face against that man, and will make him a sign and a proverb, and I will cut him off from the midst of my people; and ye shall know that I *am* the LORD" (Ezekiel 14:1-8).

This is why we can say that the absence of holiness is not because people go to movies, smoke, drink, view pornography, dance, etc. These visible practices are just the symptoms of a serious heart problem. They are the outward exhibitions of idols of the heart. You can stop all of these visible outward practices and still leave the idols standing in your heart. That is the definition of externalism. That is why so many professing Christians have just enough *Christianity* to make them miserable. They struggle with keeping their sepulchers whitewashed, but do not really learn to die to the inner fountain of sin in their hearts.

Jude
Contending for the Faith
Chapter Five
Filthy Dreamers

Unbelief creates delusional people. People who refuse to believe, acknowledge, and understand that there is a God to which we are all accountable live in a *fantasy world* where there is no Hell, no judgment, and no accountability to the God they reject. This happens within both complete atheism and agnosticism. It also happens when a person has any one of the varying degrees of rejection of the inspired Word of God or believes false doctrines.

This is what Jude addresses in Jude 8 in the words *"filthy dreamers."* There are real outcomes in life's practices and attitudes due to any degree of unbelief and any degree of heterodoxy. This universal spiritual principle is found in Galatians 6:7, "Be not deceived; God is not mocked: for **whatsoever a man soweth**, that shall he also reap."

"[8] **Likewise** also these *filthy* **dreamers defile the flesh**, despise dominion, and speak evil of dignities. [9] Yet Michael the archangel, when contending with the devil he disputed about the body of Moses, durst not bring against him a railing accusation, but said, The Lord rebuke thee. [10] But these speak evil of those things which they know not: but what they know naturally, as brute beasts, in those things they corrupt themselves. [11] Woe unto them! for they have gone in the way of Cain, and ran greedily after the error of Balaam for reward, and perished in the gainsaying of Core" (Jude 8-11).

The word "likewise" that starts Jude 8 is a translation of two Greek words, *homoíōs* (hom-oy'-oce) and *méntoi* (men'-toy). *Homoíōs* (hom-oy'-oce) means *similarly*, referring to those to which the three warnings apply in Jude 5-7. *Méntoi* (men'-toy) means *nevertheless* or *indeed though*. The meaning then is that regardless of these warnings from God in God's historical dealings with various levels of unbelief, unbelievers blindly continue to traverse on a pathway leading to their own self-destruction.

Their unbelief determines the beginning of their ultimate and horrendous destiny with innumerable unpleasantries on the way. When one chooses the beginning of a way, he chooses the predestined end of that way. All roads lead to somewhere, especially unbelief and unfaithfulness. This is the meaning of the word "likewise."

Like those exemplified in Jude 5-7, these unfaithful or unbelieving "dreamers" live in a fantasy existence where there is no God to Whom they are accountable. Their lives are merely lived in a dream world of sinful pleasures and self-indulgence. **To hold the "eat, drink, and be merry" philosophy of life is a radical manifestation of unbelief.**

"*32* If after the manner of men I have fought with beasts at Ephesus, what advantageth it me, if the dead rise not? {*if there is no resurrection*} **let us eat and drink; for to morrow we die.** *33* **Be not deceived: evil communications** {*worthless companionships*} **corrupt** {*defile or destroy*} **good manners** {*moral habits lived within a view of God's judgments*}. *34* **Awake** {*out of spiritual lethargy and the stupor of carnality*} **to** righteousness {*from occupation with one things TO occupation with the other*}, and sin not; for some have not the knowledge {*agnosia means ignorance*} of God: I speak *this* to your shame" (I Corinthians 15:32-34).

"*Filthy*" (italicized) in Jude 8 is added because it connects to the three defiling outcomes of living in a fantasy world where God does not exist or does not care about how one lives life. Unbelievers and carnal believers must be called to awaken to the reality of God's existence and pending judgment upon unbelief and unfaithfulness. The outcomes of living in this fantasy world ignorant of God and His will is that these "dreamers . . . **defile** the flesh, **despise** dominion, and **speak evil** of dignities." The intent here is to cause reflection on both the temporal outcomes of unbelief and unfaithfulness as well as the pending eternal consequences for which every person must answer to God.

The purpose of this exhortation in Jude 8-11 is to ensure that "born again" people do not slip into this careless mindset of living in a dream world where God does not care and where there is no accountability for life choices. In I Thessalonians 5:6 those that "sleep" are those that live in careless worldly apathy being slothful about the obligations of the Christian life. These types of people are not "awake to righteousness" (I Corinthians 15:34). The same Greek word translated "awake" in I Corinthians 15:34 is translated "watch" in I Thessalonians 5:6. The idea is *being spiritually alert.*

"*6* Therefore **let us** **not sleep, as** *do* **others** *{unbelievers and carnal believers}*; but **let us** **watch** *{vigilantly stay awake and alert}* **and be sober** *{abstain from alcohol to keep the mind clear and alert}*. *7* For they that sleep sleep in the night; and they that be drunken are drunken in the night. *8* But **let us**, **who are of the day**, be sober, putting on the breastplate of faith and love; and for an helmet, the hope of salvation. *9* For God hath not appointed us to wrath, but to obtain salvation by our Lord Jesus Christ, *10* Who died for us, that, **whether we wake** *{are living at the time of the resurrection/translation}* **or sleep** *{are in the grave at the time of the resurrection/translation}*, **we should live together with him**" (I Thessalonians 5:6-10).

These "*filthy* dreamers **defile** the flesh, **despise** dominion, and **speak evil** of dignities" (Jude 8). The intent here is that unbelievers and unfaithful people are spiritually untrustworthy and are particularly *egregious* (noticeably, purposefully, and flagrantly bad people). "Defile the flesh" is certainly connected to the warning about the Sodomites of "Sodom and Gomorrha" (Jude 7).

"Dispise dominion" is certainly connected to the warning about the fallen angels of Jude 6. "Speak evil of dignities" is certainly connected to the warning of the murmuring and complaining against the goodness of God's intentions and against the leadership of Moses as God's representative at Kadesh-Barnea in Jude 5. These three *characteristics* are consistent with apostates and unfaithful people.

"*3* But fornication *{sexual impurity}*, and all **uncleanness** *{moral impurity}*, or **covetousness** *{fraudulent greedy extortion}*, **let it not be once named** *{assigned to you as an appellation descriptor of character}* among you, **as becometh** *{suitable or proper}* saints; *4* Neither **filthiness** *{vulgar obscenity}*, nor **foolish talking** *{talking like a fool or moron}*, nor **jesting** *{vulgar joking}*, which are **not convenient** *{not fitting of being* *a child of God}*: but **rather giving of thanks**. [5] For this ye know, that **no** whoremonger, **nor** unclean person, **nor** covetous man, who is an idolater, **hath any inheritance in the kingdom of Christ and of God**. [6] Let no man deceive you with vain words: for because of these things cometh the wrath of God upon the children of disobedience. [7] Be not ye therefore partakers with them. [8] For ye were sometimes darkness, but now *are ye* light in the Lord: walk as children of light: [9] (For the fruit of the Spirit *is* in all goodness and righteousness and truth;) [10] Proving what is acceptable unto the Lord. [11] And **have no fellowship with the unfruitful works of darkness, but rather reprove them**. [12] For it is a shame even to speak of those things which are done of them in secret. [13] But all things that are reproved are made manifest by the light: for whatsoever doth make manifest is light. [14] Wherefore he saith, **Awake thou that sleepest, and arise from the dead, and Christ shall give thee light**. [15] See then that ye walk circumspectly, not as fools, but as wise, [16] **Redeeming the time** *{using every moment of life for the cause of Christ wasting no time on foolishness}*, **because** the days are evil" (Ephesians 5:3-16).

The *"filthy* dreamers" of Jude 8 refers to an attitude about God that is created by the false doctrines of those that "crept in unawares" in Jude 4. False doctrines warp, distort, and corrupt God's expectations, creating fantasy ideas about God and distorting reality by degree of corruption.

The point is that such distortions cannot be tolerated by the faithful just to ensure people do not leave a local church. Without loyalty to God and to truth all other loyalties are inconsequential to the reality faith sees and knows.

"[9] Yet Michael the archangel, when contending with the devil he disputed about the body of Moses, durst not bring against him a railing accusation, but said *{with the authority of God}*, The Lord rebuke thee. [10] But these speak evil of those things which they know not: but what they know naturally, as brute beasts, in those things they corrupt themselves" (Jude 9-10).

"Archangel" simply means God's chief angel. Michael is the angel in charge of all other angels that have not fallen in sin and rebellion with Satan. Lucifer was the "archangel" before he fell and before he led one-third of the angels to follow him in his rebellion. We would not understand the tension and contest mentioned in Jude 9 if we do not understand Lucifer's fall and his replacement with Michael. There is but one "archangel" and now it is Michael.

The name "Michael" simply means *one like God.* **This name Michael means he operates with the authority of God, which authority has been delegated to him.** Angels are not omnipresent, omnipotent, or omniscient. Lucifer lost this position of authority in his rebellion and became Satan. The name Satan means *opponent* or *opposer.* Satan became the *archenemy* of God and all that seek to do God's will.

"¹² How art thou fallen from heaven, **O Lucifer**, son of the morning! *how* art thou cut down to the ground, which didst weaken the nations! ¹³ For thou hast said in thine heart, I will ascend into heaven, I will exalt my throne above the stars of God: I will sit also upon the mount of the congregation, in the sides of the north: ¹⁴ I will ascend above the heights of the clouds; I will be like the most High. ¹⁵ Yet thou shalt be brought down to hell, to the sides of the pit" (Isaiah 14:12-15).

Michael as the "archangel" of God is God's first (*árchō*) messenger/pastor (*ángelos*), which simply means he is *the first to speak for God to anyone.* Needless to say, a great tension exists between Michael and Satan throughout the Bible. This tension exists because their loyalties are antagonistic to one another. Satan and his fallen angels *oppose* (stand against) everything Michael and the righteous angels *appose* (stand for). Satan opposes God's blessing upon the nation of Israel while Michael defends the nation of Israel against Satan's attempts at her destruction.

"And Satan stood up against Israel, and provoked David to number Israel" (I Chronicles 21:1).

There is little doubt that Revelation chapter twelve gives us an overview of Satan's opposition against the nation of Israel and against

God's purpose in electing the nation of Israel to manifest His sovereignty over this world. Satan thinks he is sovereign, but God clearly establishes His sovereignty through the nation of Israel and the establishment of the Kingdom Age. **This is the second fold of redemption.**

"**1** And there appeared a great wonder in heaven; **a woman clothed with the sun, and the moon under her feet, and upon her head a crown of twelve stars** {*the nation of Israel*}: **2** And **she being with child** {*Messiah/Christ*} cried, travailing in birth, and pained to be delivered. **3** And there appeared another wonder in heaven; and **behold a great red dragon** {*Satan*}, having seven **heads** and ten horns, and seven crowns upon his **heads** {*world empires and leaders*}. **4** And his tail drew the **third part of the stars** {*other angels*} of heaven, and did cast them to the earth: and the dragon stood before the woman which was ready to be delivered, for to devour her child as soon as it was born. **5** And **she brought forth a man child** {*birth of Jesus*}, who was **to rule all nations with a rod of iron** {*Kingdom Age*}: and her child was **caught up** {*resurrected, glorified, and ascended to the right hand of God*} unto God, and *to* his throne. **6** And **the woman fled into the wilderness** {*during the last part of the Tribulation*}, where she hath a place prepared of God, that they should feed her there **a thousand two hundred *and* threescore days** {*1,260 days, the last 3 and a half years of the Tribulation*}. **7** And there was war in heaven: **Michael and his angels** {*the faithful angels led by the archangel Michael*} fought against the dragon; and the dragon fought and his angels, **8** **And prevailed not** {*they could not defeat Satan and his fallen angels, which defeat can only be accomplished by Christ and His death, burial, and resurrection/glorification*}; neither was their **place found any more in heaven** {*for the Devil*}. **9** And **the great dragon was cast out**, that old serpent, called the Devil, and Satan, which deceiveth the whole world: **he was cast out into the earth, and his angels were cast out with him.** **10** And I heard **a loud voice saying in heaven** {*probably Michael as the first to speak for God to anyone*}, **Now is come salvation** {*this refers to the second part of redemption in the restoration of dominion lost by Adam and restored by the God/Man Jesus the Christ*}, and strength, and the kingdom of our God, and the power of his Christ: **for the accuser of our brethren is cast down** {*will be bound for the Kingdom Age*}, which accused them before our God day and night. [11] And **they** {*saved Jews forming the restored nation of Israel during the Kingdom Age*} overcame him by the blood of the Lamb, and by the word of their testimony; and **they loved not their lives unto the death** {*many will be martyred for Christ by the Antichrist*}" (Revelation 12:1-11).

As God's first ambassador, the archangel Michael often was sent by God to give God's messages to His prophets for those prophets to then relay those messages to God's people and to the world. We are told in two verses (Daniel 10:13 and 21) in Daniel chapter ten that the archangel Michael ("chief prince") was the messenger that spoke with the prophet Daniel along with the preincarnate Christ (Christophany).

"[1] In the third year of Cyrus king of Persia **a thing was revealed unto Daniel**, whose name was called Belteshazzar; and the thing *was* true, but the time appointed *was* long: and he understood the thing, and had understanding of the vision. [2] In those days I Daniel was mourning three full weeks. [3] I ate no pleasant bread, neither came flesh nor wine in my mouth, neither did I anoint myself at all, till three whole weeks were fulfilled. [4] And in the four and twentieth day of the first month, as I was by the side of the great river, which *is* Hiddekel; [5] Then I lifted up mine eyes, and looked, and behold **a certain man** {*Christophany*} **clothed in linen**, whose loins *were* girded with fine gold of Uphaz: [6] His body also *was* like the beryl, and his face as the appearance of lightning, and his eyes as lamps of fire, and his arms and his feet like in colour to polished brass, and the voice of his words like the voice of a multitude. [7] And **I Daniel alone saw the vision**: for the men that were with me saw not the vision; but a great quaking fell upon them, so that they fled to hide themselves. [8] Therefore I was left alone, and **saw this great vision**, and there remained no strength in me: for my comeliness was turned in me into corruption, and I retained no strength. [9] Yet heard **I the voice of his words**: and when I heard the voice of his words, then was I in a deep sleep on my face, and my face toward the ground. [10]

And, behold, **an hand touched me** {*Christophany*}, which set me upon my knees and *upon* the palms of my hands {*on all fours*}. [11] And **he said unto me**, O Daniel, a man greatly beloved, understand the words that I speak unto thee, and stand upright: for **unto thee am I now sent**. And when he had spoken this word unto me, I stood trembling. [12] Then said he unto me, **Fear not, Daniel: for from the first day that thou didst set thine heart to understand, and to chasten thyself before thy God, thy words were heard, and I am come for thy words**. [13] But the prince of the kingdom of Persia withstood me one and twenty days: but, lo, **Michael, one of the chief princes** {*as the patron guardian angel of Israel*}, came to help me; and I remained there with the kings of Persia. [14] **Now I** {*Christophany*} **am come to make thee understand what shall befall thy people in the latter days: for yet the vision *is* for *many* days**. [15] And when he had spoken such words unto me, I set my face toward the ground, and I became dumb. [16] And, behold, ***one*** {*Christophany*} **like the similitude of the sons of men touched my lips:** then I opened my mouth, and spake, and said unto him that stood before me, O my lord, by the vision my sorrows are turned upon me, and I have retained no strength. [17] For how can the servant of this my lord talk with this my lord? for as for me, straightway there remained no strength in me, neither is there breath left in me. [18] Then there came again and touched me *one* like the appearance of a man, and he strengthened me, [19] And said, O man greatly beloved, fear not: peace *be* unto thee, be strong, yea, be strong. And when he had spoken unto me, I was strengthened, and said, Let my lord speak; for thou hast strengthened me. [20] Then said he, Knowest thou wherefore I come unto thee? and **now will I return to fight with the prince of Persia**: and when I am gone forth, lo, the prince of Grecia shall come. [21] But I will shew thee that which is noted in the scripture of truth: **and *there is* none that holdeth with me in these things, but Michael your prince** {*as the patron guardian angel of Israel*}" (Daniel 10:1-21).

"Disputed about the Body of Moses"

The "body of Moses" is not the physical body of the man named Moses. The "body of Moses" is the nation of Israel (Old Covenant

Church) as the wife of God just as "the body of Christ" is the New Covenant Church as the espoused "bride of Christ." The dispute is about the resurrection/glorification of the nation of Israel. Paul answers this theological dilemma in Romans chapter nine by differentiating between those who are merely physical descendants of Abraham and those who are "born again" descendants of Abraham because of their faith in the Promise (Messiah; Galatians 3:16).

"[1] I say the truth in Christ, I lie not, my conscience also bearing me witness in the Holy Ghost, [2] That **I have great heaviness and continual sorrow in my heart**. [3] For I could wish that myself were accursed from Christ **for my brethren, my kinsmen according to the flesh**: [4] **Who are Israelites**; to whom *pertaineth* the adoption, and the glory, and the covenants, and the giving of the law, and the service *of God*, and the promises; [5] Whose *are* the fathers, and of whom as concerning the flesh Christ *came*, who is over all, God blessed for ever. Amen. [6] Not as though the word of God hath taken none effect. For they *are* not all Israel, which are of Israel: [7] **Neither, because they are the seed of Abraham, *are they* all children**: but, In Isaac shall thy seed be called. [8] That is, **They which are the children of the flesh, these *are* not the children of God**: but **the children of the promise are counted for the seed**" (Romans 9:1-8).

"[30] What shall we say then? That the Gentiles, which followed not after righteousness, have attained to righteousness, **even the righteousness which is of faith** *{justification, which is the gift of God-kind righteousness in the indwelling Spirit of Christ}*. [31] But Israel, which followed after the law of righteousness, **hath not attained to the law of righteousness**. [32] Wherefore? **Because *they sought it* not by faith, but as it were by the works of the law**. For they stumbled at that stumblingstone; [33] As it is written, Behold, I lay in Sion a stumblingstone and rock of offence: and whosoever believeth on him *{the Promised Messiah Jesus}* shall not be ashamed" (Romans 9:30-33).

Of course, God's defined solution to the election of the nation of Israel when many of the Jews were lost is found in Romans 10:1-13. Because of their false trust in "the works" of the Mosaic Covenant regarding God's expectation of perfect and righteousness and ignorance of being gifted that perfect righteousness through the instrumentality of faith in their Promised Messiah, the Jews hopelessly pursued righteousness through the "works of the Law."

"[1] **Brethren** {*'kinsmen according to the flesh', Romans 9:3*}), my heart's desire and prayer to God for Israel is, **that they might be saved**. [2] **For** {*because*} I bear them record that they have a zeal of God, but **not according to knowledge**. [3] For {*because*} **they being ignorant of God's righteousness, and going about to establish their own righteousness, have not submitted themselves unto the righteousness of God**. [4] For Christ *is* **the end** {*telos, the point aimed at or the bullseye of the target*} of the law for righteousness to every one that believeth. [5] For Moses describeth the righteousness which is of the law, That the man which doeth those things shall live by them. [6] **But the righteousness which is of faith speaketh on this wise, Say not in thine heart** {*deciding who has or has not been righteous enough*}, Who shall ascend into heaven? (that is, to bring Christ down *from above*:) [7] Or, Who shall descend into the deep? (that is, to bring up Christ again from the dead.) [8] **But what saith it** {*the Law*}? The word is nigh thee, *even* in thy mouth, and in thy heart: that is, **the word of faith**, which we preach; [9] That if thou shalt confess with thy mouth the Lord Jesus, and shalt believe in thine heart that God hath raised him from the dead, thou shalt be saved. [10] For **with the heart man believeth unto righteousness**; and with the mouth confession is made unto salvation. [11] For the scripture saith, Whosoever believeth on him shall not be ashamed. [12] For there is no difference between the Jew and the Greek: for the same Lord over all is rich unto all that call upon him. [13] **For whosoever shall call upon the name of the Lord shall be saved**" (Romans 10:1-13).

What then is the dispute "about the body of Moses"? The nation of Israel is an earthly nation and is related to the second part of the doctrine of redemption in the *Promised Seed*. The second part of the doctrine of redemption is the **redemption of lost dominion** restored through the Messiah (God/man} at the beginning of the Kingdom Age.

Why then are angels disputing "about the body of Moses"? Angels do not understand the doctrine of redemption. They desire to know about redemption, but it appears to be beyond their grasp. They surround the throne of God while He sits upon His Judgment Seat while longing to peer inside the Ark of the Covenant to understand how the justice of God can be reconciled with the broken Law.

Angels surround the heavenly throne of God in the Ark of the Covenant, whose covering lid is the Mercy Seat. The lid covers the broken law manifesting the longsuffering grace of God. They look in the hope and expectation of complete propitiation of God's wrath in the death, burial, and resurrection of the Promised Messiah.

Angels cannot comprehend the spiritual truths in the type of Aaron's "rod that budded" (Hebrews 9:4), which is the archetype of the priesthood of Christ as the God/man Redeemer fulfilling the offices of Prophet, High Priest, and King during the Kingdom Age.

"[1] And the LORD spake unto Moses, saying, [2] Speak unto the children of Israel, and **take of every one of them a rod according to the house of *their* fathers**, of all their princes according to the house of their fathers twelve rods: **write thou every man's name upon his rod.** [3] And thou shalt **write Aaron's name upon the rod of Levi**: for one rod *shall be* for the head of the house of their fathers. [4] And thou shalt **lay them up in the tabernacle of the congregation** before the testimony, where I will meet with you. [5] And it shall come to pass, *that* **the man's rod, whom I shall choose, shall blossom:** and I will make to cease from me the murmurings of the children of Israel, whereby they murmur against you. [6] And Moses spake unto the children of Israel, and every one of their princes gave him a rod apiece, for each prince one, according to their fathers' houses, *even* **twelve rods: and the rod of Aaron *was* among their rods**. [7] And Moses laid up the rods before the LORD in the tabernacle of witness. [8] And it came to pass, that on the morrow Moses went into the tabernacle of witness; and, behold, **the rod of Aaron for the house of Levi was budded**, and brought forth buds, and bloomed blossoms, and yielded almonds. [9] And Moses brought out all the rods from before the LORD unto all the children of Israel: and they looked, and took every man his rod. [10] And the LORD said unto Moses, Bring Aaron's rod again before the testimony, **to be kept for a token against the rebels**; and thou shalt quite take away their murmurings from me, **that they die not**. [11] And Moses did *so*: as the LORD commanded him, so did he. [12] And the children of Israel spake unto Moses, saying, Behold, we die, we perish, we all perish. [13] Whosoever cometh any thing near unto the tabernacle of the LORD shall die: shall we be consumed with dying" (Numbers 17:1-13)?

Numerous Scriptures describe the curiosity of angels regarding the doctrine of redemption.

"[6] Wherein ye greatly rejoice, though now for a season, if need be, ye are in heaviness through manifold temptations: [7] That the trial of your faith, being much more precious than of gold that perisheth, though it be tried with fire, might be found unto praise and honour and glory at the appearing of Jesus Christ: [8] Whom having not seen, ye love; in whom, though now ye see *him* not, yet believing, ye rejoice with joy unspeakable and full of glory: [9] Receiving the end of your faith, *even* the salvation of *your* souls. [10] Of which salvation the prophets have inquired and searched diligently, who prophesied of the grace *that should come* unto you: [11] Searching what, or what manner of time the Spirit of Christ which was in them did signify, when it testified beforehand the sufferings of Christ, and the glory that should follow. [12] Unto whom it was revealed, that not unto themselves, but unto us they did minister the things, which are now reported unto you by them that have preached the gospel unto you with the Holy Ghost sent down from heaven; **which things the angels desire to look into**" (I Peter 1:6-12).

"[14] These things write I unto thee, hoping to come unto thee shortly: [15] But if I tarry long, that thou mayest know how thou oughtest to behave thyself in the house of God, which is the church of the living God, the pillar and ground of the truth. [16] And **without controversy great is the mystery of godliness**: God was manifest in the flesh, justified in the Spirit, seen of angels, preached unto the Gentiles, believed on in the world, received up into glory" (I Timothy 3:14-16).

The issue of Michael the archangel "contending with the devil" disputing "about the body of Moses" (Jude 9) refers to nation of Israel as the "body of Moses" represented before God by the priesthood of Israel. The theological issue is that the Levitical priesthood representing the nation of Israel before God was cast away by God.

The theological question then was the nation of Israel (the "body of Moses) cast away also? Paul states emphatically that the nation of Israel and God's promises to the nation are not "cast away."

"[1] I say then, Hath God cast away his people? God forbid. For I also am an Israelite, of the seed of Abraham, *of* the tribe of Benjamin. [2] God hath not cast away his people which he foreknew. Wot ye not what the scripture saith of Elias? how he maketh intercession to God against Israel, saying, [3] Lord, they have killed thy prophets, and digged down thine altars; and I am left alone, and they seek my life. [4] But what saith the answer of God unto him? I have reserved to myself seven thousand men, who have not bowed the knee to *the image of* Baal. [5] Even so then at this present time also there is a remnant according to the election of grace" (Romans 11:1-5).

Romans 11:1-5 speaks to what the prophet Zechariah addresses by the inspiration of the Spirit in Zechariah chapter three. In Zechariah chapter three, Joshua is the High Priest of Levitical priesthood of Israel. He has defiled himself and the priesthood of Israel before the Lord.

God informs Zechariah that the Levitical priesthood will be replaced with a new priesthood with the "BRANCH" as the new High Priest. This replacement is Christ and the Melchizedekian priesthood of all New Covenant "born again" believers.

The BRANCH and the Stone

We know from history that the priesthood of Israel would ultimately fail regarding the very warning given in Zechariah 3:6-7 to Joshua. Joshua's sons would intermarry with pagans. The priesthood of Israel would be Joshua's descendants who would plot lies and deceptions to have Jesus crucified to manipulate the situation, so they might keep their power and prestigious positions in Israel.

Pilate immediately saw through their lies and deception but gave them what they demanded anyway, washing his hands of their corruption (Matthew 27:24). It is sad when God's appointed spiritual leaders become traitors to the responsibilities given them as they rebel against the God they swore to serve. It is to this very issue of the betrayal of the Messiah by the priesthood of Israel that the LORD addresses in Zechariah 3:8.

"[8] Hear now, O Joshua the high priest, thou, **and thy fellows** that sit before thee: for they *are* men wondered at: for, behold, I will bring forth my servant the BRANCH" (Zechariah 3:8).

The message is to Joshua and his "fellows," the *remnant priesthood of Israel* from the captivity, as he stands before the eternal Son of God, continues in verses eight through ten of Zechariah chapter three. The rest of Israel's priesthood had apostatized and abandoned their commission to serve God faithfully. The testimony of the faithfulness of men who wait long and live faithfully in anticipation of the fulfilment of the prophetic promises of God, amazes the unbelieving people of this world.

These people of faith believe that all that the Bible says the Messiah will do, He will do. If these truths are believed, every believer lives in the shadow of expectation of the fulfillment of these momentous events of future history.

Jesus was born of a virgin just as the Scriptures foretold. Jesus was vicariously offered for the sins of the world to satisfy God's wrath upon sin and to justify believing sinners "by grace" and "through faith" just as Psalm twenty-two and Isaiah chapter fifty-three said He would do. He rose from the dead on the third day just as He said He would do. Just as sure as all those things were fulfillments of prophetic announcements, **all the things prophecy says Jesus will do yet in the future, HE WILL DO!**

People who believe these prophetic truths about Jesus, live like they believe these things will happen. They also believe that all the promises to the faithful connected to these fulfilled events will happen. The world may mock the idea of faith, but at the same time they are amazed at the people who live by faith. They are amazed by the people who give their lives to be ambassadors of these truths and ministers of the message of eternal reconciliation with God (II Corinthians 5:17-21).

Zechariah 3:8 records the LORD saying, "behold, **I will** bring forth my servant the BRANCH." Zechariah 3:8-10 is obviously chronologically Kingdom Age and **beyond**. God called Jesus forth from the grave to be seated at His right hand in glory for the whole Church Age.

However, God will **"bring forth"** Jesus to conquer Satan's world and remove Satan as the "prince of the power of the air" (Ephesians 2:2). The Hebrew word translated "BRANCH" means a *bud* or *new sprout* (Aaron's rod that budded). The intent is a new, eternal, sovereign line of humanity created through faith in the death, burial, resurrection, and glorification of Jesus.

The continuum of the New Creation happens when believers begin to reproduce in others what Jesus produced in their lives. Salvation is not merely a gift to receive. Salvation is a message to share and communicate with others. **The gift of salvation comes with an *obligation of communication.***

Believers are obligated to communicate the Gospel because that is the only way people will hear and understand to become part of this new eternal line of humanity. They are "born again" by trusting in the substitutionary work of Jesus to satisfy the wrath of God upon their sin. They receive the gift of His righteousness given to them in the Person of the indwelling Holy Spirit (Romans 10:14). Therefore, believers are "born again" into this unfolding *New Genesis* offered "by grace" and received "through faith."

The "bud" or "sprout" (BRANCH) of the new covenant priesthood begins to grow like the mustard seed grows into a tree (Matthew 13:31-32). The Vine bears a branch (John 15:1-8) and the branch bears fruit, which continues the growth of the *New Genesis* beginning with the ONE growing into millions of millions. The "BRANCH" represents the beginning of a new *family tree* of "born again" humanity disconnected from the curse and connected to the *New Genesis* in Christ, the "last Adam" (I Corinthians 15:45).

The word "BRANCH" in Zechariah 3:8 is a word that connects to many aspects of the character, nature, and purposes of the Messiah in Jesus. When we think of the "BRANCH," we should see God connecting many truths together throughout Scripture.

These many truths are all fulfilled in the birth, death, burial, resurrection/glorification, and second coming of Jesus. The 1917 Scofield Reference Bible gives four different main connecting points throughout Scripture referring to Jesus Christ. Each point connects to hundreds, perhaps thousands, of other portions of Scripture, which develop the doctrine of Christology (the doctrine of Christ) throughout Scripture. The metaphor of the "BRANCH" are truths all growing from the same source in the prophecies of Scripture by inspiration of God.

"**Branch**
A name of Christ, used in fourfold way:

(1) 'The Branch of Jehovah' (Isa 4:2), that is, the 'Immanuel' character of Christ Isa 7:14 to be fully manifested to restored and converted Israel after His return in divine glory Mt 25:31.
(2) The 'Branch of David' Isa 11:1; Jer 23:5; 33:15 that is, the Messiah, 'of the seed of David according to the flesh' Ro 1:3 revealed in His earthly glory as King of kings, and Lord of lords;
(3) Jehovah's 'Servant, the Branch' Zec 3:8 Messiah's humiliation and obedience unto death according to Isa 52:13-15; 53; Php 2:5-8.
(4) The 'man whose name is the Branch' Zec 6:12-13 that is His character as Son of man, the 'last Adam,' the 'second Man' 1Co 15:45-47 reigning, as Priest-King, over the earth in the dominion given to and lost by the first Adam. Matthew is the Gospel of the 'Branch of David'; Mark of 'Jehovah's Servant, the Branch'; Luke of 'the man whose name is the Branch'; John of 'the Branch of Jehovah.'"[8]

With the Scriptures being so redundant with these connecting truths about the promised Messiah, why were the priests of Israel ignorant and deceived about His coming? We know the people of Israel were ignorant because the priests were ignorant, but why were the priests ignorant? Why didn't Nicodemus,

---

[8] C. I. Scofield, Notes from the Scofield Reference Bible, 1917, Module file location: C:\Program Files (x86)\SwordSearcher\Modules\Scofield.ss5cmty, Module file time: 7/31/2011 8:15:28 PM UTC.

the "teacher of Israel," know that we all "must be born again" to even be able to "see" and understand the "Kingdom of God" (John 3:3).

False doctrine is simply *educated ignorance*, lacking the *continuity of the harmony* of the Scriptures. False doctrine is always the outcome of lazy, superficial, and often convoluted Bible study. This is what happens when spiritual leaders become disconnected to the big picture provided through inductive Bible study (accurately putting all the pieces together).

Ignorance of Biblical prophecy is the outcome of lazy Bible study. God does not give us truths He does not intend for us to understand. "[9] But as it is written, Eye hath not seen, nor ear heard, neither have entered into the heart of man, the things which God hath prepared for them that love him. [10] But God hath revealed *them* unto us by his Spirit: for the Spirit searcheth all things, yea, the deep things of God" (I Corinthians 2:9-10).

Scripture interprets Scripture. Yes, there will always be details we will not be able to fully grasp about which we can only speculate, but the big picture of prophecy is clearly presented. The term "BRANCH" is a term that connects our understanding to hundreds, thousands, of verses of Scripture about Christ. Peter warns of the ignorance of prophecy in the third chapter of his second epistle.

"[11] ***Seeing* then** {*through the prophecies of Scripture*} *that* all these things shall be dissolved {*vs 10; 'the heavens shall pass away with a great noise, and the elements shall melt with fervent heat, the earth also and the works that are therein shall be burned up'*}, what manner *of persons* **ought ye to be in *all* holy conversation and godliness**, [12] **Looking for and hasting unto** the coming of the day of God, wherein the heavens being on fire **shall be dissolved**, and the elements **shall melt with fervent heat**? [13] Nevertheless we, according to his promise, **look for new heavens and a new earth, wherein dwelleth righteousness.** [14] Wherefore, beloved, **seeing that ye look for such things**, be diligent that ye may be found of him in peace, without spot, and blameless. [15] And account *that* the longsuffering of our Lord *is* salvation; even as our beloved brother Paul also according to the wisdom given unto him hath written unto you; [16] As also in all *his* epistles, speaking in them of these things; in which are some things hard to be understood, **which they that are unlearned** *{uneducated or ignorant}* **and unstable** *{vacillating, or without foundations}* **wrest, as** *they do* **also the other scriptures**, **unto their own destruction**. [17] Ye therefore, beloved, **seeing ye know** *these things* **before**, beware lest ye also, being led away with the error of the wicked, fall from your own stedfastness. [18] But grow in grace, and *in* the knowledge of our Lord and Saviour Jesus Christ. To him *be* glory both now and for ever. Amen" (II Peter 3:11-18).

Why is this warning about the "body of Moses" given here in the context of contending "for the faith" in Jude 3? The warning is in this context because it is a warning to the New Covenant priesthood of all believers who are individually responsible for preserving "the faith" by contending for every "jot and title.

Just like the Old Covenant Levitical priesthood as the representatives of the "body of Moses (the nation of Israel) failed and were defiled; they were *cast away as a priesthood.* The warning is to individual believer-priests in the New Covenant who will be *cast away* in their intended Kingdom Age rule with Christ because of their individual unfaithfulness in contending "for the faith".

"[13] For I speak to you Gentiles, inasmuch as I am the apostle of the Gentiles, I magnify mine office: [14] If by any means I may provoke to **emulation** *{jealousy}* *them which are* **my flesh** *{the Jews}*, and might save some of them. [15] For if **the casting away of them** *be* **the reconciling of the world**, what *shall* the receiving *of them be*, but life from the dead? [16] For if the firstfruit *be* holy, the lump *is* also *holy*: and if the root *be* holy, so *are* the branches. [17] And **if some of the branches be broken off**, and thou, being a wild olive tree, wert graffed in among them, and with them partakest of the root and fatness of the olive tree; [18] Boast not against the branches. But if thou boast, thou bearest not the root, but the root thee *{ 'salvation is of the Jews,' John 4:22}*. [19] Thou wilt say then, The branches were broken off, that I might be graffed in. [20] Well; **because of unbelief they were broken off, and thou standest by faith**. Be not highminded, but fear: [21] For **if God spared not the natural branches,** *take heed* **lest he also spare not thee.** [22] Behold therefore the goodness and severity of God: on them which fell, severity; but toward thee, goodness, **if thou continue in** *his* **goodness: otherwise thou also shalt be cut off**" (Romans 11:13-22).

Many will read losing one's salvation into being a *cast away* **priests. This is certainly NOT the case and is not to what being** *cast away* **in Romans 11:22 means.** Granted, the *cast away* priests of Israel were *cast away* because they made keeping the Law the means to achieve righteousness (Romans 10:3). That is equal to "unbelief."

Being a *cast away* **priest is the loss of POSITION because of unfaithfulness.** Even in the Church Age, pastors and deacons can lose their positions by becoming disqualified for the positions in specified areas of unfaithfulness (I Timothy 3:1-13 and Titus 1:5-16).

When Bible truths are lost or corrupted among *theological academia***, these corruptions are propagated and compounded because they are then taught to people who trust their** *academic authorities.* These corruptions cannot be corrected without condemning the corrupted authorities teaching them. People tend to protect and defend their trusted authorities. This is what happened during the four-hundred years of silence from God in the inter-testament period between Malachi and John the Baptist.

The remnant of Israel, returning to rebuild the Temple in Jerusalem under the direction of Ezra, Nehemiah, and Haggai, were mostly faithful priests from the faithful line of Zadok. Joshua of Zechariah 3:1-8 is the son of the High Priest Josedech (Haggai 1:1), taken into the Babylonian captivity by Nebuchadnezzar. These were descendants of the line of priesthood from Eleazer fulfilling God's prophecy regarding the casting away of the descendants of Eli as High Priests (I Samuel 2:22-33). Abiathar would be the last High Priest from the line of Eli (I Kings 2:26-27) when Zadok was appointed High Priest by king Solomon.

The point of the warning of Zechariah 3:8 is that even though Joshua was a faithful High Priest to Israel, his faithfulness did not guarantee the faithfulness of his progeny. Children MUST be trained to know the Scriptures and live the Scriptures. The prophecies of Ezekiel confirm this faithful line of priests will be restored during the Kingdom Age. The Zadokien priesthood of the Kingdom Age will be Church Age believers.

"*¹³ And they {*vs.10; 'the Levites that are gone away far from me, when Israel went astray, which went astray away from me after their idols'*} shall not come near unto me, to do the office of a priest unto me, nor to come near to any of my holy things, in the most holy *place*: but they shall bear their shame, and their abominations which they have committed. ¹⁴ But I will make them keepers of the charge of the house, for all the service thereof, and for all that shall be done therein. ¹⁵ **But the priests the Levites, the sons of Zadok, that kept the charge of my sanctuary when the children of Israel went astray from me**, they shall come near to me to minister unto me, and they shall stand before me to offer unto me the fat and the blood, saith the Lord GOD: ¹⁶ They {*the Zadokites*} shall enter into my sanctuary, and they shall come near to my table, to minister unto me, and they shall keep my charge" (Ezekiel 44:13-16).

The application of these truths is very apparent. Every believer will be rewarded for his/her faithfulness in obedience to the commands of Scripture. However, the only way to ensure our children and grandchildren are faithful is consistency in studying the Scriptures, teaching them the Scriptures, and living the Scriptures before them **just like** we live them before God. The thousands of little inconsistencies, hypocrisies, and duplicities in our lives will be the ropes that bind our next generations in spiritual death. This truth has been prevalent throughout thousands of years of recorded history from the beginning of time.

Jesus Confirms the Failure of the Levitical Priesthood

"*⁷ But when he saw many of the Pharisees and Sadducees come to his baptism, he said unto them, **O generation of vipers**, who hath warned you to flee from the wrath to come? ⁸ **Bring forth therefore fruits meet for repentance** {*context implies repentance of 'dead works' that precedes salvation; in other words, they needed to get saved first*}: ⁹ And think not to say within yourselves, We have Abraham to *our* father {*belief that they were saved because of their genetic connection to Abraham rather than their faith connection to Abraham; Galatians 3:16*}: for I say unto you, that God is able of these stones to raise up children unto Abraham. [10] **And now** {*right now the prophecies about the casting away of the apostate priesthood of Israel was being fulfilled in that generation*} also the axe is laid unto the root of the trees: **therefore** every tree which bringeth not forth good fruit is hewn down, and cast into the fire. [11] I indeed baptize you with water unto repentance {*sanctificationally*}: but he that cometh after me is mightier than I, whose shoes I am not worthy to bear: he shall baptize you with the Holy Ghost, and *with* fire: [12] Whose fan {*a tool to separate chaff from wheat*} *is* in his hand, and he will throughly purge {*cleanse or purify*} his floor {*the nation of Israel at His second coming*}, and gather his wheat into the garner; but he will burn up the chaff {*lost Christ-rejecting Jews; especially the apostate priests*} with unquenchable fire" (Matthew 3:7-12).

"[9] For behold the stone that I have laid before Joshua; upon **one stone** *shall be* seven eyes: behold, I will engrave the graving thereof, saith the LORD of hosts, and **I will remove the iniquity of that land in one day** {*the purging with the fire of God descending from heaven at the end of the Kingdom Age*}. [10] In **that day**, saith the LORD of hosts, shall ye call every man his neighbour under the vine and under the fig tree" (Zechariah 3:9-10).

Zechariah 3:9-10 is a remarkable text that looks beyond this creation to the New Genesis "in Christ." The Kingdom Age is but a small representation of the ultimate living Temple of God where all the redeemed become one with the Lord in perfect harmony of eternal existence. **The text is difficult to understand because the truths to which it speaks are unfathomable to the human mind.**

The fact that this prophecy is future should be evident by the twice repeated "I will" words of "the LORD of hosts." The "one stone" is Jesus Christ.** He is the "cornerstone" upon which all aspects of the *New Genesis* rests. Every "born again" believer is created to be a *living stone* at present and is built upon this *Cornerstone*.

However, "one day" every believer will literally and spiritually become part of this "one stone" in the living Temple of the *New Genesis* in the new Heaven/Earth created after the Kingdom Age.

"Him that overcometh will I make a pillar in the temple of my God, and he shall go no more out: and I will write upon him the name of my God, and the name of the city of my God, *which is* new Jerusalem, which cometh down out of heaven from my God: and *I will write upon him* my new name" (Revelation 3:12).

At the dissolution of the first creation after the Kingdom Age, the redeemed of God will experience for the first time a cohabitation with God hitherto never imagined, nor could it be because it is unfathomable.

This is the fulfillment of what I Corinthians 2:9 speaks; **"But as it is written, Eye hath not seen, nor ear heard, neither have entered into the heart of man, the things which God hath prepared for them that love him."**

The fact that this engraved stone with seven eyes is God and the New Genesis in Christ is revealed by Zechariah 4:10, representing the omniscience of the all-seeing and all-knowing God; "For who hath despised the day of small things? for they shall rejoice, and shall see the plummet in the hand of Zerubbabel *with* **those seven; they *are* the eyes of the LORD, which run to and fro through the whole earth**."

The "stone" is a metaphor for God representing His unchanging eternality. However, the living stone metaphor that we find elsewhere speaks of a union of the redeemed with their Redeemer in the *New Genesis*, which will ultimately be joined with the Father in the *New Genesis*.

Zechariah 3:9-10 is speaking of the "consuming fire" of God's presence, returning to His first creation to purify it in judgment and destroy it. This is the context of Isaiah 64:1-5 from which Paul quotes in I Corinthians 2:9. The material first creation will literally melt away at the presence of God at the end of the Kingdom Age.

"[1] Oh that thou wouldest rend the heavens, that thou wouldest come down, that the mountains might flow down at thy presence, [2] As *when* the melting fire burneth, the fire causeth the waters to boil, to make thy name known to thine adversaries, *that* the nations may tremble at thy presence! [3] When thou didst terrible things *which* we looked not for, thou camest down, the mountains flowed down at thy presence. [4] For since the beginning of the world *men* have not heard, nor perceived by the ear, neither hath the eye seen, O God, beside thee, *what* he hath prepared for him that waiteth for him. [5] Thou meetest him that rejoiceth and worketh righteousness, *those that* remember thee in thy ways: behold, thou art wroth; for we have sinned: in those is continuance, and we shall be saved" (Isaiah 64:1-5).

II Peter chapter three gives us considerable expansion upon our understanding of what Isaiah 64:1-5 speaks. The interpretation of Scripture is corrupted if we do not understand the inductive methodology. Inductive simply means the whole is equal to the sum of its parts.

In other words, we must gather all *the parts and put them together to understand the whole.* This is tedious and laborious work that few will take the time to do. It is often the outcome of a lifetime of diligent Bible study. God has given us the prophetic pieces of a gigantic puzzle and He expects we will be curious enough to work at putting it all together. **This is a labor of love.**

The second coming of Jesus is the "day of the Lord." The "day of the LORD" is the day of JEHOVAH. Jehovah is the Name of God the Redeemer. This is Jesus, the eternal Son of God as the second person of the Trinity. Jesus came to redeem lost souls and humanity's dominion lost to Satan in the fall into sin.

Satan will be bound for the one-thousand-year Kingdom Age period. The earth will be restored ecologically and topographically to the way it was prior to the great flood. The people entering the Kingdom Age will live for the whole one-thousand-year period. Death and disease will be eliminated. The earth will experience peace with King Jesus ruling the world.

However, the Kingdom Age is not the ultimate utopia. Although Satan and his fallen demons will be bound, the Earth will still be filled with unglorified sinners. They will marry and give birth to children needing to repent and be "born again." Many of those born into the Kingdom Age will reject Jesus as their Savior.

When Satan is loosed for a "little season" at the end of the Kingdom Age, they will join Satan in an attack against the Lord Jesus. Then they will experience the "day of God." The ultimate utopia will be created in "one day" called the "day of God." In that same day, the whole of the first creation will be "dissolved with fervent heat" at the very presence of Elohim.

"[3] Knowing this first, that there shall come in the last days scoffers, walking after their own lusts, [4] And saying, Where is the promise of his coming? for since the fathers fell asleep, all things continue as *they were* from the beginning of the creation. [5] For this they willingly are ignorant of, that by the word of God the heavens were of old, and the earth standing out of the water and in the water: [6] Whereby the world that then was, being overflowed with water, perished: [7] But the heavens and the earth, **which are now, by the same word are kept in store, reserved unto fire** against the day of judgment and perdition of ungodly men. [8] But, beloved, be not ignorant of this one thing, that one day *is* with the Lord as a thousand years, and a thousand years as one day. [9] The Lord is not slack concerning his promise, as some men count slackness; but is longsuffering to us-ward, not willing that any should perish, but that all should come to repentance. [10] But the day of the Lord will come as a thief in the night; in the which the heavens shall pass away with a great noise, and the elements shall melt with fervent heat, the earth also and the works that are therein shall be burned up. [11] *Seeing* then *that* all these things shall be dissolved, what manner *of persons* ought ye to be in *all* holy conversation and godliness, [12] **Looking for and hasting unto the coming of the day of God**, wherein the heavens being on fire shall be dissolved, and the elements shall melt with fervent heat? [13] Nevertheless **we**, according to his promise, **look for new heavens and a new earth**, wherein dwelleth righteousness" (II Peter 3:3-13).

On the "day of Pentecost" the New Covenant practically began to unfold. Every believer was indwelled by the Holy Spirit of God creating a theanthropic union with every believer. Those believers were sealed with the Holy Spirit "unto the day of redemption" of their bodies (Ephesians 4:30). That union is an eternal union that will never be broken (Hebrews 13:5).

However, that was just the beginning of our redemption, not its end. The next phase of "the regeneration" is the glorification of the believer's body when the believer is removed from his *sin nature* and the "old man" is left behind in the resurrection/glorification.

The next phase of "the regeneration" is the Kingdom Age when Jesus returns to Earth with His glorified redeemed to restore

dominion to humanity as He rules Earth from Jerusalem through a worldwide network of glorified believers dispersed into the cities through the world. We can only imagine the extent of the *theanthropic union* of the glorified believer with the heart and mind of Christ during this period of world history.

Will we know what Christ knows? Will we see what Christ sees? Will we feel what Christ feels? Is the "filling of the Spirit" during the Church Age intended to represent a small embryonic sense of the believer's glorification in the Kingdom Age?

Can we even imagine what it would be like to exist without the constant convolution of a *sin nature*? Can we imagine constantly being filled with the Spirit of God? Yet, as wonderful as this new extension of "the regeneration' will be, it is not the end of our transfiguration. There is a new last and eternal day dawning on the horizon of eternity.

"[1] And **I saw a new heaven and a new earth**: **for the first heaven and the first earth were passed away**; and there was no more sea. [2] And I John saw the holy city, new Jerusalem, **coming down from God out of heaven**, prepared **as a** bride adorned for her husband. [3] And I heard a great voice out of heaven saying, **Behold, the tabernacle of God** *is* **with men, and he will dwell with them**, and they shall be his people, and **God himself shall be with them**, *and be* their God. [4] And God shall wipe away all tears from their eyes; and there shall be no more death, neither sorrow, nor crying, neither shall there be any more pain: for the former things are passed away. [5] And he that sat upon the throne said, **Behold, I make all things new**. And he said unto me, Write: for these words are true and faithful. [6] And he said unto me, It is done. I am Alpha and Omega, the beginning and the end. I will give unto him that is athirst of the fountain of the water of life freely. [7] **He that overcometh shall inherit all things; and I will be his God, and he shall be my son**. [8] But the fearful, and unbelieving, and the abominable, and murderers, and whoremongers, and sorcerers, and idolaters, and all liars, shall have their part in the lake which burneth with fire and brimstone: which is the second death" (Revelation 21:1-8).

"Woe unto Them!"

"[8] **Likewise** {*just like the disobedient Jews in the wilderness*} also these *filthy* dreamers **defile the flesh** {*Sodomites*}, **despise dominion** {*angels that rebelled*}, and **speak evil of dignities** {*like the Jews murmured against Moses*}. [9] Yet Michael the archangel, when contending with the devil he disputed about the body of Moses, durst not bring against him a railing accusation, but said, The Lord rebuke thee. [10] But **these** {*'filthy dreamers', vs 8; who were the false teachers against which the faithful were to contend*} speak evil of those things which they know not: but what they know naturally, as brute beasts, in those things they corrupt themselves. [11] Woe unto them! for **they have gone in the way of Cain**, and **ran greedily after the error of Balaam** for reward, and **perished in the gainsaying of Core**. [12] These are spots in your feasts of charity, when they feast with you, feeding themselves without fear: clouds *they are* without water, carried about of winds; trees whose fruit withereth, without fruit, twice dead, plucked up by the roots; [13] Raging waves of the sea, foaming out their own shame; wandering stars, to whom is reserved the blackness of darkness for ever" (Jude 8-13).

"The Way of Cain"

"The way of Cain" is hatred and murder. This is true of all those who love false doctrine. Such people hate those that contend against false doctrine regardless that those contending do so merely by obedience or by exposing the false teacher. Their hatred will seek to silence the witness for truth even to the degree of murder. **The history of Christianity bears testimony to this fact.** Every person contending for the faith will experience this hatred at some point in their ministry.

Cain infected most of humanity with his false doctrine and hatred for the truth. The Roman Catholic Inquisition is an example of "the way of Cain." This hatred for the truth is very much part of the *seed of Satan* planted within the fallen natures of all those born of Adam (Romans 5:12).

Cain resisted the truth in the most heinous way possible. He simply eliminated the one that was right, his own brother. The war against truth and the enmity against God was started by Satan in the

Garden. Yet, that war was continued and propagated by Cain infecting most of humanity with a love for the false way and a hatred for the true way, by grace through faith.

All Cain needed to do was repent. Instead, he murdered. When anyone contends for the faith, he engages the enmity against God and puts himself at risk of attack.

"[14] And the LORD God said unto the serpent, Because thou hast done this, thou *art* cursed above all cattle, and above every beast of the field; upon thy belly shalt thou go, and dust shalt thou eat all the days of thy life: [15] And **I will put enmity between thee and the woman, and between thy seed and her seed**; it shall bruise thy head, and thou shalt bruise his heel" (Genesis 3:14-15).

"[6] For to be carnally minded *is* death; but to be spiritually minded *is* life and peace. [7] Because **the carnal mind *is* enmity against God**: for it is not subject to the law of God, neither indeed can be" (Romans 8:6-7).

"The Error of Balaam"

There are also those who hold to the "doctrine of Balaam," "the way of Balaam," and "the error of Balaam." These are detailed in the Old Testament in Numbers 22:5 through 23:24. Balaam was a prophet of God. He is the typical hireling prophet. The Bible has much to say about Balaam. In II Peter 2:15, it speaks of "the way of Balaam."

"The way of Balaam" is reflected in the modern preacher who will compromise the Word of God ("the faith") to gather a following of people, to keep his/her position as a pastor, or to increase the numbers of people attending their church services. This encompasses most of modern-day professing *Christianity*, which is not Christianity at all.

"Which have forsaken the right way, and are gone astray, following the way of Balaam *the son* of Bosor, who loved the wages of unrighteousness" (II Peter 2:15).

Balaam was a spiritual hireling. He used his God given gift to gain power and position in the world. He made merchandise of both his ministry and the people God called him to serve. The "way of Balaam" is the person who views people as the means to advance himself.

"¹¹ I am the good shepherd: the good shepherd giveth his life for the sheep. ¹² But **he that is an hireling**, and not the shepherd, whose own the sheep are not, seeth the wolf coming, and leaveth the sheep, and fleeth: and the wolf catcheth them, and scattereth the sheep. ¹³ The hireling fleeth, **because he is an hireling, and careth not for the sheep"** (John 10:11-13).

"And through covetousness shall they **with feigned words make merchandise of you**: whose judgment now of a long time lingereth not, and their damnation slumbereth not" (II Peter 2:3).

The "error of Balaam" is the false thinking of the false prophet who believes he exists to be served rather than to serve. The false prophet uses his position for self-glorification, rather than God-glorification. He wants to be exalted before men, rather than exalt God before men and edify men before God.

"For as he thinketh in his heart, so *is* he: Eat and drink, saith he to thee; but **his heart *is* not with thee"** (Proverbs 23:7).

Then there is the "doctrine of Balaam" that Christ speaks of in Revelation 2:14. The Christian is called to preach the *doctrine of Christ*. In other words, we are to seek to reproduce Christ in others by "renewing" their minds and allowing the Holy Spirit to "transform" their lives from the inside out. **A man reproduces what he is. He is what he believes. The "doctrine of Balaam" reproduces what Balaam was.**

Balaam taught the Moabite king Balak to corrupt God's children. King Balak wanted Balaam to curse the Israelites so that they wouldn't occupy his land, but Balaam could not. He wanted to, but he could not. **So, Balaam taught king Balak to seduce the children of Israel into compromise so that God would chastise Israel rather than bless them.**

The "doctrine of Balaam" was that he taught the men of Israel to marry Moabite women and defile their separation unto God. Paul had a similar problem with the believers at Corinth and so admonishes them:

"[11] O *ye* Corinthians, our mouth is open unto you, our heart is enlarged. [12] Ye are **not straitened in us** {*affectionately affected, love is not narrow or restricted*}, but **ye are straitened in your own bowels** {*they were restricting Paul's love towards them by resisting in their hearts what he taught*}. [13] Now for a recompense in the same, (I speak as unto *my* children,) be ye also enlarged. [14] Be ye not unequally yoked together with unbelievers: for what fellowship hath righteousness with unrighteousness? and what communion hath light with darkness? [15] And what concord hath Christ with Belial? or what part hath he that believeth with an infidel? [16] And what agreement hath the temple of God with idols? for ye are the temple of the living God; as God hath said, I will dwell in them, and walk in *them*; and I will be their God, and they shall be my people. [17] Wherefore **come out from among them, and be ye separate, saith the Lord, and touch not the unclean** *thing*; and I will receive you, [18] And will be a Father unto you, and ye shall be my sons and daughters, saith the Lord Almighty. [1] Having therefore these promises, dearly beloved, **let us cleanse ourselves from all filthiness of the flesh and spirit, perfecting holiness in the fear of God**" (II Corinthians 6:11-7:1).

As a result of Balaam's doctrine (a similar problem at Corinth), God's children became involved in pagan worship and the fornication of Baalism. This doctrine always begins with toleration and ends with a rapid slide into practice. What you begin to fix your eyes on will eventually become what you practice.

Who was Balaam? Balaam was an Old Testament prophet of God (Jude 11). We know a lot of things he wasn't, but it is apparent from Numbers 22:5 through 24:25 that Balaam was given visions and messages from God for the children of Israel and for king Balak (Numbers 22:12, 20, 32-33, 38, 23:5, 12, 16, 18-24, 26; 24:2-9, 15-25).

Balaam was an integrationist. It is obvious from Numbers 23:23 and 24:1 that he was accustomed to practicing "divination" and "enchantments."

"Surely *there is* no enchantment against Jacob, neither *is there* any divination against Israel: according to this time it shall be said of Jacob and of Israel, What hath God wrought" (Numbers 23:23)!

"And **when Balaam saw that it pleased the LORD to bless Israel**, he went not, **as at other times**, to seek for enchantments, but he set his face toward the wilderness" (Numbers 24:1).

God calls Balaam a "soothsayer" in Joshua 13:22.

"Balaam also the son of Beor, the soothsayer did the children of Israel slay with the sword among them that were slain by them" (Joshua 13:22).

Although it seems apparent that Balaam believed in Jehovah, it is also apparent that he was integrating the practices of heathenism. Pagans manipulated their gods to get those gods to do what he wanted them to do. Therefore, Balaam's understanding of Who God is was greatly corrupted.
This fact is obvious because after Balaam was directly instructed of God about what God wanted from him, he began to try to manipulate the situation to be able to have what he wanted anyway. **Balaam wanted his way, not God's way.** To the pagan mindset there were no absolutes of their gods, so they could manipulate them to change their god's minds to give the person what he wanted.
They also used "divination" and "enchantments" to see into the future and to manipulate it, people, and circumstances. Divination was the *magician's art.* Other terms for these people were a Medium, a Necromancer, a Familiar Spirit, a Wizard, and a Soothsayer. Their practices were those of witchcraft and sorcery.
The very term *divination* presumes that some *divine/deity* (at least supernatural) being would be providing the information. To the heathens, any supernatural being was considered divine even if it was Satan himself.

Divination sought knowledge of the spiritual realm through various methods, while *enchantment* sought to produce certain effects or manipulate circumstances through magic. **Balaam apparently practiced both.**

Balaam was an integrationist because he believed in the true God but used pagan practices to determine His will. In Numbers 23:3 he had offered sacrifice. Perhaps this was *Haruspicy* involved here. Balaam then went to "an high place" to look for a sign in the sky (*Augury*, to interpret as an *Omen* or *Portent*).

The "error of Balaam" is defined by two phrases in Jude 1:11, "ran greedily" and "for reward." Central to the error in the practice of Balaam was his error in thinking. His paganized mind allowed him to manipulate his position to his own benefit. He believed he existed to be served, rather than to serve. He was pre-occupied with "reward" and his heart was filled with greed. Balaam was one of the first *health and wealth* preachers.

"For as he thinketh in his heart, so *is* he: Eat and drink, saith he to thee; but his heart *is* not with thee" (Proverbs 23:7).

Balaam lived under the false assumption that God would curse Israel just to meet his selfish wants and desires. God's will *(as is evident from Balaam's responses to God's direct instruction)* was not his real concern.

The "way of Balaam" was his own way. He had his own agenda and his own methodology. For him, it was tried and proved by his own experiences, and therefore *it worked* (Pragmastism). That is, until he met with the God of Israel "in the plains of Moab on this side Jordan by Jericho (Num. 22:1)." **The "way of Balaam" is an attitude towards God that results in false practice (this practice is called a "way").**

"Every way of a man *is* right in his own eyes {*he rationalizes and justifies his false ways*}: but the LORD pondereth the hearts" (Proverbs 21:2).

The "way of Balaam" is defined by two phrases. He has "forsaken the right way, and are gone astray" and "who loved the

wages of unrighteousness.” This is also defined to some extent by God's actions in Numbers 22 in the following verses:

"And **God's anger was kindled because he went**: and the angel of the LORD stood in the way **for an adversary against him**. Now he was riding upon his ass, and his two servants *were* with him" (Numbers 22:22).

"And **the ass saw** the angel of the LORD standing in the way, and his sword drawn in his hand: and **the ass turned aside** out of the way, and went into the field: and Balaam smote the ass, **to turn her into the way** {*the way of Balaam*}" (Numbers 22:23).

God's way is always well defined if man will only *stop*, *look*, and *listen*.

"But the angel of the LORD stood in a path of the vineyards, wall *being* on this side, and a wall on that side" (Numbers 22:24).

It is amazing how blind people are to God's leading and direction and to what extremes they will go to have their own way. Remember, sometimes others see things you do not see.

"[25] And when the ass saw the angel of the LORD, she thrust herself unto the wall, and crushed Balaam's foot against the wall: and **he smote her again**. [26] And the angel of the LORD went further, and stood in a narrow place, where *was* no way to turn either to the right hand or to the left. [27] And when the ass saw the angel of the LORD, she fell down under Balaam: and Balaam's anger was kindled, and **he smote the ass with a staff**. [28] And the LORD opened the mouth of the ass, and she said unto Balaam, What have I done unto thee, that thou hast smitten me these three times? [29] And Balaam said unto the ass, Because thou hast mocked me: I would there were a sword in mine hand, for now would I kill thee. [30] And the ass said unto Balaam, *Am* not I thine ass, upon which thou hast ridden ever since *I was* thine unto this day? was I ever wont to do so unto thee? And he said, Nay" (Numbers 22:25-30).

Balaam is God's example of the need of the Christian servant to be patient with "those that oppose themselves."

"In meekness **instructing those that oppose themselves**; if God peradventure will give them repentance to the acknowledging of the truth" (II Timothy 2:25).

Only God was finally able to open Balaam's eyes:

"[31] Then **the LORD opened the eyes of Balaam** and he saw the angel of the LORD standing in the way, and his sword drawn in his hand: and he bowed down his head, and fell flat on his face. [32] And the angel of the LORD said unto him, Wherefore hast thou smitten thine ass these three times? behold, I went out to withstand thee, **because *thy* way is perverse before me.** [33] And the ass saw me, and turned from me these three times: **unless she had turned from me, surely now also I had slain thee, and saved her alive**. [34] And Balaam said unto the angel of the LORD, I have sinned; for I knew not that thou stoodest in the way against me: now therefore, **if** it displease thee, I will get me back again" (Numbers 22:31-34).

Balaam's response ("if it displease thee, I will get me back again") shows he saw, but still interpreted what he saw from his own agenda. Reception is not the same as perception. Balaam would simply seek another of his own ways to get where he wanted to be.

"But I have a few things against thee, because thou hast there them that hold the doctrine of Balaam, who taught Balac to cast a stumblingblock before the children of Israel, to eat things sacrificed unto idols, and to commit fornication" (Revelation 2:14).

Who is Balaam?

Balaam could not get God to curse Israel, so he taught Balak what to do to get Israel to bring God's hand of correction against them. What happened is detailed in Numbers 25: 1-18. The "way of

Balaam" is the "broad way." It is the way of the hireling prophet who makes merchandise of his gift and the people of God.

"[1] But there were false prophets also among the people, even as there shall be false teachers among you, **who privily shall bring in damnable heresies**, even **denying the Lord that bought them**, and bring upon themselves swift destruction. [2] And **many shall follow their pernicious ways**; by reason of whom the way of truth shall be evil spoken of. [3] And through covetousness shall they with feigned words make merchandise of you: whose judgment now of a long time lingereth not, and their damnation slumbereth not" (II Peter 2:1-3).

Twenty-four thousand people of the congregation of Israel died because of the "way of Balaam." *Laodiceanism* **will bear a heavy toll in souls.**

"Balaam also the son of Beor, the soothsayer, did the children of Israel slay with the sword among them that were slain by them" (Joshua 13:22).

"[1] And it came to pass after the plague, that the LORD spake unto Moses and unto Eleazar the son of Aaron the priest, saying, [2] Take the sum of all the congregation of the children of Israel, from twenty years old and upward, throughout their fathers' house, all that are able to go to war in Israel. [3] And Moses and Eleazar the priest spake with them in the plains of Moab by Jordan *near* Jericho, saying, [4] *Take the sum of the people*, from twenty years old and upward; as the LORD commanded Moses and the children of Israel, which went forth out of the land of Egypt. [5] Reuben, the eldest son of Israel: the children of Reuben; Hanoch, *of whom cometh* the family of the Hanochites: of Pallu, the family of the Palluites: [6] Of Hezron, the family of the Hezronites: of Carmi, the family of the Carmites. [7] These *are* the families of the Reubenites: and they that were numbered of them were forty and three thousand and seven hundred and thirty. [8] And the sons of Pallu; Eliab. [9] And the sons of Eliab; Nemuel, and Dathan, and Abiram. This *is that* Dathan and Abiram, *which were* famous in the congregation, **who strove against Moses and**

against Aaron in the company of Korah, when they strove against the LORD: [10] And the earth opened her mouth, and swallowed them up together with Korah, when that company died, what time the fire devoured two hundred and fifty men: and they became a sign. [11] Notwithstanding the children of Korah died not. [12] The sons of Simeon after their families: of Nemuel, the family of the Nemuelites: of Jamin, the family of the Jaminites: of Jachin, the family of the Jachinites: [13] Of Zerah, the family of the Zarhites: of Shaul, the family of the Shaulites. [14] **These *are* the families of the Simeonites, twenty and two thousand and two hundred**" (Numbers 26:1-14).

"And those that died in the plague were **twenty and four thousand**" (Numbers 25:9).

There is something revealed here (Numbers 25:14) that shows that is was not the entire congregation of Israel that was deceived by this false doctrine of Balaam. "Zimri, the son of Salu" was the man killed by "Phinehas" (25:11). **Zimri was a Simeonite.** If we compare the numbers of the Simeonites in Numbers 1:23 (59,300) with that of Numbers 26:14 (22,200) we find a loss of 37,100 people. The probability is that **the majority of the 24,000 killed in the plague were Simeonites**.

Today, the doctrine of Balaam is what is called *New Evangelicalism*. The harlot daughter of New Evangelicalism is the illegitimate *birth child* is called the *Emergent Church*.

One thing we can learn from this is that once you start down the *slide of compromise*, it is a steady, progressive movement out of and away from the circle of truth. The first step for the children of Israel was to begin to take Midianite women for their wives. It was not long before they were eating meat sacrificed to the idols of their wives and becoming involved in the pagan sexual rituals of the Baalistic practices of temple prostitution.

They didn't think they would be leaving the *righteous circle of truth*. They thought they would be just bringing these others (non-covenant people) into the *righteous circle of truth* with them. The reality was that as soon as they compromised the truth, they moved outside of the *righteous circle of truth*. What began as unscriptural "fellowship," ended in disaster.

"And have **no** fellowship with the unfruitful works of darkness, but rather reprove *them*" (Ephesians 5:11).

There are those that teach separation is only an Old Testament doctrine. They believe Christians are all people that believe in Jesus, regardless of what they believe or how they live. They teach we are at *liberty* today because we are not under Law, but under grace. Is that really what the New Covenant teaches?

"Now I beseech you, brethren, **mark them** {*watch for them as you would watch for an enemy*} which cause divisions and offences contrary to the doctrine which ye have learned; and **avoid them** {*shun or deviate your pathway away from them*}" (Romans 16:17).

The intent of these commands in Romans 16:17 is to keep the churches pure of various degrees of integrated paganism. Did the churches receive this warning in the seriousness of its commands? History bears record to this failure, and it continues by degree in every generation since the birth of the Church in Acts chapter two on the day of Pentecost.

This historical record of failure exists because it is easier to compromise the faith than to contend for the faith. Church history is written with the blood of the martyrs who refused to compromise and contended to their own death. There are numerous other similar texts commanding separation.

"[11] O *ye* Corinthians, our mouth is open unto you, our heart is enlarged. [12] Ye are not straitened in us, but ye are straitened in your own bowels. [13] Now for a recompence in the same, (I speak as unto [my] children,) be ye also enlarged. [14] Be ye not unequally yoked together with unbelievers: for what fellowship hath righteousness with unrighteousness? and what communion hath light with darkness? [15] And what concord hath Christ with Belial? or what part hath he that believeth with an infidel? [16] And what agreement hath the temple of God with idols? for ye are the temple of the living God; as God hath said, I will dwell in them, and walk in *them*; and I will be their God, and they shall be my people. [17] **Wherefore come out from among them, and be ye**

separate, saith the Lord, and touch not the unclean *thing*; **and I will receive you**, [18] And will be a Father unto you, and ye shall be my sons and daughters, saith the Lord Almighty. [1] Having therefore these promises, dearly beloved, let us cleanse ourselves from all filthiness of the flesh and spirit, perfecting holiness in the fear of God" (II Corinthians 6:11-7:1).

"[3] If any man teach otherwise, and consent not to wholesome words, *even* the words of our Lord Jesus Christ, and to **the doctrine which is according to godliness** {*Biblical separation*}; [4] He is proud, knowing nothing, but doting about questions and strifes of words, whereof cometh envy, strife, railings, evil surmisings, [5] **Perverse disputings of men of corrupt minds, and destitute of the truth**, supposing that gain is godliness: **from such withdraw thyself** {*remove yourself from the interaction and do not fellowship with them*}" (I Timothy 6:3-5).

"Having a **form** {*present tense; outward appearance or semblance*} **of godliness**, but **denying** {*perfect tense; therefore, apostate in that this ia a once forever act having fully denied*} **the power thereof: from such turn away** {*have no interaction with them in that they are dangerous people*}" (II Timothy 3:5).

"For the time will come when they **will not endure** {*forbear, suffer for*} **sound doctrine**; but after their own lusts shall they heap to themselves teachers, having itching ears" (II Timothy 4:3).

"[10] For there are many unruly and vain talkers and deceivers, **specially they of the circumcision**: [11] Whose mouths must be stopped, who subvert whole houses, teaching things which they ought not, for filthy lucre's sake. [12] One of themselves, *even* a prophet of their own, said, The Cretians *are* alway liars, evil beasts, slow bellies. [13] This witness is true. Wherefore rebuke them sharply, that they may be sound in the faith; [14] **Not giving heed to Jewish fables**, and **commandments of men, that turn from the truth**" (Titus 1:10-14).

"A man that is an heretick **after the first and second admonition reject** {*shun, avoid, discontinue fellowship because such a person is very dangerous*}" (Titus 3:10).

"And if any man **obey not our word by this epistle**, note that man {*mark for the purpose of avoidance; it would appear the intent is publicly*}, and have no company with him, that he may be ashamed" (II Thessalonians 3:14).

"Beloved, **believe not every spirit**, but try the spirits **whether they are of God**: because many false prophets are gone out into the world" (I John 4:1).

"[10] If there come any unto you, and **bring not this doctrine** {*of Christ, vs 9*}, **receive him not into** *your* **house** {*church house*}, neither bid him God speed: [11] For he that biddeth him God speed is partaker of his evil deeds" (II John 1:10-11).

"[3] Beloved, when I gave all diligence to write unto you of **the common salvation, it was needful for me to write unto you**, and exhort you that ye should earnestly contend for the faith which was once delivered unto the saints. [4] For there are certain men crept in unawares, who were before of old ordained to this condemnation, ungodly men, **turning the grace of our God into lasciviousness, and denying the only Lord God, and our Lord Jesus Christ**" (Jude 1:3-4).

The modern-day *Billy Balaams* would tell us that separation is an unbiblical doctrine. The example of Scripture is that thousands upon thousands will die and go to hell because of this *broad way* (and *Broadway*) approach to the things of God. Look at church history. What were the times that God blessed the most? **True revival has always come when God's people sought after holiness, not when they compromised it for convenience.**

"Perished in the Gainsaying of Core" (Jude 11)

Insurrection against God's anointed is a dangerous endeavor in which to involve oneself. The account of "Korah" in

Numbers 16:1-3 is especially grievous because in questioning and challenging God's appointed and anointed spokesman, Korah was questioning God's calling, undermining the authority of the Word of God spoken to God's people by Moses, and questioning the veracity of Moses' claim to lead the children of Israel through the Words of God given only to him.

However, the second level of Korah's sin and doubtful questioning initiated an insurrection against Moses and Aaron as High Priest where Korah gathered two other men who were leaders of the tribe of Reuben. Then they increased the insurrection against God's ordained leadership by gathering another two-hundred and fifty well known and respected "princes of the assembly" (Numbers 16:2). This is what defines *heresy*, which is dividing God's people into opposing sects based mostly on mere opinions.

"[1] Now **Korah**, the son of Izhar, the son of Kohath, the son of Levi, and **Dathan and Abiram**, the sons of Eliab, and On, the son of Peleth, sons of Reuben, took *men*: [2] And they rose up before Moses, with certain of the children of Israel, **two hundred and fifty princes of the assembly, famous in the congregation, men of renown**: [3] And they gathered themselves together against Moses and against Aaron, and said unto them, *Ye take* too much upon you, **seeing all the congregation *are* holy, every one of them** {*the ground of their heresy is that all the children of Israel were qualified to be priests*}, and the LORD *is* among them: wherefore then lift ye up yourselves above the congregation of the LORD" (Numbers 16:1-3)?

Why single out "Core" as the example? In every insurrection, there is always a primary instigator. The instigator usually works covertly until he has gathered a large enough following to seek to overthrow those he opposes. His real agenda is to take all or some of the authority for himself. Often the instigator stays covert and gets others to be his instruments of insurrection and rebellion. This was the case with Korah in Numbers chapter sixteen. **However, God sees the hearts.**

The point of Jude 11 is that those that sow the same seed of corruption as those sown by "Core" will bear the same fruit borne by "Core." "Core" sowed corruption and reaped its judgment.

Korah, Dathan, and Abiram opposed the divine authority given to Moses and Aaron by God.

Moses and Aaron spoke for God to the people. Moses and Aaron spoke the Words of God. Therefore, when "Core" raised up an insurrection against Moses and Aaron, he was opposing the Word of God thereby rejecting the Words of God through Moses. The word "gainsaying" is from the Greek word *antilogía* (*an-tee-log-ee'-ah*), which basically means *against the word*.

The use of this comparison in Jude 8 in the words "these *filthy* dreamers defile the flesh, despise dominion, and speak evil of dignities," is that such people reject or corrupt the authority of the inspired Words of God when they reject the authority of the Apostles and those God used to teach those inspired Words.

The damage that these insurrectionists can do in a local church can impact thousands of people in succeeding generations. Spiritual leaders must deal with these types of insurrectionists in no uncertain terms lest those not grounded in the Word are led astray and follow them. Remember, deceived people deceive.

This is the story of Korah in Numbers chapter sixteen. The heresy began in the heart of Korah, and he began to spread it until he had generated enough people who now shared his *opinion*.

However, as his *heretical opinion* spread it gathered momentum, because every new proselyte then covertly convinced someone else, who then covertly convinced others. All those convinced of this *heretical opinion* became *Kohathites* (followers/disciples of Korah without even being directly connected to Korah). Numbers 16:11 refers to this following as a "company." Another translation of "company" could be *congregation*.

The Judgment of Korah

There are always consequences for insurrection against God's commands. Some of those consequences are immediate as in the case of Korah and his congregation. Other consequences are merely the natural consequences of lost blessings and loss of spiritual potential due to making an allegiance choice contrary to God's will.

The judgment of Korah and his *congregation of carnality* is the substance of the reminder in Jude 11. Similar insurrections will result in similar judgments.

Although these judgments may not happen immediately as in the case of Korah and his congregation, the surety of judgment awaits it execution as a cloud of doom upon that person's future.

"*4* And **when Moses heard *it*, he fell upon his face**: *5* And he spake unto Korah and unto all his company, saying, Even to morrow **the LORD will shew who *are* his**, and *who is* holy; and will cause *him* to come near unto him: even *him* **whom he hath chosen** will he cause to come near unto him. *6* **This do**; Take you censers, Korah, and all his company; *7* And put fire therein, and put incense in them before the LORD to morrow: and it shall be *that* the man whom the LORD doth choose, he *shall be* holy: *ye take* too much upon you, ye sons of Levi. *8* And Moses said unto Korah, Hear, I pray you, ye sons of Levi: *9* ***Seemeth it but* a small thing unto you, that the God of Israel hath separated you from the congregation of Israel, to bring you near to himself to do the service of the tabernacle of the LORD, and to stand before the congregation to minister unto them?** *10* And he hath brought thee near *to him*, and all thy brethren the sons of Levi with thee: and seek ye the priesthood also? *11* For which cause *both* thou and all thy company *are* **gathered together against the LORD**: and what *is* Aaron, that ye murmur against him" (Numbers 16:4-11)?

Complicity in insurrection would be the cause of the death of a very large number of people. The insurrection did not begin with these people, but nonetheless they bore the consequences of judgment. The warning Jude 11 extrapolates from this event is that God acts consistently against those that oppose His ordained leaders and who distort His Words to justify their own purposes and ungodly lifestyles. This is no small matter.

We see the patience of Moses and God with these people as their accusations are put to the test defined in Numbers 16:16-22. The intent of the test is to give anyone that has aligned himself with the congregation of Korah to repent and separate from that "company." **Be careful with whom you keep company**!

"*16* And Moses said unto Korah, **Be thou and all thy company <u>before the LORD</u>, thou, and they, and Aaron, to morrow**: *17*

And take every man his censer, and put incense in them, and bring ye before the LORD every man his censer, two hundred and fifty censers; thou also, and Aaron, each *of you* his censer. [18] And they took every man his censer, and put fire in them, and laid incense thereon, and stood in the door of the tabernacle of the congregation with Moses and Aaron. [19] And Korah gathered all the congregation against them unto the door of the tabernacle of the congregation: and the glory of the LORD appeared unto all the congregation. [20] And the LORD spake unto Moses and unto Aaron, saying, [21] **Separate yourselves from among this congregation, that I may consume them in a moment.** [22] And they fell upon their faces, and said, O God, the God of the spirits of all flesh, shall one man sin, and wilt thou be wroth with all the congregation" (Numbers 16:16-22)?

The consequences of theological rebellion are far more serious than the consequences of civil rebellion. Civil rebellion may cause local skirmishes or even wars. Yes, people die in wars, but the consequences do not end at the sunset of their lives. **Souls are eternal.**

Death ends an "under the sun" existence, but there are also the consequences of divine judgment upon the eternal existence. Secondly, theological rebellion creates converts to that rebellion and carries those converts into the same eternal destiny. **Be careful with whom you align yourself!**

Why did "everyman" have a "censer" (Numbers 16:17)?

Prior to the institution of the Mosaic Covenant and the establishment of the Levitical priesthood of that covenant, Jews functioned under the patriarchal (head of house) priesthood of the home. Every household offered sacrifices to God and every household had a censer on which incense was offered to God to represent prayer.

The expectation of answered prayer was based upon sanctification because the incense was burned from the coals of the sacrificial fire. The potential for answered prayers and blessing was of faith in the sanctifying offering of a proper sacrifice. This was a universal practice even among the Egyptians who had their own *firepans* (censers) from their paganism.

It is highly probable that the "censers" mentioned in Numbers 16:17 were part of the spoils taking from the Egyptians upon Israel's departure.

"^{35} And the children of Israel did according to the word of Moses; and they borrowed of the Egyptians jewels of silver, and jewels of gold, and raiment: ^{36} And the LORD gave the people favour in the sight of the Egyptians, so that they lent unto them *such things as they required*. And **they spoiled the Egyptians**" (Exodus 12:35-36).

After the institution of the Mosaic Covenant through Moses, only the Levitical priests were to offer incense before God and all sacrifices were to be offered by these priests <u>in the Tabernacle</u>. This was a change in covenant responsibilities between the dispensation (*stewardship of the covenant*) of Promise (Abrahamic Covenant) and the dispensation of the Law (Mosaic Covenant).

Under the Mosaic Covenant, the fire to light and burn the incense had to be taken from the fire of the offering in the Tabernacle. Both the fire, the altar, and the incense were now *holy to the Lord* and could only be offered by a sanctified and consecrated Levitical priest. There was an extensive examination of each priest as well as rituals for his personal cleansing before he was consecrated by the High Priest to serve.

Korah's *heresy* was that he believed it was still acceptable for anyone to offer sacrifices and to burn incense in his *household censer*. God said through Moses, No! Korah responded with the accusation that Moses just made this up to take power and authority over the people. This was Korah's accusation against Moses and Aaron. He was saying that they selfishly conspired together to become *lords* over the children of Israel and invented the Mosaic Covenant to put themselves in power over the people.

In Numbers 16:22, God was about to eliminate the whole "company" of Korah instantly because of their rebellion and insurrection. Moses pleads for mercy. "O God, the God of the spirits of all flesh, shall one man sin, and wilt thou be wroth with all the congregation." There are always simple ignorant people carried along in insurrections because of loyalties to friends. Such people are easily caught up in group think and peer pressure mob mentality. Korah was the cause of the problem.

Moses' argument was that Korah alone should bear the judgment. Yet, God says no! If people heretically gather in an insurrection, whether they are simpletons or not, they will be judged as insurgents and die as insurgents, for they have declared war on God's will.

When reading Numbers 16:23-40, read it with this context in mind. We must maintain this context to understand the full ramifications of the warning in Jude 11 about "the gainsaying of Core." The word "gainsaying" is from the Greek word *antilogía (an-tee-log-ee'-ah)*, which basically means *against the word*.

Therefore, to join oneself with the likes of people like Korah is to join oneself with someone who is standing *against the word* of God taught and spoken through God's ordained messenger. When anyone joins himself to such a person, he also joins himself to the ordain consequences of that insurrection in the pending judgment of God upon the insurrection and insurgents.

This is the warning of Jude 11, very similar to God's warnings in II Peter chapter two, to all professing believers in Jesus Christ thinking they have equal authority with those God has ordained to be leaders in the local churches.

Another level of responsibility is revealed when we understand that Korah did not yet have the written words of God (the Pentateuch) that would later be recorded by Moses. Therefore, to reject Moses as God's spokesman was to reject the Word of God and all the Words of God that would later be recorded in written form in the first five books call the Law.

This historical context must be given consideration when reading Numbers chapter sixteen. If Korah is successful in his insurrection, the veracity of the first five books of the Bible would be destroyed and rejected as the Word of God. This is another satanic "hath God said" attack against the veracity of the Word of God.

Under the Abrahamic Covenant, all the faith descendants of Abraham were chosen by God and consecrated to offer sacrifice and prayer to God. In this sense, every descendant of Abraham were priests before God. God intended this to continue in the Mosaic Covenant, but the children of Israel recused themselves from this responsibility at Mt. Sinai.

Moses was told this by God, "And ye shall be unto me a kingdom of priests, and an holy nation. These *are* the words which thou shalt speak unto the children of Israel" (Exodus 19:6).

Under the Mosaic Covenant, only sanctified Levitical priests could offer sacrifice or approach the Ark of the Covenant. Only the High Priest was allowed inside the Holy of Holies and then only one a year on the Day of Atonement. Should the children of Israel and Korah have known that Moses spoke for God?

"[9] And the LORD said unto Moses, **Lo, I come unto thee in a thick cloud, that the people may hear when I speak with thee, and believe thee for ever.** And Moses told the words of the people unto the LORD. [10] And the LORD said unto Moses, Go unto the people, and sanctify them to day and to morrow, and let them wash their clothes, [11] And be ready against the third day: for the third day the LORD will come down **in the sight of all the people upon mount Sinai**" (Exodus 19:9-11).

From this point forward, when Moses said *thus saith the Lord*, every Jew needed to know that Mose's mouth was moving and words that came forth from that mouth were (and still are) **God's Word** (I Peter 4:11). Korah rejected that and therefore led people astray.

"[23] And the LORD spake unto Moses, saying, [24] Speak unto the congregation, saying, **Get you up from about the tabernacle of Korah, Dathan, and Abiram.** [25] And Moses rose up and went unto Dathan and Abiram; and the elders of Israel followed him. [26] And he spake unto the congregation, saying, Depart, I pray you, from the tents of these wicked men, and touch nothing of theirs, lest ye be consumed in all their sins. [27] So they gat up from the tabernacle of Korah, Dathan, and Abiram, on every side: and Dathan and Abiram came out, and stood in the door of their tents, and their wives, and their sons, and their little children. [28] And Moses said, Hereby ye shall know that the LORD hath sent me to do all these works; for *I have* not *done them* of mine own mind. [29] If these men die the common death of all men, or if they be visited after the visitation of all men; *then* the LORD hath not sent me. [30] But if the LORD make a new thing, and the earth open her mouth, and swallow them up, with all that *appertain* unto them, and they go down quick into the pit; then ye shall understand that these men have provoked the LORD. [31] And it came to pass, as he had made an end of speaking all these words, that the ground clave asunder that *was* under them: [32] **And the earth opened her mouth, and swallowed them up, and their houses, and all the men that *appertained* unto Korah, and all *their* goods. [33] They, and all that *appertained* to them, went down alive into the pit, and the earth closed upon them: and they perished from among the congregation.** [34] And all Israel that *were* round about them fled at the cry of them: for they said, Lest the earth swallow us up *also*. [35] **And there came out a fire from the LORD, and consumed the two hundred and fifty men that offered incense.** [36] And the LORD spake unto Moses, saying, [37] Speak unto Eleazar the son of Aaron the priest, that he take up the censers out of the burning, and scatter thou the fire yonder; for they are hallowed. [38] The censers of **these sinners against their own souls**, let them make them broad plates *for* a covering of the altar: for they offered them before the LORD, therefore they are hallowed: and they shall be a sign unto the children of Israel. [39] And Eleazar the priest took the brasen censers, wherewith they that were burnt had offered; and they were made broad *plates for* a covering of the altar: [40] *To be* **a memorial {*reminder*} unto the children of Israel, that no stranger, which *is* not of the seed of Aaron, come near to offer incense before the LORD**; that he **be not as Korah**, and **as his company**: as the LORD said to him by the hand of Moses" (Numbers 16:23-40).

The After-Effects of Insurrection: There is ALWAYS an "on the Morrow"

"[41] But **on the morrow all** the congregation of the children of Israel **murmured against Moses and against Aaron**, saying, Ye have killed the people of the LORD. [42] And it came to pass, when **the congregation was gathered against Moses and against Aaron**, that they looked toward the tabernacle of the congregation: and, behold, the cloud covered it, and the glory of the LORD appeared. [43] And Moses and Aaron came before the tabernacle of the congregation. [44] And the LORD spake unto

Moses, saying, ⁴⁵ **Get you up from among this congregation, that I may consume them as in a moment. And they** {*Moses and Aaron*} **fell upon their faces.** ⁴⁶ And Moses said unto Aaron, Take a censer, and put fire therein from off the altar, and put on incense, and **go quickly unto the congregation, and make an atonement for them: for there is wrath gone out from the LORD; <u>the plague is begun.</u>** ⁴⁷ And Aaron took as Moses commanded, and **ran** into the midst of the congregation; and, behold, the plague was begun among the people: and he put on incense, and made an atonement for the people. ⁴⁸ And **he stood between the dead and the living; and the plague was stayed.** ⁴⁹ Now they that died in the plague were **fourteen thousand and seven hundred**, beside them that died about the matter of Korah. ⁵⁰ And Aaron returned unto Moses unto the door of the tabernacle of the congregation: and **the plague was stayed**" (Numbers 16:41-50).

Jude
Contending for the Faith

Chapter Six
Apostates in the Assembly

In Jude 12-13 God gives five equivocations of allowing apostates that continue historically into all local churches. The point of these five equivocations is that the God sees compromise in a much different way than do most people.

Allowing those who teach false doctrine to remain within the local assembly is much like allowing a pedophile unmonitored oversight of children in a nursery school. Local churches are doctrinal training centers for believers who often do not yet have enough spiritual discernment to know false doctrine from right doctrine.

False teachers introduce *suppositional thinking* into the local assembly thereby causing people to read those suppositions into texts taken out of the context of a particular statement. Doing so with one verse of Scripture taken out of context can corrupt whole books of the Bible and often the teaching of a particular topic or subject.

The most dominant failure of these suppositions is the failure to see the transitional responsibilities in the different covenants of each new dispensation and that these covenants are sanctificational in their purpose. In other words, these covenants change how believers identify themselves before the world by the way they live and govern themselves according to God's ordained covenant.

Church Age believers have a different set of *qualifiers* and *identifiers* under the New Covenant than the Jews had under the Mosaic Covenant. Jews who became Christians had to abandon the Mosaic Covenant *identifiers* such as the Levitical Priesthood, the Temple and its many sacrifices, circumcision, and the numerous holy days (the liturgical calendar).

Church Age *identifiers* included aligning oneself with a local assembly to be trained doctrinally and baptized by immersion into that local assembly thereby making a personal commitment to God and the other believers in that assembly to "walk in the newness of life" (Romans 6:4). Circumcision was no longer an *identifier*.

The two ordinances (*ordained identifiers*) to be practiced were water baptism and the Lord's Supper. These ordinances were intended means to ensure that every new Christian understood New Covenant responsibilities.

Water baptism is intended to ensure believers understand their spiritual union with God through the indwelling of the Holy Spirit and their New Creation "in Christ." With that understanding came the understanding that the Christian life ("walk in the newness of life," Romans 6:4) came with obligations first to God and to other believers in the local assembly.

The Lord's Supper is intended to be a *regular refresher* and *reminder* of the incarnation of God in Jesus, His death, burial, and resurrection of Christ and WHAT HE ACCOMPLISHED on the believer's behalf. False teachers almost immediately began to corrupt the meaning of these ordinances thereby corrupting every local assembly that allowed them to continue to covertly teach those corruptions.

Eventually, these insurrectionists took over the assemblies and ousted the pastor/teachers God ordained to lead those assemblies (repeat *ad infinitum*). This is the repeated pattern of local churches on the road to apostasy. Jude 12-13 tells local churches what to do about this and seeks to give them another point of view from God's perspective.

There must be a time limit upon our patience with apostate teachers or they will undermine a local congregation by sidetracking the next generation of *baby converts*.

"[12] These are **spots in your feasts**(1) of charity, when they feast with you, feeding themselves without fear: **clouds *they are* without water**(2), carried about of winds; **trees whose fruit withereth**(3), without fruit, twice dead, plucked up by the roots; [13] **Raging waves of the sea**(4), foaming out their own shame; **wandering stars**(5), to whom is reserved the blackness of darkness for ever" (Jude 12-13).

How does God want faithful believers to see people coming into a local assembly being trained for "the work of the ministry"? God wants us to approach them with careful examination and caution.

Every local church wants to grow, and loving Christians want to reproduce the Christ-life in themselves and in others.

Christ was certainly patient with the masses (the *seekers*), but He was also very cautious with them. When the crowds grew large because they followed the miracles, Jesus delineated between following His teaching and following the miracles.

The masses wanted free food, healings, and to see miraculous events to talk about. The masses want *memorable experiences*. However, few were willing to do what Jesus said defined the requirements of true disciples. "If any *man* will come after me, let him deny himself, and take up his cross, and follow me" (Matthew 16:24).

We must always differentiate between *church building* and *crowd gathering*. Modern Evangelicalism and much of modern fundamentalism have lost this delineation between *church building* and *crowd gathering*. Church building constantly emphasizes total surrender to the will of God in doing the work of the ministry and "contending earnestly for the faith once delivered to the saints" regardless of what that "contending" cost the individual believers.

This defines true disciples of Jesus. History bears record to the fact that there have been few people belonging to the nobility of true faith and faithfulness. History bears record to the fact that almost every second generation of local assemblies depart from the faith in varying degrees.

"[1] Now the Spirit speaketh expressly, that in the latter times **some shall depart** {*desert or revolt*} **from the faith**, giving heed to seducing spirits, and doctrines of devils; [2] Speaking lies in hypocrisy; **having their conscience seared with a hot iron**; [3] Forbidding to marry, *and commanding* to abstain from meats, which God hath created to be received with thanksgiving of them which believe and know the truth" (I Timothy 4:1-3).

Jude 12-13 lists five *descriptors* of God's view of the effect of allowing those that have deserted and revolted against the faith to continue their covert corruptions within the perimeters of a local assembly. The faithful must gain God's view and act accordingly.

Paul warns of this also. "For they that are such serve not our Lord Jesus Christ, but their own belly; and by good words and fair speeches deceive the hearts of the simple" (Romans 16:18). **God wants us to see these corrupters the way God sees them.**

People naturally, but ignorantly, are drawn to the crowds like moths to the fire. People are attracted to what appears to be entertaining or something that will excite them in some experience. This is certainly true of those pursuing religious or spiritual experiences.

This is another form of Empiricism and Mysticism. These people are not content with *knowing* the truth and *living* that truth. These people want a spiritual euphoria or a sense of having been with God. They want to see, taste, and feel their experience and usually pursue such experiences with vigor with the condition that doing so is not accompanied by guilt of sin or too many commitments. They want to feel or experience for a moment and then be able to walk away from that moment and live any way they want afterwards.

This kind of religion comes without any spiritual obligations or sense of sinfulness before a holy God. Such people rush headlong into such adventures with little or no discernment as to the fact they are not pursuing God, but *experiences*.

Unfortunately, there are hundreds of religious charlatans ready and willing to cater to their carnality and entertain them with a momentary mystical religious experience. This fiasco will awe them and give them their momentary spiritual fix from which the charlatans can profit.

However, such people leave that *exciting adventure* unrepentant and unchanged in their relationship with God. This is because their experience was merely manufactured and artificial. Feelings change no one. True encounters with God have ALWAYS been encounters with truth that are accompanied with deep conviction of sin and strong desires to please God.

Dealing with the Charlatans

The obvious fact of the warnings about the charlatan false teachers addressed in Jude 8-14 is that they are self-serving. They certainly are not putting the spiritual interests of those they teach first in their priorities. They are making merchandise out of people to advance themselves in position, power, and filthy lucre.

These manipulative charlatans addressed in Jude use the same tactics as the pagans. Two governing principles are given in I Corinthians chapter fourteen establishing God's methods in everything He does. If we understand these two governing principles, we will readily be enabled to discern when a charlatan is trying to manipulate us into some false religious euphoria without any genuine spiritual outcome.

1. "For God is not *the author* of confusion" (I Corinthians 14:33). If a state of disorder exists, it is not of God ("confusion" is from the Greek word *akatastasia* {ak-at-as-tah-see'-ah} meaning *a state of disorder*). When God does something, it is always done in an orderly fashion:

"Let all things be done decently and in order" (I Corinthians 14:40).

2. Whatever God does, ALWAYS edifies. I Corinthians 14:12 states God's purpose is "edification"; the act of one who promotes another's **growth** in Christian **wisdom**, **piety**, **joy**, and **holiness**. If what someone says or does is not edifying, it **is not of God** (a key word in I Corinthians 14:2-22 is the word "understanding," or a derivative thereof, used nine times). **Spiritual growth ALWAYS results in CHANGE that makes a person more *Christ-like*.**

Understanding what Paul was dealing with at Corinth must be understood from its historical context. The church at Corinth was a carnal lot. The majority of those in the church at Corinth were saved out of the pagan mystery religions (I Corinthians 12:2). These people were incorporating some of the religious practices of the pagan mystery religions within their Christianity (*Syncretism*).

This Mysticism was a common problem being integrated into Christianity through the pagans that professed faith in Christ but had not repented of their pagan worship practices. This is like the "mixed multitude" (Exodus 12:38) that came out of Egypt with the Jews and influenced Aaron into building a golden calf to represent Jehovah and then worship Him with pagan worship practices (Exodus 32:1-6).

"Ye know that ye were Gentiles, **carried away unto these dumb idols**, even as ye were led" (I Corinthians 12:2).

Most of the predominantly Gentile churches struggled with separating themselves and their local churches from the integration of pagan worship practices. **The pagan *mystery religions* all evolved out of Babylon from the occult practices of Nimrod. This resulted in the building of the Tower of Babel and God's confounding of the languages ending in the dispersal of the people into different nations (language groups).** The origins of the mystery religions were demonic. The supernatural happenings of the mystery religions were demonic.

Common to the mystery religions was the practice of *Ecstasism* and *Enthusiasm.* S. Angus, in his book **The Mystery Religions** (New York: Dover Publications, 1975), details these two practices.

"...Ecstasy (*ekstasis*) and Enthusiasm (*enthusiasmos*), both of which might be induced by vigil and fasting, tense religious expectancy, whirling dances, physical stimuli, the contemplation of sacred objects, the effect of stirring music, inhalation of fumes, revivalistic contagion (such as happened in the church at Corinth), hallucination, suggestion, and other means belonging to the apparatus of the Mysteries."

These are the types of things that Jude addresses that were the advancing influence of the charlatans within the churches and drawing away people "after their own lusts." "These are murmurers, complainers, walking after their own lusts; and their mouth speaketh great swelling *words*, having men's persons in admiration because of advantage" (Jude 16).

"Spots in Your Feasts of Charity"

This statement should not be confused with the practice of the ordinance of the Lord's Supper. "Feasts of charity" refers to the wealthier of the early Christians generously and lovingly providing a community meal that included all the poor, orphans, and widows in the local assembly. They would all gather in the local assembly and share a meal.

This was a way for Christians to show that the "body of Christ" was a community without class divisions. True believers willfully and lovingly cared for one another.

The word "spots" is translated from the Greek word *spilás* (spee-las'), which was a word describing *a hidden rock* or *rock shelf* under the sea that caused shipwrecks if a ship captain was unaware of its location.

Although the "feasts of charity" were pure in their motives and objectives, there will always be people who take advantage of the loving generosity of others. Such people have ulterior motives in joining a "feast of charity." They may even participate in providing a large portion of the "feast."

Politics in the Church?

However, the motive of some people selfishly seeks to earn the ear and sympathy of those they want to get to listen to their teaching and to gain their sympathies. Not everyone doing good things have the spiritual interests of others as their motivation. Some are just *playing politics* with the souls of people.

A gift of love expects nothing in return. The point is that believers must be careful about forming alliances with people who expect loyalties to them over loyalties to God's Word and His ordained leadership in the pastor/teachers of a local assembly.

These political manipulators gather political popularity for the purpose of overthrowing the leadership of the local assembly and replacing those men with their own *spiritual puppets*. Under the guise of feeding the needy, these people are actually "feeding themselves without fear." This is the *hidden reef* ("spots") that will reduce the noble purpose of the "feasts of charity" to carnal competition for the loyalties of those being fed.

Each of the five *similes* of Jude 12-13 warn about false hope in empty promises offered by manipulators trying to garner loyalties to people above loyalties to truth and "the faith." Unfortunately, being careful requires a certain degree of cynicism when it comes to evaluating the seemingly noble purposes and generosity of some people. A few people can generate this cynicism that is then applied even to people without hidden and ulterior motives in their generosity.

Therefore, truly generous people seek to conceal their identity in gifts of generosity so those receiving the gift with give the glory to the Lord. Those who are pure in their motives take steps to ensure their generosity is anonymous because they want no recognition from those receiving. Jesus gave specific instruction regarding this because He understands that false loyalties can easily be created by such gifts. Those with pure motives will carefully guard against such things.

"[1] Take heed that ye **do not your alms before men, to be seen of them**: otherwise ye have no reward of your Father which is in heaven. [2] Therefore when thou doest *thine* alms, do not sound a trumpet before thee, as the hypocrites do in the synagogues and in the streets, **that they may have glory of men.** Verily I say unto you, They have their reward. [3] But **when thou doest alms, let not thy left hand know what thy right hand doeth**: [4] That thine alms may be in secret: and thy Father which seeth in secret himself shall reward thee openly" (Matthew 6:1-4).

"Clouds *They are* Without Water"

Only those living in the parched and arid geography of the Middle East or other dessert areas of the world can really understand this simile. Clouds promise refreshing rain which then waters the crops, grows the pastures for the livestock, and replenishes the water reservoirs in the wells and pools.

The words "clouds" is a simile for promises. False doctrine and false gospels claim God makes promises that He has not made. Therefore, these false teachers create a false hope. False teachers like these "clouds" promise water but never deliver except to themselves.

This is the thrust of *Prosperity Theology* also known as Health and Wealth Gospel, *Name it and Claim it* theology, Seed Faith Giving, Word of Faith, and other deceptive titles. These are all forms of Mammonism disguised as Christianity and wrapped in an alluring package of giving to gain profit. These charlatans profess to be God's prophets, but they spell the word differently: **Profits.**

A few of these wicked millionaire charlatans are Joel Osteen, Kenneth Copeland, Creflo Dollar, Joyce Meyers, Benny Hinn, and Paula White.

They live opulent lives on the gifts of others having multiple mansions, private jets, huge bank accounts, and lavish yachts. Under the guise and false promise of helping others, they just *help themselves*. Their theology is little more than a *lottery philosophy* where one person out of billions gives testimony to God making the charlatan wealthy.

All the charlatan needs are a few *success stories* to keep the deception going. Every derivation of the *Word of Faith* movement is created from a noxious concoction of innumerous doctrinal corruptions and is just another *Ponzi scheme* built upon the human desire for *wealth without work*.

Withering Fruit

"trees whose fruit withereth, without fruit, twice dead, plucked up by the roots;" (Jude 12)

In late autumn, fruit trees begin to wither and go into dormancy for the winter. This is the simile of those moving into Apostasy. Liberalism continues to gradually kill every hope of lasting/eternal fruit or any hope of spiritual prosperity until it kills the tree and plucks up that tree by its roots.

The tree is a metaphor of a local church. Liberalism and its false doctrines progressively and doctrinally disconnect people from the Church as the "pillar and ground of the truth" thereby disconnecting people from any hope of producing genuine followers of Jesus Christ ("born again" disciples). It is sad to see ripened fruit begin to rot on the trees due to the lack of harvesters and disciple makers.

God raised up Amos to speak to the children of Israel in a similar period of history. This spoke to the similar problems of eroding loyalty to the Word of God and paganization of worship into idolatry. Amos was neither a professional prophet nor the son of a professional prophet (Amos 7:14). Amos was a herder and a fruit picker (sycamore husbandman; a kind of fig).

There were schools of professional prophets in Israel, but they could not be trusted. There was a tribe of priests who were supposed to be separated from worldliness and unto God, but they were compromising and integrating paganism into the lives of the Jews. So, God used nonprofessional and untrained but godly men like Amos instead.

"[11] And I raised up of your sons **for prophets** {*to proclaim God's will and what God was doing*}, and of your young men **for Nazarites** {*separatists to holiness*}. *Is it* **not even thus, O ye children of Israel** {*you know this is true because you see it*}? saith the LORD. [12] But **ye gave the Nazarites wine to drink** {*defiling their separation*}; and commanded the prophets, saying, **Prophesy not** {*silencing God's voice of correction and rebuke*}" (Amos 2:11-12).

There are times throughout history when God has *ripened* the people of the world to listen to His "ambassadors." These times have almost always been times of famine or plagues where large numbers of people faced imminent death. The world offered them no hope for even survival, let alone thriving. This is what it was like under the overbearing dominance of the Roman Empire. Taxation was so burdensome it left most people with barely enough for their own sustenance.

The Roman Empire was an oligarchy ruled by *Martial Law*. An oligarchy is a society controlled and organized by a small class of privileged people, with no possibility of intervention from the most part of society. This *ruling class* governed through military terrorism rapidly evolving into an autocracy.

An autocracy is a society controlled and organized by a small class of privileged people, with no intervention from the larger populace of society. Rome began as a democracy ruled by laws passed by their senate. The senators evolved into an oligarchy, which was later overthrown by the military power of a dominant emperor evolving into an autocracy like a dictatorship.

These types of governments create hopeless atmospheres of existence that long for something better and create times of spiritual awakenings. Unfortunately, these times also create an atmosphere of self-protection where those who can provide answers to those seeking spiritual awakening and hope are silent and therefore never enter the harvest fields even though the "fruit" is ripe.

This is what it was like for the Jewish people under the Roman oligarchy. The United States is rapidly moving into an oligarchy progressively moving to an autocracy.

"[35] And Jesus went about all the cities and villages, teaching in their synagogues, and preaching the gospel of the kingdom, and healing every sickness and every disease among the people. [36] But when he saw the multitudes, he was moved with compassion on them, because they fainted, and were scattered abroad, as sheep having no shepherd. [37] **Then** {*after seeing the hopelessness of the people*} saith he unto his disciples, **The harvest truly *is* plenteous** {*people are spiritually ripe*}, but the labourers *are* few; [38] **Pray ye therefore the Lord of the harvest, that he will send forth labourers into his harvest**" (Matthew 9:35-38).

True Christianity has historically grown and advanced more while under adversity than it has under prosperity. During these times of adversity, Christians cease putting their hope in the things "under the sun" and begin to live and think about eternal priorities beyond this life and this world. Faith must be real if death becomes an imminent possibility every day. If faith in the eternal is not real, despair will dominate, and selfishness rather than self-sacrifice will dominate.

Real threats to personal survival "under the sun" create real people with real faith. The phonies do not speak out in these kinds of threatening cultures. Helping people to make a faith decision to be "born again" becomes a priority of purpose for living during these difficult times. For those with real faith silence is not an option. Sacrificing their temporal lives to help others gain eternal life through evangelism and discipleship is their daily priority choice.

Progressive Christianity (liberalism) like progressive politics evolves into the abstract. Notice the progressive steps listed in Jude 12; "[1]fruit withereth, [2]without fruit, [3]twice dead, [4]plucked up by the roots."

Why keep a fruit tree that produces no fruit? What would any wise husbandman do if he had a fruit tree that never produced fruit? Of course, the answer is he would dig it out by the roots and plant a tree that produced fruit. God expects fruit!

"[18] Now in the morning as he returned into the city, he hungered. [19] And when he saw a fig tree in the way, he came to it, and **found nothing thereon, but leaves only,** and said unto it, **Let no fruit grow on thee henceforward for ever.** And **presently** {*instantly*} *or immediately}* the fig tree withered away. [20] And when the disciples saw *it*, they marvelled, saying, **How soon is the fig tree withered away!** [21] Jesus answered and said unto them, Verily I say unto you, If ye have faith, and doubt not, ye shall not only do this *which is done* to the fig tree, but also if ye shall say unto this mountain, Be thou removed, and be thou cast into the sea; it shall be done. [22] And **all things, whatsoever ye shall ask in prayer, believing, ye shall receive**" (Matthew 21:18-22).

"[1]There were present at that season some that told him of the Galilaeans, whose blood Pilate had mingled with their sacrifices. [2] And Jesus answering said unto them, **Suppose ye that these Galilaeans were sinners above all the Galilaeans, because they suffered such things?** [3] I tell you, Nay: but, **except ye repent, ye shall all likewise perish**. [4] Or those eighteen, upon whom the tower in Siloam fell, and slew them, **think ye that they were sinners above all men that dwelt in Jerusalem?** [5] I tell you, Nay: but, **except ye repent**, ye shall all likewise perish. [6] He spake also this parable; A **certain** *man {refers to God}* had **a fig tree** *{Israel as the visible and practical witness to God's will}* **planted in his vineyard** *{the nation of Israel}*; and he came and **sought fruit thereon, and found none.** [7] Then said he unto the dresser of his vineyard, Behold, **these three years** *{the time of Christ's ministry from His baptism}* I come seeking fruit on this fig tree, and find none: cut it down; **why cumbereth it the ground?** [8] And he answering said unto him, Lord, let it alone this year also, till I shall dig about it, and dung *it*: And **if** it bear fruit, *well*: and **if** not, *then* after that thou shalt cut it down" (Luke 13:1-9).

God was about to set the nation of Israel aside and cast away the corrupted Levitical Priesthood of Israel. The *fruitless fig tree* **in this parable is the nation of Israel that was not even able to convert and disciple its own people let alone the nations of the world.**

Biblical truth is not only to be known, understood, and lived; Biblical truth is to be proclaim to the world without compromise or reservation. Jonah, in the book of Jonah, represents the heart and burden of the nation of Israel for the pagans that persecuted them. They did not have a heart for their conversion. They wanted them destroyed.

Jonah hated the Assyrians so badly that he ran away from God's command to go to them and preach repentance. Jonah would rather be cast into the sea to die than go to Nineveh and preach repentance. "Take me up, and cast me forth into the sea; so shall the sea be calm **unto you**: for **I know** that for my sake this great tempest *is* upon you" (Jonah 1:12).

In most part, except for a small remnant of faithful believers, the Church has utterly failed to evangelize our world and make disciple for Jesus Christ. In most part, except for a small remnant of faithful believers, the Church has failed to "contend earnestly for the faith once delivered unto the saints" (Jude 3).

Although Israel had a faithful remnant at the end of the Age of the Law, Israel utterly failed to be the godly influence on the rest of the world after the establishment of the Davidic throne. Solomon brought the world to the feet of the Temple during his early reign. However, **Solomon became so worldly and compromised that the nation of Israel lost the "book of the Law," and the temple fell into ruin during the next three-hundred years.**

"[1] **Josiah** *was* **eight years old** {*about 314 years after the beginning of Solomon's reign*} when he began to reign, and he reigned thirty and one years in Jerusalem. And **his mother's name** *was* **Jedidah** {*the name given by God to Solomon after his birth to represent God's gracious forgiveness and restoration of David after his sin with Bethsheba; the name means 'beloved of Jehovah'*}, the daughter of Adaiah of Boscath. [2] And **he** {*Josiah*} **did** *that which was* **right in the sight of the LORD, and walked in all the way of David his father**, and turned not aside to the right hand or to the left. [3] And it came to pass in the eighteenth year of king Josiah, *that* the king sent Shaphan the son of Azaliah, the son of Meshullam, the scribe, to the house of the LORD, saying, [4] Go up to Hilkiah the high priest, that he may sum the silver which is brought into the house of the LORD, which the keepers of the door have gathered of the people: [5] And **let them deliver it into the hand of the doers of the work, that have the oversight of the house of the LORD: and let them give it to the doers of the work which** *is* **in the house of the LORD, to**

repair the breaches {*gaps in the walls*} **of the house**, [6] Unto carpenters, and builders, and masons, and to buy timber and hewn stone to repair the house. [7] Howbeit there was no reckoning made with them of the money that was delivered into their hand, **because they dealt faithfully.** [8] And Hilkiah the high priest said unto Shaphan the scribe, **I have found the book of the law in the house of the LORD**. And Hilkiah gave the book to Shaphan, and he read it" (II Kings 22:1-8).

"Raging Waves of the Sea" (Jude 13)

In this verse, Jude is applying Isaiah 57:20 as a descriptor of the effects of false doctrine that allows false teachers to continue. For any congregation to allow false teachers to continue teaching is sin and unfaithfulness of that local church.

Although Christ writes His seven epistles of Revelations 1:9 through 3:22 to the "angels" (*messengers* or *pastors*) of seven local churches, He holds the congregations of those local churches individually responsible for the deviations from the truths He addresses. There are responsibilities that accompany congregational polity.

There are two categories of people being addressed in Isaiah 57:20. There are unfaithful believers who are not doing what they should be doing for the sake of peace keeping through compromise disguised as loving toleration.

God will work through chastisement in the lives of unfaithful believers to show them that they are foolishly compromising the truth to placate unbelievers. God will not allow believers to continue compromising truth without chastisement.

Second, there is also the category of the deceivers disguising themselves as believers that requires a harsh and uncompromising treatment. The faithful must be discerning enough to know the difference and thereby not slip into the area of unfaithfulness by seeking to placate these unbelievers.

The faithful must remember that faithfulness is to God first, before it extends to our dealings with those trying to teach false doctrines. God is involved in keeping things pure and will hold the unfaithful accountable. Only believers can be faithful or unfaithful.

Unbelievers are lost and no one should expect anything from them other than what lost unbelievers do.

"[17] For the iniquity of his covetousness was I wroth, and smote him: I hid me, and was wroth, and **he went on frowardly in the way of his heart**. [18] I have seen his ways, and will heal him: I will lead him also, and restore comforts unto him and to his mourners. [19] I create the fruit of the lips; Peace, peace to *him that is* far off, and to *him that is* near, saith the LORD; and I will heal him. [20] **But the wicked** *are* **like the troubled sea**, **when it cannot rest**, whose waters cast up mire and dirt. [21] *There is* no peace, saith my God, to the wicked" (Isaiah 57:17-21).

"Covetousness" here is addressed as a nameless personality. The text is addressing a believer who possesses the personality or characteristic of "covetousness." With that person, God is "wroth" and promises to smite him. We might say that God will seek to slap some sense into him through chastisement.

God promises to "work good" through chastisement in this misdirected believer. "Covetousness" is not always about material things such as money, houses, boats, horses, tractors, and cars. A person can covet the relationships another person has. We can covet another man's wife or covet another woman's husband.

"Covetousness" is basically a misplaced desire that leads a person into sinful thinking and possibly even sinful acts. "Covetousness" begins in the heart as a wrong desire, moves into the mind to form fantasies, and then may even act to bring those fantasies into reality.

Jude 13 is addressing the "covetousness" that wants to be accepted or that wants peace with the unfaithful over and above being faithful to God by dealing with false teachers. Being faithful in this arena must still be kind and gentle like a father should be when disciplining his child. However, a congregation must be firm and dogmatic in their communication and actions when dealing with a heretic teaching false doctrine.

"The wicked" of Isaiah 57:20 is another category of individuals which will require a different approach by God and a congregation in hope in might turn their hearts in repentance. This is God's warning in Hebrews chapter twelve to a hypothetical group of Jews who professed faith in Christ but who were considering "drawing back" to the beliefs and practices of the Mosaic Covenant. God will not let this happen to believers without chastisement. This hypothetical is posited in Hebrews 12:4-8.

"⁴ Ye have not yet resisted unto blood, striving against sin. ⁵ And ye have forgotten the exhortation **which speaketh unto you <u>as</u> unto children**, My son, despise not thou the chastening of the Lord, nor faint when thou art rebuked of him: ⁶ For whom the Lord loveth he chasteneth, and scourgeth every son whom he receiveth. ⁷ **If** ye endure chastening, God dealeth with you as with sons; for what son is he whom the father chasteneth not? ⁸ But **if** ye be without chastisement, whereof all are partakers, then are ye bastards, and not sons" (Hebrews 12:4-8).

God is faithful and righteous. This means God will ALWAYS act in accordance with His Inspired Word. Second, God will always do what is right regardless of the consequences. God never compromises or acts out of alignment with His Inspired Words.

This pattern established by God is the believer's example of what defines faithfulness. Any distortion of our understanding of what God wants or what God would do in any given situation or choice of life will cause the believer to act in accordance with that distortion and thereby become unfaithful to God.

Under congregational polity (local church membership government), God expects the faithful of a local church to deal with the unfaithful. Many local churches fail to Biblically practice congregational polity and local church discipline and by that failure are soon captured by false teachers or defiled by the sinful practices of the membership.

Congregational polity is clearly defined in I Corinthians chapters five and six and Matthew 18:15-20. This certainly is a contradiction against the *don't judge me* crowd. **To point out that something is sinful, wrong, or is false teaching is not judgment.** This is *discernment* and is an act of loving kindness if done properly.

Judgment is the power to pass a sentence of punishment. Individual believers do not have this authority over anyone, certainly not over unbelievers or those who are not members of their local congregation. However, a local congregation has both the right and responsibility to judge the disobedient within their membership.

"¹⁵ Moreover if thy brother {*congregational polity*} shall trespass against thee, **go and tell him his fault between thee and him alone**: if he shall hear thee, thou hast gained thy brother. ¹⁶ But **if he will not hear** *thee, then* take with thee **one or two more** {*congregational polity*}, that in the mouth of **two or three witnesses every word may be established**. ¹⁷ And **if he shall neglect to hear them**, tell *it* unto the church: but **if he neglect to hear the church** {*congregational polity*}, lct him bc unto thee as an heathen man and a publican. ¹⁸ Verily I say unto you, Whatsoever ye shall bind on earth shall be bound in heaven: and whatsoever ye shall loose on earth shall be loosed in heaven. ¹⁹ Again I say unto you, That if two of you shall agree on earth as touching any thing that they shall ask, it shall be done for them of my Father which is in heaven. ²⁰ For where two or three are gathered together in my name, there am I in the midst of them {*congregational polity judges with the authority of Christ*}" (Matthew 18:15-20).

I Corinthians 5:9 through 6:10 is Paul's rebuke of the Corinthian local church for failing to practice church discipline as defined by Matthew 18:15-20. The reason a local church loses its Biblical values and compromises the doctrines of the Word of God is because local congregations become slack in their responsibilities to contend "for the faith once deliver" into their care to obey and preserve. Local church is an expected responsibility of faithfulness in all matters of sin, doctrine, and social disagreements.

"⁹ I wrote unto you in an epistle **not to company with fornicators**: ¹⁰ Yet not altogether with the fornicators of this world, or with the covetous, or extortioners, or with idolaters; **for then must ye needs go out of the world**. ¹¹ But now I have written unto you **not to keep company** {*mix up together, the idea is not to allow these types of people to be members of a local congregation*}, if any man that is called a brother be a fornicator, or covetous, or an idolater, or a railer, or a drunkard, or an extortioner; with such an one no not to eat. ¹² For what have I to do to judge them also that are without? **do not ye judge them that are within** {*the question is rhetorically answered, of course we do*}? [13] But **them that are without** {*church membership*} God judgeth. **Therefore put away from among yourselves that wicked person**. [1] Dare **any of you** {*who are part of a local congregation*}, **having a matter against another** {*personal disagreements that need resolution*}, go to law **before the unjust** {*civil courts*}, and **not before the saints** {*the local congregation*}? [2] **Do ye not know that the saints shall judge the world?** {*During the Kingdom Age.*} and if the world shall be judged by you, **are ye unworthy to judge the smallest matters?** {*civil disagreements between believers*} [3] Know **ye not that we shall judge angels**? how much more things that pertain to this life? [4] If then ye have judgments of things pertaining to this life, **set them to judge who are least esteemed in the church**. [5] I speak to your shame. Is it so, that there is not a wise man among you? no, **not one that shall be able to judge between his brethren?** [6] But brother goeth to law with brother, and that before the unbelievers. [7] Now therefore there is utterly a fault among you, because ye go to law one with another. Why do ye not rather take wrong? why do ye not rather *suffer yourselves to* be defrauded? [8] Nay, ye do wrong, and defraud, and that *your* brethren. [9] Know ye not that the unrighteous shall not inherit the kingdom of God? Be not deceived: neither fornicators, nor idolaters, nor adulterers, nor effeminate, nor abusers of themselves with mankind, [10] Nor thieves, nor covetous, nor drunkards, nor revilers, nor extortioners, **shall inherit the kingdom of God** {*and the responsibility of judging all matters during the Kingdom Age*}" (I Corinthians 5:9 - 6:10).

"Raging waves of the sea" (Jude 13) communicates both the destructive power of the sea and the purification of the sea by the waves driving everything that does not belong in the sea to the shore. This is a local congregational polity issue of faithfulness. This is the substance of what Jude is saying in this epistle. Christ has set every believer on watch over the purity of the Church, His bride. He has trusted each of us with His most precious love in this world. **Put a stop to this nonsense Jude is addressing! Be a purifier, not a contributor to the pollution.**

"Raging waves of the sea, foaming out their own shame[s];" (Jude 13a).

Everything in the sea that does not belong in the sea is eventually brought to the shores of the world and deposited there as refuse of the sea. **God has built into the dynamic of nature the ability to purify itself from pollutants.**

This is the point of the phrase, "foaming out their own shame[s] *{actually plural}*." This reality should be a major part of the understanding of congregational polity. **Keeping the lives and doctrines of a local church pure from false doctrine and worldliness is one of the purposes for which congregational polity exists and for which it is ordained by God.** Since this simile describes a natural process of fallen creation, it certainly should have a supernatural expectation in the New Creation. **Live pure and keep your local church pure!**

"Foaming out" is from the Greek word *epaphrízō* (ep-af-rid'-zo). The *epa* prefix heightens the meaning of *aphrízō*, adding *passion to the action*. The verb is a present, active, participle, meaning this is a state of constant action in nature.

This purification process is part of God's physical design within nature. Nature normally and naturally, is constantly purifying itself, healing itself, and renewing itself. **Therefore, God's use of this simile in Jude 13 is this process of constant purification, healing, and renewing that should be an ongoing normal part of congregational polity.**

This is the same meaning conveyed in Isaiah 57:20, "But the wicked *are* like the troubled sea, when it cannot rest, whose waters cast up mire and dirt." The "mire and dirt" is the "wicked," which "the troubled sea" removes from itself. Paul uses a similarity in Philippians 3:17-19.

"[17] Brethren, be followers together of me, and **mark them** *{the faithful, meaning to focus your attention upon them like an archer at his bullseye}* **which walk so as ye have us for an ensample.** [18] (For **many walk** *{unfaithful}*, of whom I have told you often, and now tell you even weeping, *that they are* the **enemies of the cross of Christ**: [19] Whose end *is* destruction, **whose God *is their* belly** *{carnal appetites}*, and *whose* **glory** *{in sensuality in food,* *wine, and sex, 'eat, drink, and be merry' said the rich man in Luke 12:19}* **is** **in their shame**, who **mind earthly things** *{'under the sun' considerations dominate their thinking and therefore their motivations}*" (Philippians 3:17-19).

Every congregational member of a local church must be able to distinguish between being faithful and being unfaithful, *beginning with themselves.*

Although the sea purifies itself of impurities naturally, the simile means that a local church must act according to truth and love when dealing with false teachers within its congregational membership. We cannot just let false doctrine and immoral, carnal lives continue, thinking God will take care of the problem.

"Wandering Stars, to Whom is Reserved the Blackness of Darkness for Ever" (Jude 13b).

Just like the "raging *{wild and untamable}* **waves" of the first part of this first, "wandering stars" are not fixed in space.** By man's evaluation "wandering stars" are uncontrolled. However, we must understand "wandering stars" are still under the sovereignty of God.

This most probably refers to *shooting stars,* or what we know to be comets. The point of both these similes together is referring to things that cannot and will not be controlled by human efforts.

"Wandering stars" describes the heart of the rebel who will not be controlled by either laws, government, or even by God (*apart from judgment***).** Compromise in any degree is rebellion. Compromise steals liberty when none is given.

"For rebellion *is as* the sin of witchcraft, and **stubbornness** *{unrepentance} is as* iniquity and idolatry. **Because thou hast rejected the word of the LORD** *{that rebukes and corrects}*, he hath also rejected thee from *being* king" (I Samuel 15:23).

We must study the Scriptures carefully and meticulously to know God's commands and obey them with equal fervor. This was expected of every individual Jew within the nation of Israel as they corporately practiced congregational polity.

Congregational polity existed under their original theocracy with God-chosen judges and a God-chosen priesthood and later as they evolved in disobedience into a theonomy with a God-chosen king and a God-chosen priesthood.

As a nation, every individual was responsible to keep the "statues and judgments," even taking part in executions through stoning after an individual was found guilty of capital punishment offenses. Local church congregational polity has no such continuing obligation beyond excommunication (I Corinthians 5:5; although a similar outcome was expected).

"**Ye** {*corporately as a nation of individuals, every individual that forms the corporate nation*} **shall therefore keep all my statutes, and all my judgments**, and **do them**: that the land, whither I bring you to dwell therein, spue you not out" (Leviticus 20:2).

One of the first examples of the children of Israel practicing congregational polity was in dealing with the family of Achan in Numbers chapter seven. In this text, the children of Israel were forbidden to take of the spoils of the war, because the victories were God's and not theirs.

Therefore, the spoils belonged to God. These spoils were *chêrem* (khay'-rem). **Every act of disobedience is similar in that people take liberty that God forbids.** Faith understands that God is sovereign, and the human will of the faithful must be yielded to God's will. This defines obedience.

Rebellion and willful disobedience are always a rejection of God's sovereign Lordship over the heart. Achan's sin was a willful rebellion of unbelief, thinking he could hide his sin from God's eyes if it was hidden from man's eyes.

"[1] But **the children of Israel committed a trespass in the accursed thing**: <u>for Achan</u>, the son of Carmi, the son of Zabdi, the son of Zerah, of the tribe of Judah, **took of the accursed thing**: and the anger of the LORD was kindled against the children of Israel. [2] And Joshua sent men from Jericho to Ai, which *is* beside Beth-aven, on the east side of Beth-el, and spake unto them, saying, Go up and view the country. And the men went up and viewed Ai. ³ And they returned to Joshua, and said unto him, Let not all the people go up; but let about two or three thousand men go up and smite Ai; *and* make not all the people to labour thither; for they *are but* few. ⁴ So there went up thither of the people about three thousand men: and they fled before the men of Ai. ⁵ And the men of Ai smote of them about thirty and six men: for they chased them *from* before the gate *even* unto Shebarim, and smote them in the going down: wherefore the hearts of the people melted, and became as water. ⁶ And **Joshua rent his clothes, and fell to the earth upon his face before the ark of the LORD until the eventide, he and the elders of Israel, and put dust upon their heads.** ⁷ And Joshua said, Alas, O Lord GOD, wherefore hast thou at all brought this people over Jordan, to deliver us into the hand of the Amorites, to destroy us? would to God we had been content, and dwelt on the other side Jordan! ⁸ O Lord, what shall I say, when Israel turneth their backs before their enemies! ⁹ For the Canaanites and all the inhabitants of the land shall hear *of it*, and shall environ us round, and cut off our name from the earth: and what wilt thou do unto thy great name? ¹⁰ And **the LORD said unto Joshua, Get thee up; wherefore liest thou thus upon thy face?** ¹¹ **Israel hath sinned**, and they have also transgressed my covenant which I commanded them: for **they** have even taken of the accursed thing, and have also stolen, and dissembled also, and **they** have put *it* even among their own stuff. ¹² **Therefore the children of Israel could not stand before their enemies, *but* turned *their* backs before their enemies, because they were accursed: neither will I be with you any more, except ye destroy the accursed from among you.** ¹³ Up, sanctify the people, and say, Sanctify yourselves against to morrow: for thus saith the LORD God of Israel, *There is* an **accursed thing** {*chêrem*} in the midst of thee, O Israel: thou canst not stand before thine enemies, **until ye take away the accursed thing** {*chêrem*} from among you. ¹⁴ In the morning therefore ye shall be brought according to your tribes: and it shall be, *that* the tribe which the LORD taketh shall come according to the families *thereof*; and the family which the LORD shall take shall come by households; and the household which the LORD shall take shall come man by man. ¹⁵ **And it shall be, *that* he that is taken with the accursed thing shall be**

burnt with fire, he and all that he hath: because he hath transgressed the covenant of the LORD, and because he hath wrought folly in Israel. [16] So Joshua rose up early in the morning, and brought Israel by their tribes; and the tribe of Judah was taken: [17] And he brought the **family of Judah**; and he took the family of the Zarhites: and he brought the family of the Zarhites man by man; and Zabdi was taken: [18] And he brought his household man by man; **and Achan**, the son of Carmi, the son of Zabdi, the son of Zerah, of the tribe of Judah, was taken. [19] And Joshua said unto Achan, My son, give, I pray thee, glory to the LORD God of Israel, and make confession unto him; and tell me now what thou hast done; hide *it* not from me. [20] And **Achan answered Joshua, and said, Indeed I have sinned against the LORD God of Israel, and thus and thus have I done**: [21] When I saw among the spoils a goodly Babylonish garment, and two hundred shekels of silver, and a wedge of gold of fifty shekels weight, then I coveted them, and took them; and, behold, they *are* hid in the earth in the midst of my tent, and the silver under it. [22] So **Joshua sent messengers** {*congregational polity*}, and they ran unto the tent; and, behold, *it was* hid in his tent, and the silver under it. [23] And they took them out of the midst of the tent, and brought them unto Joshua, and **unto all the children of Israel** {*congregational polity*}, and **laid them out before the LORD.** [24] And Joshua, and **all Israel with him** {*congregational polity*}, took Achan the son of Zerah, and the silver, and the garment, and the wedge of gold, and **his sons**, and **his daughters**, and **his oxen**, and **his asses**, and **his sheep**, and **his tent**, and **all that he had**: and **they** {*congregational polity*} brought them unto the valley of Achor. [25] And Joshua said, **Why hast thou troubled us** {*congregational polity*}? the LORD shall trouble thee this day. And **all Israel** stoned him with stones {*congregational polity*}, and burned them with fire, after they had stoned them with stones. [26] And **they** {*congregational polity*} raised over him a great heap of stones unto this day. So the LORD turned from the fierceness of his anger. Wherefore the name of that place was called, The valley of Achor, unto this day" (Joshua 7:1-26).

To understand the *chêrem* (khay'-rem) **command to the nation of Israel, we must understand who and what God chooses to be His is sanctified.** In other words, a sanctified thing or person cannot be used for purposes other than what God allows. A sanctified thing or person is to be kept sanctified and holy.

God chose some real estate and promised that real estate to the children of Israel. God chose the children of Israel (the Jews) to be the nation through which He would interact and reveal Himself to the world. Therefore, they too were sanctified by God for that purpose.

God had already spent forty years in the wilderness sanctifying His chosen nation to prepare them to enter His Promised Land to sanctify it. Faith here means believing AND living God's commandments given at Mt. Sinai. During those forty years in the wilderness, God purged the "mixed multitude" from the congregation and sanctified the nation to enter the Promised Land under Joshua's leadership.

When the children of Israel began to enter the promised Land, God went before them to purify the land and remove any thing or peoples that desecrated His sanctifying it. The unsanctified people either completely abandoned the land and left it or they were to be "utterly destroyed" by the children of Israel. This **all** defines **the** *chêrem* (khay'-rem) command to the nation of Israel.

Understanding Joshua chapter seven, we then understand that God continued His *chêrem* (khay'-rem) command to the nation of Israel when they crossed the Jordan into the Holy Land to *"utterly destroy"* every man, woman, child, and livestock that did not leave the promised land and surrender it to God's people. God addresses this again in I Samuel chapter fifteen where Saul was supposed to correct the failure to execute the *chêrem* against the Amalekites.

Samuel spoke to king Saul about this issue of his heart in I Samuel 15:23. Saul compromised God's command to "utterly destroy" (Samuel 15:3) the Amalekites for their treachery against the children of Israel. Saul was commanded to "slay both man and woman, infant and suckling, ox and sheep, camel and ass."

God had put a divine curse upon the Amalekites when they attacked the rear of the procession of Israel when they were wandering in the wilderness. The rear of Israel's procession was for the elderly, weak, and sickly that could not keep pace with the rest of the nation. They were extremely vulnerable and unable to defend themselves. ***The***

***Treasury of Scripture Knowledge* makes the following comment on this historical event.**

"The Amalekites, a people of Arabia Petræa, who inhabited a tract of country on the frontiers of Egypt and Canaan, had acted with great cruelty towards the Israelites on their coming out of Egypt, and God then purposed that Amalek, as a nation, should be blotted out from under heaven; but it had been spared till it had filled up the measure of its iniquities, and now this purpose is carried into effect by Saul, upwards of 400 years afterwards! Nothing could justify such an exterminating decree but the absolute authority of God; and this was given: all the reasons of it we do not know; but this we know well, the Judge of all the earth doeth right."[9]

In I Samuel chapter twelve, we are given the record of the events surrounded the appointment of Saul as king over Israel. This was not something God wanted, but what the people wanted. God permitted it with a warning.

"[1] And **Samuel** {*appointed by God to be a prophet and judge over Israel*} **said** {*speaking for God*} unto all Israel, **Behold, I have hearkened unto your voice in all that ye said unto me, and have made a king over you** {*thereby rejecting Samuel as God's appointed judge over them*}. [2] And now, behold, the king walketh before you: and I am old and grayheaded; and, behold, my sons *are* with you: and I have walked before you from my childhood unto this day. [3] **Behold, here I *am*: witness against me before the LORD**, and before his anointed: whose ox have I taken? or whose ass have I taken? or whom have I defrauded? whom have I oppressed? or of whose hand have I received *any* bribe to blind mine eyes therewith? and I will restore it you. [4] And they said, Thou hast not defrauded us, nor oppressed us, neither hast thou taken ought of any man's hand. [5] And he said unto them, **The LORD *is* witness against you, and his anointed *is* witness this day, that ye have not found ought in my hand.**

---

[9] **The Treasury of Scripture Knowledge,**
SwordSearcher\Modules\TSK.ss5cmty,Module file time: 1/19/2017 6:14:42 PM UTC.

And they answered, *He is* **witness.** ⁶ And Samuel said unto the people, *It is* the LORD that advanced Moses and Aaron, and that brought your fathers up out of the land of Egypt. ⁷ **Now therefore stand still, that I may reason with you before the LORD of all the righteous acts of the LORD, which he did to you and to your fathers.** ⁸ When Jacob was come into Egypt, and your fathers cried unto the LORD, then the LORD sent Moses and Aaron, which brought forth your fathers out of Egypt, and made them dwell in this place. ⁹ And **when they forgat the LORD their God**, he sold them into the hand of Sisera, captain of the host of Hazor, and into the hand of the Philistines, and into the hand of the king of Moab, and they fought against them. ¹⁰ **And they cried** {*repented*} **unto the LORD, and said** {*confessed*}, We have sinned, because **we have forsaken the LORD**, and have served Baalim and Ashtaroth: but now deliver us out of the hand of our enemies, **and we will serve thee**. ¹¹ And the LORD sent Jerubbaal, and Bedan, and Jephthah, and Samuel, and delivered you out of the hand of your enemies on every side, and ye dwelled safe. ¹² And when ye saw that Nahash the king of the children of Ammon came against you, **ye said unto me, Nay; but a king shall reign over us: when the LORD your God** *was* **your king.** ¹³ **Now therefore behold the king whom ye have chosen**, *and* whom ye have desired! and, behold, the LORD hath set a king over you. ¹⁴ If ye will fear the LORD, and serve him, and obey his voice, and not rebel against the commandment of the LORD, then shall both ye and also the king that reigneth over you continue following the LORD your God: ¹⁵ **But if ye will not obey the voice of the LORD, but rebel against the commandment of the LORD, then shall the hand of the LORD be against you, as** *it was* **against your fathers.** ¹⁶ Now therefore stand and see this great thing, which the LORD will do before your eyes. ¹⁷ *Is it* not wheat harvest to day? I will call unto the LORD, and he shall send thunder and rain; **that ye may perceive and see that your wickedness** *is* **great, which ye have done in the sight of the LORD, in asking you a king.** ¹⁸ So Samuel called unto the LORD; and the LORD sent thunder and rain that day: and all the people greatly feared the LORD and Samuel. ¹⁹ And all the people said unto Samuel, Pray for thy servants unto the LORD thy God, that we die not: **for we have**

added unto all our sins *this* **evil, to ask us a king.** [20] And Samuel said unto the people, Fear not: ye have done all this wickedness: yet turn not aside from following the LORD, **but serve the LORD with all your heart;** [21] And turn ye not aside: for *then should ye go* after vain *things*, which cannot profit nor deliver; for they *are* vain. [22] **For the LORD will not forsake his people for his great name's sake: because it hath pleased the LORD to make you his people.** [23] Moreover as for me, God forbid that I should sin against the LORD in ceasing to pray for you: but **I will teach you the good and the right way:** [24] Only fear the LORD, and serve him in truth with all your heart: for consider how great *things* he hath done for you. [25] **But if ye shall still do wickedly, ye shall be consumed, both ye and your king**" (I Samuel 12:1-25).

As the newly appointed *populist* **king of Israel, Saul was to become God's appointed** *executor* **of the** *chêrem* **(khay'-rem).** The Amalekites had not been "utterly" destroyed as God commanded. The land of the Amalekites was outside of the Promised Land, but they had committed an atrocious trespass against the children of Israel. Almost five-hundred years had passed since God had cursed them as a nation and promised He would "utterly destroy" them (*the chêrem*).

"[16] For all that do such things, *and* all that do unrighteously, *are* an abomination unto the LORD thy God. [17] **Remember what Amalek** {*king of the Amalekites*} **did unto thee by the way, when ye were come forth out of Egypt;** [18] **How he met thee by the way, and smote the hindmost of thee,** *even* **all** *that were* **feeble behind thee, when thou** *wast* **faint and weary; and he feared not God.** [19] Therefore it shall be, when the LORD thy God hath given thee rest from all thine enemies round about, in the land which the LORD thy God giveth thee *for* an inheritance to possess it, *that* **thou shalt blot out the remembrance of Amalek from under heaven; thou shalt not forget** *it*" (Deuteronomy 25:16-19).

I Samuel chapter fifteen records the time of God's intended execution of His *chêrem.* **The king of the Amalekites was currently**

Agag. Saul executed the *chêrem* against all the Amalekites, but pardoned Agag and let him live.

Partial obedience is equal to disobedience. Saul failed to execute Agag and thereby failed to keep sanctity in the nation of Israel by keeping fully God's commands.

"[1] Samuel also said unto Saul, The LORD sent me to anoint thee *to be* king over his people, over Israel: **now therefore hearken thou unto the voice of the words of the LORD.** [2] Thus saith the LORD of hosts, **I remember *that* which Amalek did to Israel**, how he laid *wait* for him in the way, when he came up from Egypt. [3] Now go and smite Amalek, and **utterly destroy** {*khaw-ram'*} all that they have, and **spare them not; but slay both man and woman, infant and suckling, ox and sheep, camel and ass**. [4] And Saul gathered the people together, and numbered them in Telaim, two hundred thousand footmen, and ten thousand men of Judah. [5] And Saul came to a city of Amalek, and laid wait in the valley. [6] And Saul said unto the Kenites, Go, depart, get you down from among the Amalekites, lest I destroy you with them: for ye shewed kindness to all the children of Israel, when they came up out of Egypt. So the Kenites departed from among the Amalekites. [7] And Saul smote the Amalekites from Havilah *until* thou comest to Shur, that *is* over against Egypt. [8] And he took Agag the king of the Amalekites alive, and **utterly destroyed** all the people with the edge of the sword. [9] **But Saul and the people spared Agag, and the best of the sheep, and of the oxen, and of the fatlings, and the lambs, and all *that was* good, and would not utterly destroy them**: but every thing *that was* vile and refuse, that they destroyed utterly. [10] Then came the word of the LORD unto Samuel, saying, [11] **It repenteth me that I have set up Saul *to be* king: for he is turned back from following me, and hath not performed my commandments.** And it grieved Samuel; and he cried unto the LORD all night. [12] And when Samuel rose early to meet Saul in the morning, it was told Samuel, saying, Saul came to Carmel, and, behold, he set him up a place, and is gone about, and passed on, and gone down to Gilgal. [13] And Samuel came to Saul: and Saul said unto him, **Blessed *be* thou of the LORD: I have performed the commandment of the LORD** {*no one has the right to show* *mercy when God demands death}*. ¹⁴ And Samuel said, **What meaneth** then this bleating of the sheep in mine ears, and the lowing of the oxen which I hear?** ¹⁵ And Saul said, **They** {*blame shifting*} have brought them from the Amalekites: for **the people spared** the best of the sheep and of the oxen, **to sacrifice unto the LORD thy God**; and the rest we have utterly destroyed. ¹⁶ Then Samuel said unto Saul, Stay, and I will tell thee what the LORD hath said to me this night. And he said unto him, Say on. ¹⁷ And Samuel said, When thou *wast* little in thine own sight, *wast* thou not *made* the head of the tribes of Israel, and the LORD anointed thee king over Israel? ¹⁸ And the LORD sent thee on a journey, and said, **Go and utterly destroy the sinners the Amalekites, and fight against them until they be consumed.** ¹⁹ Wherefore then didst thou not obey the voice of the LORD, but didst fly upon the spoil, and **didst evil in the sight of the LORD?** ²⁰ And Saul said unto Samuel, Yea, I have obeyed the voice of the LORD, and have gone the way which the LORD sent me, and have brought Agag the king of Amalek, and have utterly destroyed the Amalekites. ²¹ But **the people took of the spoil, sheep and oxen, the chief of the things which should have been utterly destroyed, to sacrifice unto the LORD thy God in Gilgal.** ²² And Samuel said, **Hath the LORD *as great* delight in burnt offerings and sacrifices, as in obeying the voice of the LORD? Behold, to obey *is* better than sacrifice, *and* to hearken than the fat of rams.** ²³ For rebellion *is as* the sin of witchcraft, and stubbornness *is as* iniquity and idolatry. **Because thou hast rejected the word of the LORD, he hath also rejected thee from *being* king.** ²⁴ And Saul said unto Samuel, I have sinned: for I have transgressed the commandment of the LORD, and thy words: because I feared the people, and obeyed their voice. ²⁵ **Now therefore, I pray thee, pardon my sin, and turn again with me, that I may worship the LORD.** ²⁶ And Samuel said unto Saul, **I will not return with thee: for thou hast rejected the word of the LORD, and the LORD hath rejected thee from being king over Israel.** ²⁷ And as Samuel turned about to go away, he {*Saul*} laid hold upon the skirt of his {*Samuel's*} mantle, and it rent. ²⁸ And Samuel said unto him, The LORD hath rent the kingdom of Israel from thee this day, and hath given it to a neighbour of thine, *that is* better than thou. ²⁹

And also **the Strength** {*He that gives victory to Israel*} of Israel will not lie nor repent: for he *is* not a man, that he should repent. [30] Then he {*Saul*} said, I have sinned: *yet* honour me now, I pray thee, before the elders of my people, and before Israel, and turn again with me, that I may worship the LORD thy God. [31] So Samuel turned again after Saul; and Saul worshipped the LORD. [32] Then said Samuel, Bring ye hither to me Agag the king of the Amalekites. And **Agag came unto him delicately** {*cheerfully thinking he was safe because he was pardoned by king Saul*}. And Agag said, Surely the bitterness of death is past. [33] And Samuel said, As thy sword hath made women childless, so shall thy mother be childless among women. And **Samuel hewed Agag in pieces before the LORD in Gilgal.** [34] Then Samuel went to Ramah; and Saul went up to his house to Gibeah of Saul. [35] And **Samuel came no more to see Saul until the day of his death**: **nevertheless Samuel mourned for Saul**: and the LORD repented that he had made Saul king over Israel" (I Samuel 15:1-35).

Unfortunately, the two similes of Jude 13 are addressing a common failure of professing believers amongst God people similar to the failures of Achan and Saul. "Raging waves of the sea" and "wandering stars" are professing believers who do not understand complete obedience to maintain sanctity before God. The second level of the admonition is that the faithful MUST address the unfaithful and "contend for the faith."

The fact is, the Scriptures are redundant with the failure of the people of Israel and the priesthood of Israel to keep the statutes and judgments as God commanded them to do and to which they agreed. Unfortunately, this is equally true of both the pastoral leadership of local churches AND congregation polity in the priesthood of all believers during the Church Age.

Achan is an example of irresponsibility and failures of congregational polity. Saul is an example of failure in pastoral leadership in *administrating* righteousness in local churches. **Often and unfortunately, the errors pastors allow they endorse by that allowance. Their congregations then accept the allowance without question.**

The simile of "wandering stars" can refer to both fallen angels and to doctrinally corrupted pastors and their congregations. Although the highest probability is that the simile refers to fallen angels, which in turn influence pastors of local churches with various degrees of false doctrine. This is detailed in the seven local churches used as examples in Revelation chapters two and three.

"[19] Write the things which thou hast seen, and the things which are, and the things which shall be hereafter; [20] The **mystery of the seven stars** which thou sawest in my right hand, and the seven golden candlesticks. The **seven stars are the angels** {*messengers/pastors*} of the seven churches: and the seven candlesticks which thou sawest are the seven churches" (Revelation 1:19-20).

"[1] And there appeared a great wonder in heaven; a woman clothed with the sun, and the moon under her feet, and upon her head a crown of twelve stars: [2] And she being with child cried, travailing in birth, and pained to be delivered. [3] And there appeared another wonder in heaven; and **behold a great red dragon** {*Satan*}, having seven heads and ten horns, and seven crowns upon his heads. [4] And **his tail drew the third part of the stars of heaven**, and **did cast them to the earth** {*into the curse*}: and **the dragon stood before the woman** {*Israel as a nation and the virgin Mary specifically as the mother of Jesus and descendant of David in the genetical lineage of Christ*} which was ready to be delivered, for **to devour her child** {*Messiah*} as soon as it was born" (Revelation 12:1-4).

"**Wandering stars, to whom is reserved the blackness of darkness for ever**" (Jude 13).

The simile of the word "stars" is that of being lights in the darkness. This was one of the purposes God says He created stars. Our sun is a star.

"And God made two great lights; **the greater light** {*the Sun, which is a star*} <u>to</u> rule the day, and **the lesser light** {*the Moon,*} *which reflects the light of the Sun to the Earth}* <u>to</u> rule the night: *he made* **the stars also**" (Genesis 1:16).

The point in the simile is that God has created stars for a purpose for which these "wandering stars" are no longer fulfilling. This is what happens when things are corrupted by the curse or through false doctrine. The direction right doctrine gives no longer corrects once that doctrine is perverted. False doctrine misdirects and leads people astray.

"Whoso causeth the righteous to go astray in an evil way, he shall fall himself into his own pit: but the upright shall have good *things* in possession" (Proverbs 28:10).

Peter addresses false teachers in a very similar manner and tone warning both the false teachers and them that listen to them. Like fallen angels, false teachers have a placed "reserved" in "the blackness of darkness for ever" (Jude 13). However, **false teachers take their converts to hell with them.**

"[10] But chiefly **them that walk after the flesh in the lust of uncleanness, and despise government** *{authoritarian rulers as pastors are the resident theological authorities in a local church}*. **Presumptuous** *{boldly and arrogantly self-willed as they oppose their God appointed leaders}* *are they,* selfwilled, they are **not afraid to speak evil** *{blaspheme}* **of dignities** *{glories, probably referring to pastors or other Christians who will not follower their compromises because the faithful want God to be glorified}*. [11] **Whereas angels, which are greater in power and might, bring not railing accusation against them before the Lord** *{Angels are not appointed judges of false teachers and blasphemers in the local assembly. The intent of this phrase is that faithful members of a local church have more authority than faithful angels in dealing with blasphemers and false teachers through congregational polity}*. [12] **But these** *{*false teachers*}*, as natural brute beasts, made to be taken and destroyed, **speak evil of the things that they understand not;** and shall utterly perish in their own corruption; [13] And **shall receive the reward of unrighteousness,** *as* **they that count it**

pleasure to riot in the day time. Spots *they are* and blemishes, sporting themselves with their own deceivings while they feast with you; [14] Having eyes full of adultery, and that cannot cease from sin; **beguiling** {*deluding and thereby entrapping*} **unstable souls** {*unfixed; referring to doctrinally unstable or undiscipled*} : an heart they have exercised with covetous practices; cursed children: [15] Which **have forsaken** {*to leave behind; in other words having considered the right truth rejected it and took a false pathway*} the **right way**, and **are gone astray, following the way of Balaam** *the son* of Bosor, who loved the wages of unrighteousness; [16] But was rebuked for his iniquity: the dumb ass speaking with man's voice forbad the madness of the prophet. [17] These are wells without water, clouds that are carried with a tempest; to whom the mist of darkness is reserved for ever. [18] For when they **speak great swelling *words* of vanity**, they allure through the lusts of the flesh, *through much* wantonness, those that were clean escaped from them who live in error. [19] **While they promise them liberty, they themselves are the servants of corruption**: for of whom a man is overcome, of the same is he brought in bondage. [20] For if after they have escaped the pollutions of the world through **the knowledge of the Lord and Saviour Jesus Christ, they are again entangled therein**, and overcome, the latter end is worse with them than the beginning. [21] For it had been better for them not to have known the way of righteousness, than, after they have known *it*, **to turn from the holy commandment delivered unto them.** [22] But it is happened unto them according to the true proverb, **The dog *is* turned to his own vomit again; and the sow that was washed to her wallowing in the mire** {*manifesting that the nature was never changed and they were never 'born again'*}" (II Peter 2:10-22).

The word "wandering" is from the Greek word *planétēs* (plan-ay'-tace). Obviously, it is the Greek word from which we get our English word *planet*. The Greek word was also use figuratively to refer to a teacher who *erratically was constantly changing*. Therefore, the simile to false teachers is that they are like shooting stars constantly moving through space.

All truth originates with the Creator. Because God is immutable and therefore unchanging, all truth is unchanging. The immutability of God is a divine descriptor of His character. To misrepresent the character and nature of God is to blaspheme. To corrupt God's immutable truth is therefore blasphemy by its very nature of *de-glorifying* God. False doctrine does not reveal the God of the Bible but rather misrepresents Him and de-glorifies Him.

"[13] Let no man say when he is tempted, I am tempted of God: **for God cannot be tempted with evil, neither tempteth he any man**: [14] But every man is tempted, when he is **drawn away of his own lust**, and enticed. [15] Then when lust hath conceived, it bringeth forth sin: and sin, when it is finished, bringeth forth death. [16] Do not err, my beloved brethren. [17] Every good gift and every perfect gift is from above, and **cometh down from the <u>Father of lights</u>, with whom is no variableness, neither shadow of turning**. [18] Of his own will **begat he us with the word of truth**, that we should be a kind of firstfruits of his creatures" (James 1:13-18).

Jude
Contending for the Faith
Chapter Seven
False Teachers Will Be Judged

In Jude 14, Jude refers to a prophesy by Enoch. The notion that Jude is quoting the apocryphal book of Enoch and thereby giving that book canonical credibility is ludicrous. Enoch's prophecies were certainly known by God and were recorded in Israel's historical documents.

Secondly, the book of Jude is breathed out by the Holy Spirit (inspired) Who certainly could bring those prophecies to Jude's mind. Even if Jude is quoting from the apocryphal book of Enoch, this quote would only confirm God's agreement with this particular statement and not the whole of the apocryphal book of Enoch. **Jude 14-16 is stating that all false teachers and their converts will be ultimately judged.**

"¹⁴ And Enoch also, the seventh from Adam, **prophesied of these** *{types of unfaithful and self-serving men who corrupted doctrine for their personal gain}*, **saying** *{Enoch prophesying}*, Behold, the Lord cometh with ten thousands of his saints, ¹⁵ To execute judgment upon all, and to convince all that are ungodly among them of all their ungodly deeds which they have ungodly committed, and of all their hard *speeches* which ungodly sinners have spoken against him. ¹⁶ **These are murmurers, complainers, walking after their own lusts**; and their mouth speaketh great swelling *words*, having men's persons in admiration because of advantage" (Jude 14-16).

The intent of the statement of Jude 14-16 is that there is nothing new under the sun. False teachers have existed for millennia. This statement reveals the character and motivation of false teachers especially in Jude 16, "having men's persons in admiration because of advantage."

The "advantage" meaning these *admired people* would be able to advance the false teachers politically and give credence to what they say. Both the "admired people" and the false teachers thereby are advantaged due to the compromise by the false teacher. This is *you scratch my back, and I will scratch yours* philosophy of ministry. This is absolutely wicked especially when it results in the acceptance and propagation of false doctrine.

Age-old problems require age-old solutions. Showing favoritism to get favors is an age-old problem. This is how politicians work. This is NOT how faithful people work. **False teachers are NOT to be dealt with behind the scenes. False teachers are to be confronted publicly and exposed publicly.** False teachers need to be confronted publicly BEFORE they can gather a following of simpletons in a local assembly.

False teachers will always target those who are doctrinally ignorant and undiscipled. God calls these people simple. False teachers capitalize on the doctrinal ignorance of the simple to make merchandise of them.

"[20] **Wisdom crieth without**; she uttereth her voice in the streets: [21] She crieth in the chief place of concourse, in the openings of the gates: in the city she uttereth her words, *saying,* [22] **How long, ye simple ones, will ye love simplicity?** and the scorners delight in their scorning, and fools hate knowledge? [23] Turn you at my reproof: behold, I will pour out my spirit unto you, I will make known my words unto you" (Proverbs 1:20-23).

"[32] For **the turning away of the simple shall slay them**, and **the prosperity of fools shall destroy them**. [33] But whoso hearkeneth unto me shall dwell safely, and shall be quiet from fear of evil" (Proverbs 1:32-33).

"[17] Now I beseech you, brethren, **mark them which cause divisions and offences contrary to the doctrine which ye have learned**; and avoid them. [18] For they that are such serve not our Lord Jesus Christ, but their own belly; and **by good words and fair speeches deceive the hearts of the simple**" (Romans 16:17-18).

There is little doubt that false teachers depend upon simpletons and their ignorance of doctrine to gather a following of people to support their false teaching. Simpletons are easily deceived and convinced by false teachers because they have not yet been fully discipled in the Words of God. Simpletons admire people that they think are knowledgeable. "Good words and fair speeches" easily persuade simple people into allegiances with false teachers that should never happen.

Politicians give favor to get favor. Biblical truth should never be politicalized. It is equally true with false teachers. Simple people ignorantly want lives with as few restrictions upon them as possible. False teachers are willing to water down God's commands to gain the favor of simple people.

Simpletons want to believe false teachers who give liberty to the point of license in permissive teachings and lower Biblical standards of holiness. This is what was happening in early Church history by a group that taught a heresy known as *Antinomianism.* Paul addresses this heresy in Romans 6:1-2. Such a heresy is a complete contradiction against the testimony in water baptism of the expectation of living a sanctified life.

"What shall we say then? Shall we continue in sin, that grace may abound? [2] God forbid. **How shall we, that are dead to sin, live any longer therein**" (Romans 6:1-2)?

The thrust of the exhortation of Jude 14-16 is about the moral responsibility of faithful believers doing all in their power to rightly divide the Word of truth (II Timothy 2:15) and preserve that rightly divided Word of truth through faithfully living it and teaching it to another generation of believers (discipleship).

"[14] And **Enoch also**, the seventh from Adam, prophesied of these, saying, Behold, the Lord cometh with ten thousands of his saints, [15] **To execute judgment upon all, and to convince all** that are **ungodly** among them of all their **ungodly deeds** which they have **ungodly committed,** and of all their hard *speeches* which **ungodly sinners** have spoken against him. [16] These are murmurers, complainers, walking after their own lusts; and their mouth speaketh great swelling *words*, having men's persons in admiration because of advantage" (Jude 14-16).

The preservation of God's Words and their meaning/instruction has been a primary responsibility of the

faithful since those Words were first given to Moses in the first five books called the Law. Every other revelation from God in the wisdom books, poetry books, and the prophets were to be treated with the same responsibility and with equal fervor.

This would extend into the four Gospels, the book of Acts, the New Testament epistles, and the Revelation of Jesus Christ. Just as keeping (preserving) the Words of God in their meaning and purpose was the responsibility of every Old Testament Jew and the nation of Israel, this is the same responsibility of every truly "born again" Christian the makes up the "church of the firstborn" (Hebrews 12:23). The "ungodly" (Jude 15) are satanically being used to corrupt God's preservation workings through God's faithful.

This preservation of *meaning* is exactly what is taking place in the book of Deuteronomy, which is often called the *second giving of the Law.* Deuteronomy is written about forty years after Moses received the original Law. Deuteronomy does not change the original Words of God but rather gives *clarification* and *explanation* to certain truths and expectations by God. This is one of the methods God has used over the centuries to preserve the meaning of His Words with additional explanation.

This is certainly true of all the epistles of the New Testament books. When corruptions arose in history, God divinely intervened with corrections through additional Old Testament books such as the Wisdom books and the prophets and the epistles in the New Testament.

God has ordained that preaching (explanation of rightly divided Scripture) through local churches to be how God's Word would be preserved until the second coming of Jesus. Allowing false teachers to teach in a local church is a complete antithesis to God's instructions. **One generation of poorly discipled believers will not create a continuum of preservation of God's truths, which is every faithful pastor's greatest fear.**

"[1] And it shall come to pass, when all these things are come upon thee, **the blessing and the curse** {*based upon understanding and obeying God's commands*}, **which I have set before thee**, and **thou shalt call *them* to mind** among all the nations, whither the LORD thy God **hath driven thee,** [2] And **shalt return unto the LORD thy God**, and shalt obey his voice according to all that I command thee this day, thou and thy children, **with all thine**

heart, and with all thy soul; [3] That **then** the LORD thy God will turn thy captivity, and have compassion upon thee, and will return and gather thee from all the nations, whither the LORD thy God hath scattered thee. [4] If *any* of thine be driven out unto the outmost *parts* of heaven, from thence will the LORD thy God gather thee, and from thence will he fetch thee: [5] And the LORD thy God will bring thee into the land which thy fathers possessed, and thou shalt possess it; and he will do thee good, and multiply thee above thy fathers. [6] And the LORD thy God will circumcise thine heart, and the heart of thy seed, to love the LORD thy God with all thine heart, and with all thy soul, that thou mayest live. [7] And the LORD thy God will put all these curses upon thine enemies, and on them that hate thee, which persecuted thee. [8] And **thou shalt return and obey the voice of the LORD, and do all his commandments** which I command thee this day. [9] And the LORD thy God will make thee plenteous in every work of thine hand, in the fruit of thy body, and in the fruit of thy cattle, and in the fruit of thy land, for good: for the LORD will again rejoice over thee for good, as he rejoiced over thy fathers: [10] **If thou shalt hearken unto the voice of the LORD thy God, to keep** *{put a hedge about to guard or preserve}* **his commandments and his statutes which are written in this book of the law,** *and* **if thou turn unto the LORD thy God with all thine heart, and with all thy soul.** [11] For this commandment which I command thee this day, **it** *is* **not hidden from thee, neither** *is* **it far off.** [12] **It** *is* **not in heaven** *{preservation of God's Words is not needed in Heaven, but upon earth}*, that thou shouldest say, Who shall go up for us to heaven, and bring it unto us, **that we may hear it** *{with understanding}*, **and do it?** [13] Neither *is* it beyond the sea, that thou shouldest say, Who shall go over the sea for us, and bring it unto us, that we may hear it, and do it? [14] **But the word** *is* **very nigh unto thee, in thy mouth, and in thy heart, that thou mayest do it** *{personal responsibility}*" (Deuteronomy 30:1-14).

In Jude 15, God uses the word "ungodly" on four occasions. "Ungodly" is translated from the Greek word *asebēs* (as-eb-ace'), or a derivative of that word. The *a* as the beginning letter negates it meaning. It is equal to putting the prefix *non* or *un* in front of an

English word. The word means the **opposite** of reverent, devoted, holy, or pious.

Therefore, the word means irreverent, impious, and wicked. God is speaking of false teachers or false believers that do not have God or God's will anywhere near to their hearts. Such people are pure hypocrites living solely to their own advantages. Therefore, these people are compared to Cain, Balaam, and Core (Jude 11).

The epitome of hypocrisy is the pretense that deceives others to take advantage of their loyalties for personal gain or out of jealousy. This is not spiritual leadership. This is pure carnal, selfish, egotistic narcissism and self-worship. It is "ungodly" and evil wickedness. Unfortunately, the "ungodly" person is often so blinded to his own ungodliness by his own carnality so masterly disguised as spiritually he cannot see it himself.

The words "to execute judgment upon all" in Jude 15 are most probably referring to God's rejected warning to the pre-flood unbelievers at the time of Noah's preaching. Although God gave the preflood unbelievers over a hundred years to repent and believe, they hardened themselves to God's warning, mocked God's preacher, and ended up buried under the waters of God's wrath destined ultimately to Hell.

The warning of God's judgment will ultimately be executed. The word "all" extends to all those rejecting the warning. This encompasses a population in the warning of the flood to numbers of people that was universal and world-wide.

The false teacher thinks his offenses and abuses in teaching the Word of God can be done with impunity. This was the case with the motivations of all three of the men cited in Jude 11: Cain, Balaam, and Core. They each thought that God would not judge them for what they were doing.

What they did not understand was that they had already been judged by God. This is essentially what God said to Cain in Genesis chapter four. Why was Cain so upset with Abel? He wasn't. He was upset with God's rejection of his offering. Cain just directed his anger toward Abel.

"⁶ And the LORD said unto Cain, **Why art thou wroth?** and **why is thy countenance fallen?** ⁷ **If thou doest well** {*the way God says to do it*}, shalt **thou** {*not it*} not be accepted? and **if**

thou doest not well {*Can your anger and hatred for your brother correct the fact you didn't offer the offering you were instructed to offer?*}, **sin lieth at the door** {*Your solution is not to kill your brother, which is in your heart, but to repent and offer the right offering.*}. **And unto thee *shall be* his desire** {*Cain would always be the older brother with primogeniture over Abel. Why then envy him and hate him?*}, and thou shalt rule over him" (Genesis 4:6).

False teachers think they can bend and distort God's Word with impunity because such people use *religion* (belief in God) to gain advantage over people and then use those people for their own personal gain. Right doctrine is not necessary to their abuse of the Scriptures and of people.

However, the primary reason false teachers think they can do so with impunity is really because of their own unbelief in God and unbelief in God's intent to preserve the original meaning of His inspired Words. For them religion, falsely so-called, is just a vehicle for personal gain.

Bending and distorting God's Word with impunity was the outcome of the integration into Christianity of the pagan's ideas about their pagan gods. It was believed that pagan gods could be manipulated by their followers because pagan gods shared the same lusts, pride, and greed as do humans.

Pagans believed their gods could be manipulated with gifts, sacrifices, or enticements. In doing so, the pagans got what they wanted from their pagan gods and the pagans' gods got what they wanted. Therefore, in their corrupted thinking, there was no harm and no foul in these manipulations.

False doctrines are more conducive to controlling and manipulating people. Right doctrine frees people from false religious leaders who make people dependent upon them for blessings from God. Right doctrine takes a person to a personal relationship with God Himself, and instruction can come directly through God's rightly divided truth.

Always beware of spiritual leaders who never want people to mature to the place where those people can live in independence of the spiritual leader. Imagine parents who never want their children to grow to the kind of maturity that can live and reproduce independent of the parents. When spiritual leaders, parents, and governments seek to create people forever dependent upon them, there is something bizarre going on. Christ addressed the Pharisees about this.

"*31* Then said Jesus to those Jews which believed on him, **If ye continue in my word**, *then* are ye my disciples indeed; *32* And ye shall know the truth, and **the truth shall make you free** {*intent is to liberate from the protective custody and guardianship of the Law as a 'child leader', Galatians 4:2*}. *33* They answered him, We be Abraham's seed, and were never in bondage to any man: how sayest thou, Ye shall be made free? *34* Jesus answered them, Verily, verily, I say unto you, **Whosoever committeth sin is the servant of sin.** *35* And the servant abideth not in the house for ever: *but* the Son abideth ever. *36* If the Son therefore shall make you free, ye shall be free indeed. *37* I know that ye are Abraham's seed; but ye seek to kill me, because **my word hath no place in you**" (John 8:31-37).

"*17* **But** {*an adversative conjunction expressing an adverse circumstance acting against the intent of the adversary*}, beloved, **remember** {*personal responsibility necessary to counteracting the adversary*} ye **the words** {*previous Biblical instructions regarding these people*} which were spoken {*warnings*} before **of the apostles** {*multiple warnings*} **of our Lord Jesus Christ**; *18* How that **they told you** {*believers should be aware when they are warned many times*} there should be mockers in the last time, **who should walk after their own ungodly lusts**. *19* These be **they who separate themselves** {*moved away from God's specified doctrinal boundaries*}, sensual, **having not the Spirit** {*they are not truly 'born again'*}" (Jude 17-19).

"Sensual" in Jude 19 is from the Greek word *psychikós* (psoo-khee-kos'). It is almost opposite of the Greek word *pneumatikós* (pnyoo-mat-ik-os'), which is often used to describe the supernatural operations of God in regeneration through which God partners with His redeemed to generate spirituality through those believers.

Psychikós (psoo-khee-kos') is without the supernatural operations of God and is the natural, and bestial tendencies of the "natural man" who is still lost and governed by his fallen nature. We might say the lost person is spiritually *psychotic*, moving towards Amoralism and spiritual *psychosis*.

Psychosis is a serious mental illness characterized by defective thinking moving towards losing contact with reality often accompanied with hallucinations and/or delusional thinking. The mental and the spiritual are intricately connected to one another. When the mind is corrupted with false teaching (like Amoralism) the soul/spirit is affected in a downward movement away from spirituality resulting in insane outcomes.

Every local church is a guardian of the truths of the Word of God and responsible to proclaim those truths dogmatically regardless of the growing opposition of any society to those truths. False teachers oppose dogmatic truths.

False teachers do not oppose philosophical truths, because philosophical truths do not demand anything. Philosophical truths merely offer suggestions. The Bible give commands and makes demands for acceptance before God. What God says in I Timothy 3:14-16 is important as we understand His four-fold address to the "ungodly" in Jude 15.

"[14] These things write I unto thee, hoping to come unto thee shortly: [15] But if I tarry long, **that thou mayest know how thou oughtest to behave thyself in the house of God**, which is the church of the living God, the **pillar and ground of the truth**. [16] And **without controversy great is the mystery of godliness** {*'Christ in you the hope of glory,' Colossians 1:27*}: God was manifest in the flesh, justified in the Spirit, seen of angels, preached unto the Gentiles, believed on in the world, received up into glory" (I Timothy 3:14-16).

There will be a *devolution of revolution* in any culture that rejects Biblical dogmatism regarding what God says is right and wrong. There are both personal and social outcomes to the abdication of Biblical dogmatism. In other words, the abdication of Biblical dogmatism in theological orthodoxy does not exist within a vacuum of the nonexistence of a spiritual realm where there is a clear line of demarcation between black and white, good and evil, and righteousness and sin.

When a person begins to be influenced into the realm of doctrinal error, darkness begins to grow in his life. Evil grows in his life. Sin begins to expand to the place it begins to dominate and consume filling every aspect of a person's life moving this person into insanity by degrees.

Fallen people have an inclination and propensity for wickedness. The beliefs they believe and the truths they know are grand deterrents to their wicked propensities. Therefore, false teachers are so dangerous. False teachers are constantly moving and removing God's landmark truths that guard the souls of sinners from going over the cliff into the chasms of wickedness.

This is to what God spoke through Jeremiah to the rebellious children of Israel as they became increasingly involved in the licentious practices of paganism on all the high places in the land of Israel. **God's point in Jeremiah chapter seventeen is that once the declension of false doctrines begins, it takes one into the pits of degeneration where no man would think himself capable.**

"[5] **Thus saith the LORD**; Cursed *be* the man that trusteth in man, and maketh flesh his arm, and **whose heart departeth from the LORD**. [6] For he shall be **like the heath in the desert** {*naked and destitute; the heath was a viewed as an unwanted weed excluded from any spiritual purposes*}, and **shall not see when good cometh** {*totally lacking in spiritual discernment*}; but **shall inhabit the parched places in the wilderness** {*barren of spiritual potential*}, *in* **a salt land** {*barren and impossible to produce growth*} and not {*fit to be*} inhabited. [7] {*the opposite is true of the faithful believer*} **Blessed *is* the man that trusteth in the LORD, and whose hope the LORD is.** [8] For he shall be **as a** tree planted by the waters, and *that* spreadeth out her roots by the river, and shall not see when heat cometh, but her leaf shall be green; and shall not be careful in the year of drought, **neither shall cease from yielding fruit** {*spiritual prosperity is guaranteed*}. [9] {*the question*} **The heart *is* deceitful above all things,** {*the fallen nature is dominantly insidious, puffed up in selfish pursuits and fraudulent deceptions*} **and desperately wicked** {*hopeless, unfixable apart from divine help and intervention*}**: who can know it?** [10] {*the answer*} **I the LORD search the heart, *I* try the reins, even to give every man**

according to his ways, *and* according to the fruit of his doings. [11] *As* the partridge sitteth *on eggs*, and hatcheth *them* not; *so* he that getteth riches, **and not by right**, shall leave them in the midst of his days, and **at his end shall be a fool**" (Jeremiah 17:5-11).

It is absolute foolishness to profess faith in the God of the Bible and then live in contradiction of His revealed will, thinking that God does not care about what man considers *minor points* of holiness. This is the attitude that always leads a person into apostasy. The point of Jeremiah 17:9 is that all of us have a natural propensity for self-deception and giving our fallen nature what it wants.

False teachers are simply leaders in the church that are bent in this same direction. They want what they want, and they are willing to mock what they consider minor points of holiness. They think they are preaching spiritual freedom (grace) when they are in fact putting shackles upon themselves and everyone following them. **Pied Pipers have their own agendas.**

Just as Jude warns the hypothetical wanderer to "remember" in Jude 17, God does the same through Jeremiah in the words "I the LORD search the heart, *I* try the reins, even to give every man according to his ways, *and* according to the fruit of his doings" (Jeremiah 17:10).

There is nothing about us that escapes God knowledge. God knows us inside and out. He knows our rising ups and our laying downs. He knows the thoughts and motivations of our hearts. He knows our faulty inclinations and our propensity for unrighteousness. Therefore, if we believe in the God of the Bible, we would be wise to follow the leadership God gives us through His Bible. When teachers depart from the Bible, depart from them, or separate them from you.

"[20] But ye, beloved, building up yourselves on your most holy faith, praying in the Holy Ghost, [21] Keep yourselves in the love of God, looking for the mercy of our Lord Jesus Christ unto eternal life. [22] And of some have compassion, making a difference: [23] And others save with fear, pulling *them* out of the fire; hating even the garment spotted by the flesh" (Jude 20-22).

Sometimes trying to contend for the faith seems hopeless because we evaluate success in doing so by looking at the results.

We must remember (Jude 17) that results are not why we contend. Faithfulness to God and manifesting genuine worship through obedience is why we contend. When no effort is made, God cannot bless what we do not do. In our contending for the faith, God is primarily trying our faith and proving our faithfulness to Him.

In Jude 20-22, we are given seven responsibilities connected to contending for the faith. In contending for the faith there are dangers to the faithful. Therefore, these seven responsibilities prepare our minds and hearts for what would otherwise be a very discouraging ministry.

We cannot expect to engage the opposition to righteousness or involve ourselves combatting the forces of evil in the "mystery of iniquity" (II Thessalonians 2:7) as partners with the Spirit of God in His restraint upon the growth of evil in this world if we do not understand and commit to our mission. **Evil never rests.**

1. "Building up yourselves on your most holy faith"

"Building" if from the Greek word *epoikodoméō* (ep-oy-kod-om-eh'-o). The *epi* prefix heightens the intensity of responsibility to the highest degree. The second part of the verb is *oikodoméō*. This verb is used to describe the building of a house. However, the object of the verb is "your most holy faith."

Building one's faith is not about increasing our ability to believe. Building one's faith involves learning the details of what the Bible teaches (God's will) and implementing (living) the truths we learn. This is an unending lifetime process. Faithfulness involves stewardship of the house we build.

This command from Jude parallels the teaching of Christ on building our house upon a rock rather than the sand (Matthew 7:24-26). Building on a rock creates stability and solidity. Building on a rock is equal to "rightly dividing the word of truth" (II Timothy 2:15) to the point of dogmatic surety and stability of what God says and wills for our lives.

Building upon the shifting sands of ignorance and the philosophical opinions of men regarding God's will is to build upon instability with the ultimate destiny of destruction. The goal of construction is the opposite of destruction.

Construction builds to last. Therefore, "building up yourselves on your most holy faith" is intended to defend against the destructive forces of Biblical ignorance and the apathy of lazy Bible study. Every Christian is responsible to carefully build upon the foundation of salvation laid for us in Jesus Christ. **We do not build without God's help.**

"[9] For we are **labourers together with God**: ye are **God's husbandry**, *ye are* **God's building**. [10] **According to the grace of God** which is given unto me, as a wise masterbuilder, I have laid the foundation, and **another buildeth thereon. But let every man take heed how he buildeth thereupon**" (I Corinthians 3:9-10).

2. "Praying in the Holy Ghost"

Prayer is simply a one-way conversation with God. God speaks to believers through his Word and through answers to prayer. Conversationally talking with God is the primary way in which a believer expresses faith in God and His involvement in our lives.

God is constantly working in the believer and through the believer. It is wise to converse with God about what we are doing asking Him for direction and leadership as we seek to keep ourselves holy before Him and involve ourselves in the "work of the ministry."

Conversing with God defines our every moment relationship of constant communion with our Creator. God wants to use us in the good He is doing in the world (Romans 8:28). He wants to talk to us if we will read and study His Word. He wants us to talk with Him, telling Him our fears, weaknesses, and failings.

It is not that God does not already know about our fears, weaknesses, and failings. We tell God these things to humble ourselves before Him - to tell Him we know He knows. Telling these things to God declares our dependency upon His enabling grace, leadership, and empowering for the ministries He has put in our care.

Prayer is the grandest of divine privileges given to the children of God as well as the most neglected privilege. Seldom is anything accomplished through ministry apart from bathing ourselves and our hopes in prayer before God.

Revival is always born through prayer. Conversing with God about the details and confrontations of our lives should be the most natural and common experience of a life of faith in God. It would be foolish to profess faith in God and His abilities and fail to communicate with Him to ensure His participation and leadership in what we venture to do for Him.

The neglectful failure of believers to labor in prayer is often result of their failing to understand the battle going on around them. This was certainly true of the disciples the night before the crucifixion of Jesus. **Jesus knew in detail what was about to happen to Him. Therefore, He prayed through the night.**

The disciples were ignorant of the dangers that surrounded Jesus and them. Therefore, they were weary and overcome with sleep. When we are aware of the dangers involved in faithful ministry to us and our loved ones, we will be diligent in our conversations with God.

"36 Then cometh Jesus with them unto a place called Gethsemane, and saith unto the disciples, Sit ye here, **while I go and pray yonder**. 37 And he took with him Peter and the two sons of Zebedee, and began to be sorrowful and very heavy. 38 Then saith he unto them, **My soul is exceeding sorrowful, even unto death: tarry ye here, and watch with me.** 39 And he went a little further, and fell on his face, and prayed, saying, O my Father, if it be possible, let this cup pass from me: nevertheless not as I will, but as thou *wilt*. 40 And he cometh unto the disciples, and **findeth them asleep**, and saith unto Peter, What, **could ye not watch with me one hour?** 41 **Watch and pray, that ye enter not into temptation: the spirit indeed *is* willing, but the flesh *is* weak.** 42 He went away again the second time, and prayed, saying, O my Father, if this cup may not pass away from me, except I drink it, thy will be done. 43 And **he came and found them asleep again:** for their eyes were heavy. 44 And he left them, and went away again, and prayed the third time, saying the same words. 45 Then cometh he to his disciples, and saith unto them, **Sleep on now, and take *your* rest: behold, the hour is at hand, and the Son of man is betrayed into the hands of sinners.** 46 Rise, let us be going: behold, **he is at hand that doth betray me**" (Matthew 26:36-46).

"Praying in the Holy Ghost" is praying within the will of God and within the power of God. "Praying in the Holy Ghost" is to connect holy objectives with Divine influence and ability. "Praying in the Holy Ghost" is the only way our prayers reach past the ceilings of our existence.

"Praying in the Holy Ghost" is the prayer of a life confessed up, sanctified, and yielded to the indwelling Christ. Only such prayer can expect to see God in the answers. God is committed to His will being done. "Praying in the Holy Ghost" connects the believer to God's enabling power, leadership, and engages the believer in God's objectives.

3. "Keep yourselves in the love of God"

This is **not** referring to keeping ourselves in a place where God loves us, for God loves us regardless of what we do or how we live. God's actions of love to His children may change between blessings and chastisement depending upon our faithfulness or unfaithfulness, but He will always love us.

"Love" here is *agápē* (ag-ah'-pay), which is self-sacrificing love manifested by Christ as He died to pay the death sentence for the sins of sinners. To "keep" oneself "in" that "love" is a difficulty requiring extreme dedication and an eternal vision of reality. Therefore, a believer who understands the dangers of ministry and is willing to live within the constant threat of those dangers is what is necessary to keeping oneself "in the love of God."

It is the believer's responsibility to keep himself living a self-sacrificing life. Therefore, understanding that resistance to our ministry by people is the norm and our continuance in our willingness to sacrifice our safety and even lives for them is to what God refers in this text.

"[19] For I through the law am dead to the law, **that I might live unto God** {*volitionally because we love Him, not legally because of fear of condemnation*}. [20] I am crucified with Christ: **nevertheless I live**; yet not I, but Christ liveth in me: and **the life which I now live in the flesh I live by the faith of the Son of God, who loved me, and gave himself for me**" (Galatians 2:19-20).

"[20] But ye, beloved, {1} building up yourselves on your most holy faith, {2} praying in the Holy Ghost, [21] {3} Keep yourselves in the love of God, {4} looking for the mercy of our Lord Jesus Christ unto eternal life. [22] And {5} of some have compassion, making a difference: [23] And {6} others save with fear, {7} pulling *them* out of the fire; {8} hating even the garment spotted by the flesh" (Jude 20-22).

4. "Looking for the mercy of our Lord Jesus Christ unto eternal life"

"The mercy of our Lord Jesus Christ" is the believer's "blessed hope." "Mercy" is referring to the resurrection and glorification of the believer in the final act of God in the redemption of our bodies and final deliverance from and eradication of our sin natures. This is an act of mercy because it is another aspect of grace in our salvation.

"Looking" is from the Greek word prosdéchomai (pros-dekh'-om-ahee). "Pros" is a preposition of direction (forward to a future event). *Déchomai* means to accept or receive what is offered or gifted. **Therefore, the believer should maintain this vision of the future gifting of a new glorified and sinless body.** This is every believer's "blessed hope."

"[11] For the grace of God that bringeth salvation hath appeared to all men, [12] Teaching us that, denying ungodliness and worldly lusts, we should live soberly, righteously, and godly, in this present world; [13] **Looking for that blessed hope**, and the glorious appearing of the great God and our Saviour Jesus Christ; [14] Who gave himself for us, that **he might redeem us from all iniquity, and purify unto himself a peculiar people**, zealous of good works" (Titus 2:11-14).

The command to be "looking for the mercy of our Lord Jesus Christ unto eternal life" often confuses people into thinking they can never be sure they are truly "born again" and at best can only hope to be saved at the end of their lives. Of course, this is a complete falsehood.

Biblical salvation is presented throughout Scripture in three tenses. The third aspect of a believer's salvation is to what the phrase "looking for the mercy of our Lord Jesus Christ unto eternal life" refers. If believers do not understand these three tenses of their salvation used throughout Scripture, they will be greatly confused about their salvation.

1. We **were** saved (positional, i.e., the salvation of the soul from Hell).
2. We **are being** saved (practical, i.e., the salvation of the life from ruin and waste).
3. We **will be** saved (premier or ultimate, i.e., the salvation/redemption of the body).

"Looking" in this phrase is present tense and middle voice (passive deponent). The middle voice in Koine Greek is almost always understood as equal to being in the active voice. Therefore, it is the believer's responsibility to be constantly "looking for the mercy of our Lord Jesus Christ unto eternal life." This action is to what is often referred as the *imminent* (any moment) return of Jesus for His Bride, known to Bible believers as the rapture.

"⁵¹ Behold, **I shew** {*expose or reveal*} you a mystery; **We shall not all sleep** {*a common phrased used to describe a believer's body in the grave while his soul/spirit are 'with the Lord,' some believers will be translated without dying*}, but **we shall all be changed** {*glorified*}, ⁵² In a moment, in the twinkling of an eye, at the last trump: for the trumpet shall sound, and **the dead shall be raised incorruptible, and we shall be changed**. ⁵³ For this corruptible must put on incorruption, and this mortal *must* put on immortality. ⁵⁴ So when this corruptible shall have put on incorruption, and this mortal shall have put on immortality, then shall be brought to pass the saying that is written, Death is swallowed up in victory. ⁵⁵ O death, where *is* thy sting? O grave, where *is* thy victory? ⁵⁶ The sting of death *is* sin; and the strength of sin *is* the law. ⁵⁷ But thanks *be* to God, **which giveth us the victory** {*over separation from God due to sin and death*} **through our Lord Jesus Christ**" (I Corinthians 15:51-57).

"¹³ But **I would not have you to be ignorant**, brethren, **concerning them which are asleep** {*believers who have died*}, that ye sorrow not, even as others which have no hope. [14] For if we believe that Jesus died and rose again, even so **them also which sleep in Jesus will God bring with him**. [15] For this we say unto you by the word of the Lord, that we which are alive *and* remain unto the coming of the Lord **shall not prevent them which are asleep**. [16] For the Lord himself shall descend from heaven with a shout, with the voice of the archangel, and with the trump of God: and *the dead in Christ shall rise first*: [17] **Then we which are alive *and* remain shall be caught up together with them in the clouds, to meet the Lord in the air**: and so shall we ever be with the Lord. [18] Wherefore comfort one another with these words" (I Thessalonians 4:13-18).

Why must the believer be constantly "looking for the mercy of our Lord Jesus Christ unto eternal life"? This is needed because life tends to overwhelm us with moments of great stress, difficult situations, and difficult people. Keeping this pending reality as *an any moment event* helps us endure, be steadfast in our living, and not lose hope in our eternal perspective of life. One's life is but a "vapour, that appeareth for a little time, and then vanisheth away" (James 4:14). Maintaining perspective is important.

5. "Of some have compassion, making a difference"

Every compassionate person's hope is to make a difference in someone's life. Everyone wants a purpose for existence in a world cursed and destined for the "lake of fire." However, the words "making a difference" refer to differentiating between the types of individuals who are being deceived by false teachers.

Not every deceived person is to be treated in the same way. Some of those deceived by false teachers can be returned to faithfulness with tender, compassionate, and patient care. Both wisdom and compassion must be applied based upon the individuality of the person's deceived.

In many cases, novices and unlearned simpletons are easily led astray by him whose "mouth speaketh great swelling words" (Jude 16). Compassion takes every individual's circumstance into consideration. The adult who willfully commits a crime is not treated in the same manner as a child who ignorantly commits the same crime.

Mature believers differentiate people by the nature of their characters. Most people should be evaluated and carefully treated individually and not judged by the character of the one who was the deceiver. The tendency of the immature person is to lump all disagreement together and write the whole lot off as unrecoverable. This is never to be the way mature spiritual people look upon the deceived. Most deceived people are ignorant babes and may not even be "born again" people.

6. "Others save with fear"

There are many categories of deceived people and many levels of deception. Those deepest in the quicksand require greater caution lest you put yourself into an unrecoverable condition. The believer seeking to do the rescue work should not proudly leap into a situation he is not capable of handling. In dealing with deceived people, always be soul conscious. You may or may not be able to rescue someone from deception.

However, it is always wise to approach such people with caution lest you get in over your head and put yourself in danger of deception. Novices often make such foolish mistakes because they proudly think themselves to be experts when they have nothing more than the basics themselves.

Personal knowledge of someone is often miscalculated when one compares himself to the simpleton. However, deceivers are experts in the things of which they speak. When you seek to pull someone out of the fire, don't jump in with both feet yourself. This is the greatest mistake among moderately trained people (Ephesians 4:12). No one can assume himself properly prepared if he does not fully understand the positions against which he must contend.

Always be over prepared, prayer prepared, and fully yielded to the indwelling Christ. Recovery work is not for carnal and proud notices. There are eternal souls weighing in the balance.

Do not begin when you are unwilling to invest the time necessary to first train yourself. You will need to do considerable research into the areas in which these people have been deceived. You will need to read books on the subject both from the false perspective and from those who hold to that false perspective. You will need to familiarize yourself with all the arguments and there will be many levels and degrees of deception.

Books cost money and are an investment in your own education to be effective in discipleship. You will need to ask questions and understand the degree of a person's deception and be able to Scripturally lead him away from that position back to what God's Word teaches. Understanding *Biblical Hermeneutics* will be your greatest tool coupled with the filling of the Holy Spirit.

Secondly, do not begin unless you are willing to commit as much TIME AS NECESSARY to stick with the person you are trying to rescue. This kind of ministry is extremely time-consuming and is usually very inconvenient to a person's time schedules. This kind of ministry work is not for the lazy and lackadaisical students of Scripture.

"[14] Of these things put *them* in remembrance, charging *them* before the Lord that they strive not about words to no profit, *but* to the subverting of the hearers. [15] **Study** {*imperative*} <u>**to shew thyself** approved</u> {*legitimate*} unto God, a workman that needeth not to be ashamed, **rightly dividing the word of truth**. [16] But **shun** {*imperative*} **profane** {*unhallowed or unsanctified*} *and* **vain babblings** {*meaningless and empty discussions*}: for they will increase unto more ungodliness. [17] And their word will eat as doth a canker {*infectious gangrene*}: of whom is Hymenaeus and Philetus; [18] Who concerning the truth have erred, **saying that the resurrection is past already** {*their false doctrine*}; **and overthrow** {*subvert*} **the faith of some**" (II Timothy 2:14-18).

7. "Pulling them out of the fire"

The word "pulling" is translated from the Greek word *harpázō* (har-pad'-zo). The word means *to seize or catch away*. A good meaning would be to "snatch them out of the fire." This meaning fits the scenario of trying to rescue someone from "the fire" without getting yourself burned in the process. Therefore, there is a matter of urgency to rescue the person in the fire and for the person doing the snatching to take care in doing so because there are risks to oneself in doing the rescuing. The intent is to proceed with *courage* but also *caution*. There are spiritual dangers involved.

People who are loving and caring are often sympathetic and empathic to the people they seek to help and rescue from false beliefs and deceptions. Because of this, loving and caring people are often willing to soften the message needed to rescue a person from false beliefs and deceptions.** The difficulty is that the situation requires both *urgency* and *gentleness*.

Unfortunately, many zealous *rescuers* use a sword when a scalpel is needed. Others sugarcoat the message to make it more palatable. Understanding the individual, the person's spiritual age and knowledge of the Scriptures, and the circumstances of the person's life experiences can be helpful in attempting a rescue. Familiarity can help with evaluating the exact method required to attempt the rescue. Then, bathe that understanding of the person to be rescued with the precursor of much prayer. Know with whom you are speaking!

"[8] Reprove not a scorner, lest he hate thee: rebuke a wise man, and he will love thee. [9] Give *instruction* to a wise *man*, and he will be yet wiser: teach a just *man*, and he will increase in learning" (Proverbs 9:8-9).

"[1] I charge *thee* therefore before God, and the Lord Jesus Christ, who shall judge the quick and the dead at his appearing and his kingdom; [2] **Preach the word**; be instant in season, out of season; **reprove, rebuke, exhort** with all longsuffering and doctrine. [3] **For** {because} the time will come when they will not endure sound doctrine; but after their own lusts shall they heap to themselves teachers, having itching ears; [4] And **they shall turn away *their* ears from the truth**, and shall be turned unto fables. [5] But watch thou in all things, endure afflictions, do the work of an evangelist, make full proof of thy ministry" (II Timothy 4:1-5).

II Timothy 4:2 gives believers four Biblical actions necessary to dealing with those leaning toward deceptive false doctrines. Understanding what is involved in each of these four actions necessary to rescuing the deceived, or those being deceived, is essential to making a Biblical rescue. Secondly, we must know the person being rescued well enough to choose what action is best for that person.

"Preach the word"

The word translated "preach" does not mean shout at a person at the top of your lungs until they bow before you in submission to your dominant voice. The word "preach" is from the Greek word *kērýssō* (kay-roos'-so). The phrase "preach the word" means to *proclaim* and *explain* the doctrines that the Word of God gives us. The word "preach" is active voice and imperative mood, meaning this is a command we are all expected to OBEY.

Preaching first demands the dogmatic proclamation of what God has said. Then, preaching requires the careful explanation and discussion of what God has said. After which, personal application to a person's life in each situation must be made from the doctrine that has been *proclaimed* and *explained*. Application will not be accepted until understanding of the explanation has been made.

Biblically reproving, rebuking, and exhorting are extensions and *applications* of thoroughly proclaiming and explaining "the Word." However, Biblically reproving, rebuking, and exhorting **MUST** involve the proclamation and careful explanation of God's Word or Biblically reproving, rebuking, and exhorting will fall on deaf ears and hardened hearts.

There is no place in the dynamic of rescuing souls from deception for the ignorant, careless, lazy Bible student, or the angry person. This is spiritual surgery and must be done with meticulous care. If the rescuer cannot control his spirit, he/she has no business in trying to rescue people from deception. "He that *hath* no rule over his own spirit *is like* a city *that is* broken down, *and* without walls" (Proverbs 25:28).

"Reprove"

The word "reprove" is from the Greek word *elénchō* (el-eng'-kho). The word means to *confute* and *convince*. The word *confute* means to *prove a person wrong* with careful explanation of the meaning of Scripture while *appealing* to the person to repent. There is care and gentleness in reproof. Reproof communicates appealing care and gentleness intermingled with the proclamation and explanation of God's Word. Do not communicate with an uncompassionate spirit to the person being rescued by being harsh in your demeanor.

The rescuer cannot force anyone into repentance, or such action becomes merely an external control mechanism that has not enjoined the heart of the deceived into his own rescue. The first thing a lifeguard learns in rescuing someone drowning is to calm them so he/she does not drown you too.

"Rebuke"

"Rebuke" is from the Greek word *epitimáō* (ep-ee-tee-mah'-o). Rebuke takes rescue to another level of intensity. Rebuke is used when reproof has failed, and the person has rejected reproof. Rebuke is direct and straight forward commands given with the authority of the Word of God after proclamation and explanation of the Word. Rebuke usually is a warning accompanied with a call to repent. Rebuke is a no nonsense repent or else kind of action.

"Exhort with all longsuffering and doctrine"

"Exhort" is from the Greek word *parakaléō* (par-ak-al-eh'-o). "Exhort" means to call someone near to you to invite or invoke them to respond in the manner directed by the Word thoroughly proclaimed and explained. Yet the decision to respond must be a free will decision. Thoroughly proclaiming and explaining is followed with an appeal/encouragement to do what has been proclaimed and explained. We might call this an invitation to exercise the will in making the right and Biblical decision.

"Hating even the garments spotted by the flesh" (Jude 1:23)

"Flesh" is from the Greek word *sárx* (sarx). Although the word "flesh" simply means the flesh of an animal or person, theologically the word refers to the natural and unregenerate person. The word "flesh" is synonymous with the phrase "old man" in Romans 6:6 and refers to the sin nature of human beings fallen in sin. Often the word "sin" is used to describe the sin nature. The Old Scofield Reference Bible gives us the following note on the "flesh":

"Flesh, Summary: 'Flesh,' in the ethical sense, is the whole natural or unregenerate man, spirit, soul, and body, **as centered**

upon self, prone to sin, and opposed to God Ro 7:18. The regenerate man is not 'in *the sphere of* the flesh,' but in *the sphere of* the Spirit **Ro** 8:9 but the flesh is still in him, and he may, according to his choice, 'walk after the flesh' or 'in the Spirit' **1Co** 3:1-4; **Ga** 5:16-17. In the first case he is a 'carnal,' in the second a 'spiritual,' Christian. Victory over the flesh will be the habitual experience of the believer who walks in the Spirit **Ro** 8:2, 4; **Ga** 5:16-17."[10] (bolding added)

The sin nature automatically defiles everything it touches, even the good things a fallen person attempts to do. Therefore, God says: "But we are all as an unclean *thing*, and all our righteousnesses *are* as filthy rags" (Isaiah 64:6). "Hating even the garments spotted by the flesh" is to hate the defiling nature of the "old man" who motivates us into sin and selfishness. This defines our nature.

We naturally are motivated by sinful desires (lusts), selfishness, and pride. The propensity of the *sin nature* is described in Proverbs 6:12-19. Everything about the sin nature God hates. **Every "born again" believer should hate what God hates as much as God hates it. This defines genuine repentance.**

"[12] A **naughty person** {*someone without potential for profit, worthless and therefore destined to be destructive and wicked*}, a wicked man, walketh with **a froward** {*stubborn or willful*} **mouth** {*the mouth follows the heart*}. [13] **He winketh with his eyes, he speaketh with his feet, he teacheth with his fingers** {*uses secret signs to communicate covertly and deceptively*}; [14] **Frowardness** {*perversity and fraud*} is **in his heart** {*as the motivation for all he does and is in what he delights*}, **he deviseth mischief** {*as an artisan constructs his masterpieces with great pride he plans, plots, and schemes*} **continually** {*never ending and never satisfied*}; **he soweth discord** {*there is a selfish malignancy in everything and everyone he touches*}. [15] <u>**Therefore**</u> shall **his calamity** {*misfortune or destruction; the intent is that God will remove satisfaction from all this person's*

---

[10] C. I. Scofield, *Notes from the Scofield Reference Bible*, 1917, Module file location: C:\Program Files\SwordSearcher\Modules\Scofield.ss5cmty, Module file time: 7/31/2011 9:15:28 PM UTC.

pursuits; even those there might appear to be some type of temporary gratification in these sinful pursuits, they will end in emptiness and loneliness} **come suddenly** *{although sin can bring momentary pleasure, it is immediately found to be empty}*; **suddenly** *{to open the eyes}* **shall he be broken without remedy** *{no cure or deliverance apart from genuine heart felt repentance and turning to God}.* [16] These six *things* doth the LORD hate: yea, <u>**seven *are* an abomination unto him**</u>: [17] {1}**A proud look**, {2}**a lying tongue**, and {3}**hands that shed innocent blood**, [18] **An** {4}**heart that deviseth wicked imaginations,** {5}**feet that be swift in running to mischief,** [19] **A** {6}**false witness *that* speaketh lies**, and {7}**he that soweth discord among brethren**" (Proverbs 6:12-19).

"Hating even the garments spotted by the flesh" hates the actions, attitudes, and all that motivates sinners in the things God hates. Once a person is "born again," the daily manifestation of a repentant heart is that such a person hates everything God hates, especially those things about himself that defiles him before God.

"[1] What shall we say then? **Shall we continue in sin, that grace may abound?** [2] **God forbid.** How shall we, that are dead to sin, live any longer therein? [3] Know ye not, that so many of us as were baptized into Jesus Christ were baptized into his death? [4] Therefore we are buried with him by baptism into death: that like as Christ was raised up from the dead by the glory of the Father, even so we also should walk in newness of life. [5] For if we have been planted together in the likeness of his death, we shall be also *in the likeness* of *his* resurrection: [6] **Knowing this, that our old man is crucified with *him*, that the body of sin might be destroyed, that henceforth we should not serve sin.** [7] For he that is dead is freed from sin. [8] Now if we be dead with Christ, we believe that we shall also live with him: [9] Knowing that Christ being raised from the dead dieth no more; death hath no more dominion over him. [10] For in that he died, he died unto sin once: but in that he liveth, he liveth unto God" (Romans 6:1-10).

The sin nature is the by-product of Satanic deception and the fall of mankind into sin. The sin nature is the source of sin in our lives.

Temptation to sin would be ineffective if we did not possess a sin nature. That means we have an innate desire to sin. Our sin natures want that with which Satan tempts us.

"**[1] From whence *come* wars and fightings among you? *come they* not hence, *even* of your lusts that war in your members?** [2] Ye lust, and have not: ye kill, and desire to have, and cannot obtain: ye fight and war, yet ye have not, because ye ask not. [3] Ye ask, and receive not, because ye ask amiss, that ye may consume *it* upon your lusts. [4] Ye adulterers and adulteresses, know ye not that the friendship of the world is enmity with God? whosoever therefore will be a friend of the world is the enemy of God. [5] **Do ye think that the scripture saith in vain, The spirit that dwelleth in us lusteth to envy?** [6] But he giveth more grace. Wherefore he saith, **God resisteth the proud, but giveth grace unto the humble.** [7] Submit yourselves therefore to God. Resist the devil, and he will flee from you. [8] **Draw nigh to God, and he will draw nigh to you. Cleanse *your* hands, *ye* sinners; and purify *your* hearts, *ye* double minded.** [9] Be afflicted, and mourn, and weep: let your laughter be turned to mourning, and *your* joy to heaviness. [10] Humble yourselves in the sight of the Lord, and he shall lift you up" (James 4:1-10).

The struggle against sin is the struggle against our own sin nature and our desires for the things we are tempted to do. All men are by nature worldly. In the fall of man into sin, the fallen nature formulated a partnership with Satan that leads a man deeper and deeper into sin as the sinner rejects the restraining power of divinely revealed truth. We see the results of this in Romans 1:21-32.

When the believing sinner is saved (regenerated or "born again"), the Holy Spirit formulates the *potential* for an indwelling *partnership* with the believer to lead the believer into practical righteousness.

This is the transitional issue from the doctrine of justification (*imparted righteousness*) to the doctrine of sanctification (*practical righteousness*). This partnership with the Holy Spirit is activated in the believer's life when the believer learns to confess and repent of sin (I John 1:7-9) and learns to "yield" himself (his will) to the *control* of the Holy Spirit (Romans 6:11-13).

This *control* of the Holy Spirit is expressed elsewhere in the Scriptures as being "filled" with the Holy Spirit (see Ephesians 5:1-18).

"[1] **Be ye therefore followers of God, as dear children**; [2] And walk in love, as Christ also hath loved us, and hath given himself for us an offering and a sacrifice to God for a sweetsmelling savour. [3] But fornication, and all uncleanness, or covetousness, let it not be once named among you, as becometh saints; [4] Neither filthiness, nor foolish talking, nor jesting, which are not convenient: but rather giving of thanks. [5] For this ye know, that no whoremonger, nor unclean person, nor covetous man, who is an idolater, hath any inheritance in the kingdom of Christ and of God. [6] Let no man deceive you with vain words: for because of these things cometh the wrath of God upon the children of disobedience. [7] Be not ye therefore partakers with them. [8] For ye were sometimes darkness, but now *are ye* light in the Lord: walk as children of light: [9] **(For the fruit of the Spirit *is* in all goodness and righteousness and truth**;) [10] Proving what is acceptable unto the Lord. [11] **And have no fellowship with the unfruitful works of darkness**, but rather reprove *them*. [12] For it is a shame even to speak of those things which are done of them in secret. [13] But all things that are reproved are made manifest by the light: for whatsoever doth make manifest is light. [14] Wherefore he saith, Awake thou that sleepest, and arise from the dead, and Christ shall give thee light. [15] See then that ye walk circumspectly, not as fools, but as wise, [16] Redeeming the time, because the days are evil. [17] Wherefore be ye not unwise, but understanding what the will of the Lord *is*. [18] And be not drunk with wine, wherein is excess; but **be filled with the Spirit**" (Ephesians 5:1-18).

The believer who confesses, repents of sin, and is cleansed of all unrighteousness is filled with the Holy Spirit (I John 1:9). This is the basis of "fellowship" with God. To be in "fellowship" with God is to be in a *working partnership* with (*controlled by or filled to overflowing with*) the indwelling Holy Spirit in the struggle with the desires of our sin natures and the temptation to sin, as well as in a partnership with the Holy Spirit in the work of the ministry.

"²⁴ Now **unto him that is able to keep you from falling**, and to present *you* faultless before the presence of his glory with exceeding joy, ²⁵ To the only wise God our Saviour, *be* glory and majesty, dominion and power, both now and ever. Amen" (Jude 24-25).

The indwelling Spirit of Christ is "able to keep you from falling." This statement is based upon the Greek word *dýnamai* (doo'-nam-ahee), with the meaning that Christ's indwelling presence has created the *possibility for this outcome*.

This empowering is not automatic. This enabling requires a *synergism* between the yielded believer and the indwelling Spirit of Christ. The indwelling Spirit of Christ can enable the heart that has yielded the will to the Lordship of Christ. This is what defines grace enabling.

In other words, Jesus "is able," but He does not enable without the believer yielding his will (nature) to God's will in every circumstance of life. The point in this text in the words "unto him that is able to keep you from falling" is that the ability is available to every believer willing to yield his will to Christ's will, regardless of the dire circumstances that life might present when he does so.

"¹ Simon Peter, a servant and an apostle of Jesus Christ, to them that have obtained like precious faith with us through the righteousness of God and our Saviour Jesus Christ: ² Grace and peace be multiplied unto you through the knowledge of God, and of Jesus our Lord, ³ **According as his divine power hath given unto us <u>all</u> things that *pertain* unto life and godliness**, through the knowledge of him that hath called us to glory and virtue: ⁴ Whereby are given unto us exceeding great and precious promises: **that by these ye might be partakers** {*koinonos; sharer, partner, or associate*} **of the divine nature** {*the character and communicable attributes of God*}, having escaped the corruption that is in the world through lust" (II Peter 1:1-4).

Obviously, the words, "According as his divine power hath given unto us <u>all</u> things that *pertain* unto life and godliness" are not referring to anyone being made equal with God in power or knowledge.

The words speak of *potential* or *possibility* to be holy and live sanctified lives throughout our days while still living in our human bodies. Although holiness of this nature is not possible if it merely comes from our human bodies because the presence of our sin natures corrupts any righteousness sought to be produced by the mere power of the "flesh."

However, the Spirit of Christ in us is righteous and when a believer fully surrenders his will to the indwelling Spirit of Christ, Christ **in us** can produce His righteousness through us.

"¹⁷ Therefore **if** any man *be* **in Christ**, *he is* a new creature: old things are passed away; behold, all things **are become** {*perfect tense*} new. ¹⁸ And **all things *are* of God**, who hath reconciled us to himself by Jesus Christ, and hath given to us the ministry of reconciliation; ¹⁹ To wit, that God was in Christ, reconciling the world unto himself, not imputing their trespasses unto them; and hath committed unto us the word of reconciliation. ²⁰ Now then we are ambassadors for Christ, as though God did beseech *you* by us: we pray *you* in Christ's stead, be ye reconciled to God. ²¹ For he hath made him *to be* sin for us, who knew no sin; **that we might be made the righteousness of God <u>in him</u>**" (II Corinthians 5:17-21).

The word "falling" in Jude 24 is from the Greek word *áptaistos* (ap-tah'-ee-stos). It is the negative form of the word *ptaíō* (ptah'-yo), which means *to trip*. **Therefore, the meaning is that the indwelling Christ is able to keep a believer from tripping over a temptation and falling into sin. This phrase does NOT refer to a possibility of losing one's salvation.** The phrase means it is possible for a believer to live a faithful life in holiness if he lives in a *cooperative partnership* with the indwelling Christ. Christ can and will enable **if** a believer will yield to the indwelling Christ.

"⁶ Knowing this, that **our old man is crucified with *him*,** that the body of sin might be destroyed, **that henceforth we should not serve sin.** ⁷ For he that is dead is freed from sin. ⁸ Now if we be dead with Christ, we believe that we shall also live with him: ⁹ Knowing that Christ being raised from the dead dieth no more; death hath no more dominion over him. ¹⁰ For in that he died, he died unto sin once: but in that he liveth, he liveth unto God. [11] **Likewise reckon ye also yourselves to be dead indeed unto sin, but alive unto God through Jesus Christ our Lord.** [12] Let not sin therefore reign in your mortal body, that ye should obey it in the lusts thereof. [13] Neither yield ye your members *as* instruments of unrighteousness unto sin: but **yield yourselves unto God, as those that are alive from the dead, and your members *as* instruments of righteousness unto God.** [14] For sin shall not have dominion over you: for ye are not under the law, but **under grace** {*enabling*}. [15] What then? shall we sin, because we are not under the law, but under grace? God forbid. [16] Know ye not, that **to whom ye yield yourselves servants to obey, his servants ye are to whom ye obey; whether of sin unto death, or of obedience unto righteousness**? [17] But God be thanked, that ye were the servants of sin, but **ye have obeyed from the heart** that form of doctrine which was delivered you. [18] Being then made free from sin, ye became the servants of righteousness" (Romans 6:6-18).

We sing the hymn *He's Able* by Paul E. Paino without really understanding that the words of this hymn come from the context of contending for the faith in the epistle of Jude.

"He's able, He's able,
I know He's able,
I know my Lord is able
To carry me through."

The phrase "and to present *you* faultless before the presence of his glory with exceeding joy," in Jude 24 is connected to the High Priesthood of Christ as He presents the believer to God for consecration. This is not referring to the believer's position before God "in Christ" because this position has nothing to do with the believer's responsibility. This presentation of the believer "faultless" before God is practical in that it is connected with the believer's responsibility to be practically sanctified before attempting ministry before God and to men.

This connects to the previous statement in Jude 23 referring to "the garment spotted by the flesh. Priests were responsible to

keep their linen garments washed and clean before they entered their ministry cycle in the temple. This was a picture of their personal sanctification before they presented themselves to the High Priest for examination and consecration for their ministry cycle.

This is the context of Romans 12:1-8 for New Covenant believer-priests. Only in the New Covenant, the believer-priest is responsible to present himself and his heart cleansed by confessing sins and unrighteousness to God and receiving the cleansing "from all unrighteousness" (I John 1:9). Therefore, doing what I John 1:5-9 describes should precede the "reasonable service" of what Romans 12:1-2 asks the believer to do.

"[5] This then is the message which we have heard of him, and declare unto you, that God is light, and in him is no darkness at all. [6] If we say that we have fellowship with him, and walk in darkness, we lie, and do not the truth: [7] But if we walk in the light, as he is in the light, we have fellowship one with another, and the blood of Jesus Christ his Son cleanseth us from all sin. [8] If we say that we have no sin, we deceive ourselves, and the truth is not in us. [9] If we confess our sins, he is faithful and just to forgive us *our* sins, and to cleanse us from all unrighteousness" (I John 1:5-9).

"[1] I beseech you therefore, brethren, by the mercies of God, that ye present your bodies a living sacrifice, holy, acceptable unto God, *which is* your reasonable service. [2] And be not conformed to this world: but be ye transformed by the renewing of your mind, that ye may prove what *is* that good, and acceptable, and perfect, will of God" (Romans 12:1-2).

It is in understanding this context that the words, "To the only wise God our Saviour, *be* glory and majesty, dominion and power, both now and ever. Amen," in Jude 25 have their fullest understanding. Everything good or righteous that the believer does in his human body is done as enabled/empowered by the indwelling Christ. Therefore, "glory and majesty, dominion and power" are all, and always, sourced in the indwelling Christ. **Amen! So let it be!**

Bibliography

Alford, Henry, *Alford's Greek Testament, Hebrews-Revelation,* Volume I, Volume II, Volume III, Volume IV, Baker Book House; reprinted, 1980.

Archer, Gleason L., *Encyclopedia of Bible Difficulties,* The Zondervan Corporation Copyright 1982.

Armitage, Thomas, *The History of the Baptists, Volume I, Volume II,* Maranatha Baptist Press, Reprint, 1980.

Armstrong, John H. -General Editor, *The Coming Evangelical Crisis,* Moody Bible Institute, Copyright 1996.

Armstrong, Mead C., *That Ye Might Walk Worthy-Studies in Colossians,* Regular Baptist Press, Copyright 1981.

Armstrong, O.K. and Marjorie M. Armstong, *The Indomitable Baptists,* Doubleday & Company, Inc., Copyright 1967.

Baker, Don, *Finding Hope In Times of Crisis,* Inspirational Press, Copyright 1992.

Barclay, William, *The Letters of James and Peter, revised edition-The Daily Study Series,* The Westminster Press, Copyright 1975.

Barber, Cyril J., *Everyman's Bible Commentary-Habakkuk and Zephaniah,* Moody press, Copyright 1985.

Barnes, Albert, *Genesis; Barnes' Notes on the Old & New Testament, James-Jude; Barnes' Notes on the Old & New Testament,* Vol. 1, Baker Book House, twentieth printing, 1981.

Barnhart, Clarence L.-Editor, *Thorndike Barnhart Comprehensive Desk Dictionary,* Scott, Foresman and Company, Copyright 1955.

Barnhouse, Donald Grey, *God's Methods for Holy Living,* Revelation Publications, Copyright 1940.

Baumgartner, Anne S., *A Comprehensive Dictionary of the Gods,* Wings Books, 1995 Edition.

Baxter, Sidlow J., *Explore the Book-Six Volumes in One,* Zondervan Publishing House Eleventh Printing, March 1975.

Beacham, Roy E. and Bauder, Kevin T., *One Bible Only?,* William B. Eerdmans Publishing Company, Copyright 1962.

Beasley-Murray, G.R., *Baptism in the New Testament,* Jerry W. Beaver, Printed 2009.

Bednar, L., *Evidence of the Divine Hand on True Scripture,* Lawrence Bednar, Copyright 2010.

Binney, Jim, *Living Purely in an Impure World,* The Counselor's Pen Publications, Copyright 2003.

Boer, Harry R., *A Short History of the Early Church,* Wm. B. Eerdmans Pub. Co., 5th Printing, April 1981.

Boettner, Loraine, *The Millennium,* Presbyterian and Reformed Publishing Company, Revised Edition, 1984.

Boice, James Montgomery, *An Expositional Commentary-Philippians,* Zondervan Publishing House, Copyright 1971.
The Minor Prophets-Volume 2-Mich-Malachi, Zondervan Publishing House, Copyright 1986.

Bopp, Virgil W., *Confidently Committed-A Look at the Baptist Heritage,* Regular Baptist Press, Copyright 1987.

Borland, James A., *Christ In The Old Testament,* Moody Press, Copyright 1978.

Brandenburg, Kent (Editor), *Thou Shalt Keep Them-A Biblical Theology of the Perfect Preservation of Scripture,* Pillar & Ground Publishing, 2003.

Breeze, Dave, *Seven Men Who Rule the World from the Grave,* Moody Press, 8th Printing, 1995.
Satan's Ten Most Believable Lies, Moody Press, Paperback edition, 1987.

Bruce, F.F., *Jesus: Lord and Savior,* Intervarsity Press, 1966.
The Hard Sayings of Jesus, Intervarsity Press, 1983.

Bruns, Roger A., *Preacher-Billy Sunday & Big-Time American Evangelism,* W.W. Norton & Company, Copyright 1992.

Bruce, A.B, *The Training of the Twelve,* Kregel Publications, Seventh Printing, 1978.

Bruce, F.F., *What the Bible Teaches About What Jesus Did,* Tyndale House Publishers, 1979.
Bruce, F.F., *Paul Apostle of the Heart Set Free,* William B. Eerdmans Publishing Company, Reprinted 1983.
Bruce, F.F., *The Canon of Scripture,* 1988.

Brumback, Carl, *What Meaneth This?,* Gospel Publishing House, Copyright 1947.

Bucke, Emory Stevens-Editor, *The Interpreter's Dictionary of the Bible,* Abingdon, Copyright 1976.

Burgon, Dean John William, *Inspiration and Interpretation,* The Dean Burgon Society Press, Copyright 1999.
The Traitional Text of the Holy Gospels-Volume I, The Dean Burgon Society Press, Copyright 1998.

Burnham, David and Sue Burnham, *Acts the Body in Action-A Group Bible Study,* Moody Press, Copyright 1978.

Burgon, Dean John, *The Last Twelve Verses of Mark,* James Parker and Co., Copyright 1871 Reprinted.

Burgon, Dean John, *The Causes of Corruption of the Traditional Test of the Holy Gospels-Volume II,* The Dean Burgon Society Press, Copyright 1998.

Carson, D.A., *The King James Version Debate A Plea for Realism,* Baker Book House, Thirteenth Printing 1995.
Exegetical Fallacies Second Edition, Baker Book House, Seventh Printing 2002.

Central Baptist Theological Seminary-Faculty, *The Bible Version Debate-The Perspective of Central Baptist Theological Seminary,* Copyright 1997.

Chafer, Lewis Sperry, *Systematic Theology, Volume I, Volume II, Volume III, Volume IV, Volume V, Volume VI, Volume VII, Volume VIII,* Lewis Sperry Chafer, Thirteenth Printing, 1976.
Salvation, Lewis Sperry Chafer, Copyright 1917.

Charnock, Stephen, *Existence and Attributes of God-Volume I,* Baker Book House, Reprinted 1979.
Charnock, Stephen, *Existence And Attributes of God-Volume II,* Baker Book House, Third Printing, May 1981.

Chilstrom, Herbert W., *Hebrews- A New & Better Way,* Fortress Press, Copyright 1984.

Christian, John T., *A History of the Baptists, Volume I,* Bogard Press, Copyright 1922.
Volume II, Bogard Press, Copyright 1926.

Clearwaters, Richard V., *The Local Church of the New Testament,* Central Press, Copyright 1954.
The Great Conservative Baptist Compromise, Central Seminary Press.
On The Upward Road- An Autobiography, Nystrom Publishing, 1954.

Cloud, David W., *Myths about the Modern Bible Versions,* Published by Way of Life Literature, Copyright 1999 Second Edition, Sept.1999.

Cocoris, Michael G., *Evangelism: A Biblical Approach,* Moody Press, 1984.

Coder, Maxwell S., *Jude-The Acts of the Apostates,* Moody Press, Copyright 1958.

Cohen, Gary G. and Salem Kirban, *Revelation Visualized,* Salem Kirban, Copyright 1981.

Coleman, Robert E.-Editor, *Evangelism on the Cutting Edge,* Fleming H. Revell Company, Copyright 1986.

Comfort, Philip W., *Early Manuscripts & Modern Translations of the New Testament,* Tyndale House Publishers, Inc., Copyright 1990.

Comfort, Ron, *Last Things A Book on Bible Prophecy,* Ron Comfort Evangelistic Association, 2011.
Revival's Golden Key, Bridge-Logos Publisher, 2002.

Conybeare, W.J. and Howson J.S., *The Life and Epistles of St. Paul,* WM. B. Eerdmans Publishing Company, Reprinted December 1992.

Cook, Arnold L., *Historical Drift Must My Church Die?,* Christian Publications, 2000.

Corner, Daniel D., *The Believer's Conditional Security,* Evangelical Outreach, Copyright 2000.

Couch, Mal, *Dictionary of Premillennial Theology,* Kregel, 1996.
A Bible Handbook to The Acts of The Apostles, Kregel, 1999.
An Introduction to Classical Evangelical Hermeneutics, Kregel, 2000.

Cowman, Charles E., *Handfuls of Purpose,* Cowman Publications, Copyright 1955.

Cowen, Gerald, *Salvation-Word Studies From The Greek New Testament,* Broadman Press, Copyright 1990.

Criswell, W.A., *Isaiah and exposition,* Zondervan Publishing House, 1982.
The Bible for Today's World, Zondervan Publishing House, Third printing, 1966.
Why I Preach That the Bible Is Literally True, Broadman Press, Copyright 1969.

Crockett, William Day, *A Harmony of Samuel, Kings and Chronicles,* Baker Book House, Fourteenth Printing, 1978.

Crow, Paul, *Cliffs and Fences-Holiness and Personal Separation In Biblical Perspective,* Booksurge, Copyright 2008.

Dabney, Robert L., *Lectures In Systematic Theology,* Zondervan Publishing House, Third printing, 1976.

Davis, John J., *Moses and the Gods of Egypt-Studies in Exodus-second edition,* Baker Books, Copyright 1971.

DeHaan, M.R., *Coming Events in Prophecy,* Zondervan Publishing House, Tenth printing, November 1970.
Hebrews-Twenty-six Simple Studies in God's Pattern for Victorious Living, Zondervan Publishing House, Copyright 1959.

Delany, James, *Abiding in Christ-God's Plan for Spiritual Growth,* James Delany, Copyright 2000.

DeJong, Benjamin R., Director of Material, *This We Believe,* IFCA Publications, Revised 1980.

DeMar, Gary and Peter Leithart, *The Reduction of Christianity,* Dominion Press, Copyright 1988.

Dersham, James-Managing Editor, *So Great Salvation,* Regular Baptist Press, 1986.

Dollar, George W., *The New Testament and New Pentecostalism,* Central Baptist Theological Seminary, Copyright 1978.

Dowley, Tim- Organizing Editor, *Eerdmans Handbook to the History of Christianity,* William B. Publishing Co., Reprinted 1987.

Dunn, Richard S., *The Age of Religious Wars, 1559-1689,* Norton & Company, Inc., Copyright 1970.

Eaide, John, *Thessalonians,* James and Klock Christian Publishing Co., Reprint 1977.
Philippians, James and Klock Christian Publishing Co., Reprint 1977.
Galatians, James and Klock Christian Publishing Co., Reprint 1977.

Earle, Ralph, *Word Meanings in the New Testament- Volume 1, Matthew, Volume 2 Mark, Luke, Volume 3 Romans, Volume 4, 1, and 2 Corinthians, Galatians, Ephesians, Volume 5, Philippians, Colossians, 1 & 2 Thessalonians, Volume 6, 1 & 2 Timothy, Titus, Philemon,* Baker Book House Company, Reprinted 1980.

Clarke, Adam, *Adam Clarke's Commentary on the Bible,* Baker Book House Company, Fifteenth Printing 1984.

Edersheim, Alfred, *Old Testament Bible History,* William B. Eerdmans Publishing Company, Reprinted December 1982.
Practical Truths from Elisha, Kregel Publications, Copyright 1982.

Epp, Theodore H., *Volume 1 Practical Studies in Revelation,* Back to the Bible, Copyright 1969.
Present Labor and Future Reward, Back to the Bible, Copyright 1960.
Joshua Victorious by Faith, Back to the Bible, Copyright 1968.

Joseph -God planned it for good, The Good News Broadcasting Association, Copyright 1971.

Epp, Eldon Jay and Gordon D. Fee (Edited by), *New Testament Textual Criticism,* Clarendon Press, 1981.

Evans, William, *Personal Soul Winning-A Guide to Effective Methods,* Moody Press, Revised 1964.

Farison, Marquerite, *Passport to Heaven,* Barbour Books, Copyright 1989.

Farrar, Canon, *The Story of A Beautiful Life,* Dodd, Mead and Company, Copyright 1900.

Farrar, Steve, *Finishing Strong,* Dodd, Mead and Company, Copyright 1995.

Farrar, F.W., *Texts Explained or Helps to Understand the New Testament,* Dodd, Mead and Company, Copyright 1899.

Farrell, Tom, *Preaching That Pleases God The Keys to Life-Changing Bible Exposition,* Striving Together Publications, Copyright 2010.

Finney, Charles G., *Revivals,* Fleming H. Revell Company, 1965.

Fosdick, Harry Emerson, *Christianity and Progress,* Fleming H. Revell Company, Copyright 1922.

Fraser, John W. -Translator
Calvin's New Testament Commentaries-Volume 6-Acts 1-13
Calvin's New Testament Commentaries-Volume 7-Acts 14-28
Calvin's New Testament Commentaries-Volume 9- I Corinthians
Calvin's New Testament Commentaries-Volume 11-Galatians, Ephesians, Philippians, & Colossians
Calvin's New Testament Commentaries-Volume 12-Hebrews and 1 & 2 Peter, William B, Eerdmans Publishing Company, 1965.

Gaebelein, Frank E.- General Editor, *The Expositor's Bible Commentary, Ephesians-Philemon, Volume II – NIV,* Zondervan Publishing House, 1978. *Volume 7 with NIV - The Expositor's Bible Commentary,* Zondervan Publishing House, 1985.

Gardiner, Gardiner E., *The Corinthian Catastrophe,* Kregel Publications, 1974.

Garlock, Frank and Woetzel Kurl, *Music in the Balance,* Majesty Music, Inc., Second Printing 1996.

Garraty, John A. and Gay, Peter (Editors), *The Columbia History of the World,* Harper and Row Publishers, 1987.

Gaussen, L., *Divine Inspiration of the Bible,* Kregel, Copyright 1971.

Garrison, R. Benjamin, *Creeds In Collision,* Abington Books, 1967.

Gentry, Kenneth L. Jr., *The Greatness of the Great Commission,* Kenneth L. Gentry, Revised edition, 1993.

Getz, Gene A., *The Measure of a Church,* G.L. Regal Books, 7th Printing, 1979.
Sharpening the focus of the Church, Moody Press, 1974.

Gibbs, Alfred P., *The Preacher and His Preaching,* Walterick Publishers, 6th Edition.

Gillquist, Peter E., *Love Is Now,* Zondervan Publishing House, Third Printing, 1971.

Gilmore, John, *The Probing Heaven-Key Questions on the Hereafter,* Baker Book House, Copyright 1989.

Goetsch, John, *Twenty-first Century Revival (is it possible?),* West Coast Baptist College.

Good, Kenneth H., *God's Blueprint for a Church-A Study of Baptist Distinctives,* Regular Baptist Press.

Grady, William P., *Final Authority-A Christian's Guide to the King James Bible,* Grady Publications, Eighth Printing, 1997.

Grant, George, *In the Shadow of Plenty,* Christian Liberty Press, Revised Edition, 1998.

Green, Michael, *Evangelism in the Early Church,* Wm. B. Eerdmans Pub. Co., Reprinted Jan. 1985.

Greenhough, M.A., Thomas G. Selby, Albert Goodrich, Alexander Stewart, George Milligan, W.H. Selbie, J. Morgan Gibbon, Alfred Rowland, D Rowlands, *The Sermon on the Mount A Practical Exposition of St. Matthew VI 16-VII 27,* Manchester James Robinson, 1903.

Grist, William Alexander, *The Historic Christ in The Faith of To-day,* Fleming H. Revell Company, Copyright 1911.

Griswold, Roland, E., *The Winning Church,* Victor Books, Copyright 1986.

Gundry, Stanley N. and Alan F. Johnson-Editors, *Tensions In Contemporary Theology,* Moody Press, Copyright 1976.

Habershon, Ada R., *The Study of The Miracles,* Kregel, Fourth Printing 1972.

Haifley, Daniel S., *The Bible Study Toolbook-A Text on Biblical Hermeneutics,* Beams of Grace Press, Fourth Printing 2009.

Halfyard, Samuel F., *Fundamentals of the Christian Religion,* Jennings and Graham, Copyright 1911.

Hartog, John, *The Fall of a Kingdom-Jeremiah and Lamentations,* Regular Baptist Press, 1983.

Hendricks, Howard G., *Don't Fake It: Say It With Love the Art and Joy of Telling the Good News,* Victor Books, Third Printing, 1973.

Hengstenberg, E.W., *Christology of The Old Testament,* Kregel Publications, Third Printing, 1976.

Henry, Carl F.G., *Fundamentals of the Faith,* Baker Book House, 1975.

Hester, H.L., *The Heart of the New Testament,* Loizeaux Brothers, Third Edition, 1980.

Hislop, Alexander, *The Two Babylons,* Loizeaux Brothers, Third Edition, 1989.

Hoekstra, Harvey T., *The World Council of Churches and the Demise of Evangelism,* Tyndale House, Copyright 1979.

Holstad, Wayne B., *Leviticus v. Leviathan-Choosing Our Sovereign* Alethos Press, Copyright 2004.

Horne, Chevis F., *Crisis in the Pulpit,* Baker Book House, Copyright 1975.

Huffman, J.A., *Redemption Completed,* The Standard Press, Eighth Edition, 1941.
Wholly Living-Paul's Last Word for a Dynamic Lifestyle, Victor Books, 1978.

Hufhand, Lawrence D., *The Acts of the Apostates-A Study in the book of Jude,* Lift Ministries, 2011.

Hunt, Dave and McMahon, T.A., *The Seduction of Christianity,* Harvest House Publishers, 6th Printing, Feb. 1986.

Hunnex, Milton D., *Existentialism and Christian Belief-A Frank Appraisal of a Modern-Day Philosophy,* Moody Press, 1969.

Hunter, Harold F., *Revelation,* Trinty Crusades for Christ, 1984.

Hunter, John E., *Living the Christ filled Life,* Zondervan Publishing House, Tenth Printing, 1975.

Ironside, H.A., *Lectures on Levitical Offerings,* Loizeaux Brothers, Tenth Printing, 1979.
Ironside, H.A., *Holiness-The False and the True,* Loizeaux Brothers, Twenty-third Printing, 1980.

Jackson, Bill, *Battling for Eternity-The Church's Quest for Pure Evangelism,* Colonial Baptist Press, Copyright 1992.
Scriptural Evangelism, Colonial Baptist Press, Copyright 1992.

Jackson, Jeremy C., *No Other Foundation, The Church Through Twenty Centuries,* Cornerstone Books, 1980.

Jackson, Paul R., *The Doctrine and Administration of the Church,* Regular Baptist Press, Sixth Printing, 1997.

Jacobs, Jack W., *What's Right with the Church-Studies in Ephesians,* Regular Baptist Press, Copyright, 1980.

James, Edgar C., *Day of the Lamb,* Victor Books, Third Printing, 1981.

James, Kevin R., *The Corruption of the Word: The Failure of Modern New Testament Scholarship,* Micro-Load Press, Third Printing, 1995.

Jank, Margaret, *Culture Shock,* Moody Press, Copyright 1977.

Jefferson, Charles, *The Minister As Shepherd,* Scripture Truth Book Co., 2006.

Jensen, Irving L., *Romans-A Self-Study Guide,* Moody Bible Institute, Copyright 1969.

Jenson, Ron and Jim Stevens, *Dynamics of Church Growth,* Baker Book House, Copyright 1981.

Jewish Nation, *Hebrew English New Covenant-Prophecy Edition,* Hope of Israel Publications, 2003.

Johnson, Cedric B. and H. Newton Malony, *Christian Conversion: Biblical and Psychological Perspectives,* Zondervan Publishing House, Copyright 1982.

Johnson, Daniel R., *The Greatest Soldier Who Ever Lived,* Providence Publications, Fourth Printing, 2001.

Juris, Paul, *Blessed Mary,* Paul Juris, Copyright 1978.
The Other Side of Purgatory, Paul Juris, Copyright 1981.

Kaiser, Walter C. Jr., *Malachi God's Unchanging Love,* Baker Book House, Copyright 1984.

Keddie, Gordon, *Looking for The Good Life-The Search for Fulfillment in the Light of Ecclesiastes,* Presbyterian and Reformed Publishing Company, Copyright 1991.

Keller, Phillip W., *A Layman Looks at the Lord's Prayer,* World Wide Publications, Second Printing, 1976.

Kent, Homer A. Jr., *The Pastoral Epistles-Studies in 1 Timothy and 2 Timothy and Titus,* BMH Books, Copyright 1995.

Kidner, Derek, *An Introduction to Wisdom Literature-The Wisdom of Proverbs, Job & Ecclesiastes,* IVP, Copyright 1985.

Kinder, Ernst, *Evangelical-What Does It Really Mean,* Concordia Publishing House, Copyright 1968.

King, Richard and Susan, *Confusion-A Biblical Critique of the New Teaching of Dr. Peter Ruckman,* Gigatt Books, Copyright 2012.

Kistemaker, Simon J., *New Testament Commentary Acts,* Baker Book House, Copyright 1990.

Kittel, Gerhard-Editor, *Volume I-Theological Dictionary of the New Testament,* WM. B. Eerdmans Publishing Company, Reprinted September 1983.

Klimkeit, Hans-Joachim, *Gnosis on the Silk Road,* Hans J. Klimkeit, Copyright 1993.

Knauss, Keith E., *Heartbeats of the Holy-A Philosophy Of Ministry,* Dickerson Press Inc., 2009.

Kuen, Alfred F., *I Will Build My Church,* Moody Press, Translated from original French Edition, 1971.

Kuhne, Gary W., *The Dynamics of Discipleship Training-Being and Producing Spiritual Leaders,* Zondervan Publishing House, Copyright 1978

LaHaye, Tim, *Revelation,* Zondervan Publishing House, tenth printing, 1978.
The Battle for the Family, Fleming H. Revell Company, 1984.

Lawson, George, *Exposition of Proverbs,* Kregel Inc., 1980.

Lewis, C.S., *Mere Christianity,* Macmillan Publishing Co. Inc., 1986.

Lightfoot, J. B. and Harmer, J.R. (Translator), *The Apostolic Fathers (Second Edition),* Baker Book House Co., Second Printing, Aug. 1990.

Lightfoot, Neil R., *How We Got the Bible (Second Edition),* Baker Book House Co., Third Printing, Dec. 1991.

Lindsey, Hal, *The Late Great Planet Earth,* Zondervan Publishing House, 27th Printing, Feb. 1974.
The Terminal Generation, Fleming H. Revell Company, Copyright 1976.

Lloyd-Jones, Martyn D., *Life in the Spirit in Marriage, Home & Work,* Baker Book House, Reprinted 1975.

The Christian Soldier-An Exposition of Ephesians 6:10-20, Baker Book House, Reprinted 1978.

God's Ultimate Purpose-An Exposition of Ephesians One, Baker Book House, Reprinted 1979.

The Unsearchable Riches of Christ-An Exposition of Ephesians 3:1-21, Baker Book House, Reprinted 1980.

Christian Unity-An Exposition of Ephesians 4:1-16, Baker Book House, Reprinted 1981.

Romans-Atonement and Justification-Exposition of Chapters 3:20-4:25, Zondervan Publishing House, Ninth Printing, 1981.

Romans-Assurance-Exposition of Chapter 5, Zondervan Publishing House, Ninth Printing, 1980.

Romans-The New Man-Exposition of Chapter 6, Zondervan Publishing House, Ninth Printing, 1981.

Romans-The Law: It's Functions and Limits-Exposition of Chapters 7:1-8:4, Zondervan Publishing House, Ninth Printing, 1981.

Romans-The Sons of God-Exposition of Chapters 8:5-17, Zondervan Publishing House, Seventh Printing, 1981.

Romans-The Final Perseverance of the Saints-Exposition of Chapters 8:17-39, Zondervan Publishing House, Fifth Printing, 1980.

Spiritual Depression It's Causes and Its Cure, Wm. B. Eerdmans Publishing Company, Reprinted March 1987.

Lockyer, Herbert, *All the Men of The Bible,* Zondervan Publishing House, Copyright 1958.

All The Kings and Queens of The Bible, Zondervan Publishing House, Copyright 1961.

All The Miracles of The Bible, Zondervan Publishing House, Copyright 1961.

All The Doctrines of The Bible, Zondervan Publishing House, Twenty-Second Printing, 1982.

MacArthur, John Jr., *Beware The Pretenders-Who are the Spiritual Masqueraders Jude Warns Against?,* Victor Books, Copyright 1980.

Found: God's Will-God Wants to Give Your Life Direction and Purpose, Victor Books, Copyright 1973.

Our Sufficiency in Christ, John F. Macarthur Jr., Copyright 1991.

The Charismatics-Doctrinal Perspective, John F. MacArthur Jr., Copyright 1987.

Condemned and Crucified-Matthew 27:11-56, Word of Grace Communications, Copyright 1987.

Lighting The Path-How To Study The Bible, Word of Grace Communications, Copyright 1982.

Acting on the Good News-Romans 1:1-16, Word of Grace Communications, Copyright 1987.

Body Dynamics-A Blueprint for the Church as a Body-A Fresh and Exciting View of What the Church Can Be, Victor Books, Second Printing, 1983.

God, Satan and Angels, Moody Press, Sixth Printing, 1993.

Your Completeness in Christ-Colossians 1:24-2:23, Moody Press, Copyright 1985.

The Believer's Armor-Ephesians 6:10-24, Moody Press, Copyright 1985.

Priorities Of A Faithful Teacher-2 Timothy 4:1-8, Moody Press, Copyright 1991.

Church Leadership -1 Timothy 3: 1-13, John F. MacArthur Jr. Copyright 1989.

Living For Christ in A Cynical World-1 Peter 2:11-20; 3:1-7, John F. MacArthur Jr. Copyright 1989.

Unashamed-2 Timothy 1:1-18, Moody Press, Copyright 1990.

Without Excuse: Principles of God's Judgment-Romans 2:1-16, Moody Press, Copyright 1990.

To Live Is Christ-Philippians 1:12-26, Moody Press, Copyright 1990.

Triumph Over Death, Word of Grace Communications, 1982.

Introduction to Biblical Counseling, John F. MacArthur Jr., Copyright 1994.

Successful Christian Parenting, Word Publishing, 1999.

MacDonald, Charles R., *Administration of the Work of the Local Church,* Central Seminary Press, Copyright 1973.

Machen, J. Gresham, *The Origen of Paul's Religion,* Wm. B. Eerdmans Pub. Co., Reprinted August 1978.

Mack, Michael C., *The Synergy Church-A Strategy for Integrating Small Groups and Sunday School,* Baker Books, Copyright 1996.

Malphurs, Aubrey, *Ministry Nuts and Bolts: What They Don't Teach Pastors in Seminary,* Kregel, Copyright 1997.

Maring, Norman H. and Winthrop S. Hudson, *A Baptist Manual of Polity and Practice,* Revised Edition, Copyright 1991.

Marshall, Alfred, *The New International Version Interlinear Greek-English New Testament,* Zondervan Publishing House, 1976.

Matteson, Earle E., *The Job Complex,* River City Press, Copyright 2004.
The Biblical Plan for Power, Matteson Ministries, Copyright 1989.

Maynard, Michael, *A History of The Debate Over I John 5:7-8,* Comma Publications, Copyright 1995.

McCarrell, William, *The Great Shepherd in Psalm Twenty-Three,* Cicero Bible Press, 2017.

McClure, Alexander, *The Translators Revived,* Maranatha Bible Society, 2008.

McDowell, Josh, *Evidence that Demands a Verdict-Historical Evidences for the Christian Faith,* Campus Crusade for Christ, Inc., Copyright 1972. *More Evidence that Demands a Verdict,* Campus Crusade for Christ, Inc., Copyright 1975.
Answers To Tough Questions Skeptics Ask About The Christian Faith, Campus Crusade for Christ, Inc., Copyright 1980.

McGee, J. Vernon, *Volume IV-Matthew-Romans-Thru The Bible With J. Vernon McGee,* Thru The Bible Radio, 1994.

McLachlan, Douglas R., *Reclaiming Authentic Fundamentalism,* American Association of Christian Schools, 1993.

McLaughlin, Raymond W., *Communication For The Church,* Zondervan Publishing House, Copyright, 1968.

McLoughlin, William G., *Isaac Backus on Church, State, and Calvinism,* President and Fellows of Harvard Collage, Copyright 1968.

Miller, Allen O. and M. Eugene Osterhaven (Translators), *The Heidelberg Catechism,* United Church Press, 1962.

Moffatt, James, *The Expositor's Greek Testament, ed. by W. R. Nicoll, Vol. 5,* Wm. B. Eerdmans Publishing Co., November 1980 printing.

Moody, D.L., *Notes from My Bible,* Baker Book House Company, August 1979.

Moore, David L., *Galatians: Grace Alone,* Regular Baptist Press, Copyright 1979.

Morgan, Campbell, *The Acts Of The Apostles,* Fleming H. Revell Company, Copyright 1924.

Morris, Leon, *Tyndale New Testament Commentaries, ed. R.V.G. Tasker, Vol. 20,* Wm. B. Eerdmans Publishing Co., November 1980.
Galatians-Paul's Charter of Christian Freedom, InterVarsity Press, Copyright 1996.

Muck, Kenneth A., *Life and Love-Ecclesiastes and Song of Solomon,* Regular Baptist Press, 1981.

Mullen, Mickey R., *The Way The Truth and The Life,* Micky Mullen, Copyright 2001.

Murphey, Cecil B., (Compiled by), *Dictionary of Biblical Literacy,* Oliver Nelson Books, Copyright 1989.

Murry, Andrew., *Abide in Christ,* Miracle Press, 1997.

Nash, Ronald H., *Christian Faith and Historical Understanding,* Zondervan Publishing House, 1984.

Nee, Watchman, *A Balanced Christian Life,* Christian Fellowship Publishers, Copyright 1981.

Nettleton, David, *Meet the Minor Prophets-Adult Student Manual,* Regular Baptist Press, 1985.

Newell, William R., *The Book of Revelation,* Moody Press, 1978.
Hebrews Verse By Verse, Moody Press, Reprinted 1978.
Romans Verse By Verse, Moody Press, Reprinted 1978.

Nicoll, W. Robertson (Editor), *The Expositor's Greek Testament, Volume Five-First Peter, Second Peter, John, Jude & Revelation,* WM. B. Eerdmans Publishing Company, Reprinted November 1980.
The Sermon Outline Bible-Preacher's Homiletic Library-Colossians-James, Baker Book House, Reprinted 1979.

Noordtzij, A., *The Bible Student's Commentary Numbers,* Zondervan Publishing House, Copyright 1983.

North, Gary, *Millennialism and Social Theory,* Gary North, Copyright 1990.
Backward, Christian Soldiers, Institute for Christian Economics, Copyright 1984.

O'Brien, Peter T., *44 Word Biblical Commentary-Colossians, Philemon,* Word Incorporated, Copyright 1982.

Oehler, Gustave Friedrich, *Theology of the Old Testament,* Zondervan Publishing House, 2018.

Orthner, Donald, *Wellsprings of Life-Understanding Proverbs,* Adon Books, Third Printing, September 1992.

Paige, Richard L. Jr., *The Church Christ Built,* North Star Baptist Press, Reprinted 1999.

Pelikan, Jaroslav and Walter A. Hansen, *Luther's Works Volume 27 Lectures on Galatians,* Concordia Publishing House, Copyright 1964.

Pfeiffer, Charles F. and Everett F. Harrison, *The Wycliffe Bible Commentary,* Moody Press, Nineteenth Printing, 1981.

Phillips, John, *Exploring Revelation,* Loizeaux Brothers, 1991.
Exploring Acts, Loizeaux Brothers, 1991.
100 Sermon Outlines From The Old Testament, Moody Press, Second Printing, 1980.

Pickering, Ernest, *Biblical Separation-The Struggle for a Pure Church,* Regular Baptist Press, Fourth Printing, 1983.
The Theology of Evangelism, Regular Baptist Press, Copyright 1984.
The Tragedy of Compromise, Bob Jones University Press, Copyright 1994.

Phillips, John, *Exploring Revelation,* Loizeaux Brothers, 1991.

Pink, Arthur, W., *Exposition of the Gospel of John,* Zondervan Publishing House, Copyright 1975.
The Sovereignty of God, The Banner of Truth Trust, Reprinted 1972.
The Doctrine of Revelation, Baker Book House, Copyright 1975.
The Attributes of God, Baker Book House, Seventh Printing, 1980.

Piper, John, *The Passion of Jesus Christ,* Crossway Books, Copyright 2004.

Radmacher, Earl D., *What the Church Is All About,* Moody Press, 1978.

Ramm, Bernard L., *Hermeneutics,* Baker Book House, 1987.

Ravenhill, Leonard, *A Classic on Revival-Why Revival Tarries,* Bethany House Publishers, 1983.

Reid, Daniel G., Robert D. Linder, Bruce L. Shelley, Harry S. Stout (Editor), *Dictionary of Christianity in America,* InterVarsity Press, 1990.

Rice, John R., *I Am a Fundamentalist,* Sword of the Lord Publishers, 1975.
God's Work-How to Do It, Sword of the Lord Publishers, 1971.
The Golden Path To Successful Personal Soul Winning, Sword of the Lord Publishers, Copyright 1961.
Predestined for Hell? NO!, Sword of the Lord Publishers, 1953.
You Must Be Born Again, Sword of the Lord Publishers, 1953.
When Skeletons Come out of their Closets!, Sword of the Lord Publishers, Fifth Printing, July 1971.
The Rice Reference Bible, Thomas Nelson, Inc., Copyright 1981.

Richards, Lawrence O., *Expository Dictionary of Bible Worlds,* Zondervan Publishing House, 1985.

Rimmer, Harry, *The Last of The Giants,* Reprinted by Christian Book Gallery, 1948.

Robertson, Archibald T., *Word Pictures In The New Testament, Matthew Mark- Volume I,* Baker Book House, 1930.
Luke- Volume II, Baker Book House, 1930.
Acts- Volume III, Baker Book House, 1930.
Epistles of Paul- Volume IV, Baker Book House, 1931.
John Hebrews- Volume V, Baker Book House, 1932.
Volume VI, Baker Book House, 1933.

Robinson, Haddon W., *Biblical Preaching-The Development and Delivery of Expository Messages,* Baker Book House, Fourth Printing, 1981.

Rodgers, Thomas R., *The Panorama of The Old Testament,* Impact Press, Third Printing, 1991.
Strategy-A Sourcebook of Tactics For A Dynamic Ministry, Impact Press, Copyright, 1983.
Russell, D.S., *Between the Testaments,* Fortress Press, Sixth Printing, 1979.

Ryrie, Charles Caldwell, *Revelation,* Moody Press, Seventeenth Printing, 1979.
The Holy Spirit, Moody Press, Ninth Printing, 1973.
Basic Theology, Victor Books, 1999.

Saucy, Robert L., *The Church in God's Program,* Moody Press, Published 1972.

Saxe, Raymond H., *The Battle for Your Bible,* Grace Bible Publications, Second Printing, 1978.

Schaeffer, Francis A., *The God Who Is There,* Inter-Varsity Press, Copyright 1968.
He Is There and He Is not Silent, Tyndale House Publishers, Fifteenth Printing, 1981.
How Should We Then Live?-The Rise and Decline of Western Thought and Culture, Crossway Books, Copyright July 1976.

Schaff, Philip, *History of the Christian Church-Apostolic Christianity-Volume I,* W.M. B. Eerdmans Publishing Company, Reprinted July 1980.
History of the Christian Church-Ante-Nicene Christianity-Volume II, WM. B. Eerdmans Publishing Company, Tenth Printing, July 1980.
History of the Christian Church-Nicene and Ante-nicene Christianity-Volume III, WM. B. Eerdmans Publishing Company, Reprinted April 1979.
History of the Christian Church-Mediaeval Christianity-Volume IV, WM. B. Eerdmans Publishing Company, Reprinted April 1979.
History of the Christian Church-The Middle Ages-Volume V, WM. B. Eerdmans Publishing Company, Reprinted April 1979.
History of the Christian Church-The Middle Ages-Volume VI, WM. B. Eerdmans Publishing Company, Reprinted July 1980.
History of the Christian Church-Modern Christianity-Volume VII, WM. B. Eerdmans Publishing Company, Reprinted April 1979.
History of the Christian Church-Modern Christianity-Volume VIII, WM. B. Eerdmans Publishing Company, Reprinted April 1979.
A Christian Manifesto, Crossway Books, Copyright 1982.

Schein, Bruce E., *Following the Way-The Setting of John's Gospel,* Augsburg Publishing House, Copyright 1980.

Shedd, William G.T., *Shedd's Dogmatic Theology-Volume I, Shedd's Dogmatic Theology-Volume II, Shedd's Dogmatic Theology-Volume III,* Tomas Nelson Publishers, Second Edition, 1980.

Sheldon, Charles M., *In His Steps-What Would Jesus Do?,* Grosset & Dunlap, 1935.

Soltau, Henry W., *The Holy Vessels and Furniture of the Tabernacle,* Kregal Publications, Reprinted 1975.
The Tabernacle, the Priesthood and the Offerings, Kregal Publications, Second Printing, 1974.

Sproul, R.C., *Faith Alone The Evangelical Doctrine of Justification,* Baker Books Second Printing, 1996.

Spurgeon, Charles H., *The Parables of Our Lord,* Baker Book House, Six Volumes, Reprinted 1979.

Spurgeon, Charles H., *The Treasury of David,* Baker Book House, Seven Volumes, Second Printing, July 1978.

Spurgeon, Charles H., *12 Sermons on Backsliding,* Baker Book House, Reprinted 1979.
The Passion and Death of Christ, William B. Eerdmans Publishing Company, Reprinted October 1979.

Stott, John R.W., *The Message of Ephesians,* Inter-Varsity Press, 1984.

Strauch, Alexander, *Biblical Eldership-An Urgent Call to Restore Biblical Church Leadership,* Lewis and Roth Publishers, Copyright 1995.

Streeter, Lloyd L., *Seventy-five Problems,* Lloyd L. Streeter, Copyright 2001.

Sturz, Harry A., *The Byzantine Text-Type & New Testament Textual Criticism,* Biblical Viewpoints Publications, Copyright 1984.

Tasker, R.V.G General Editor, Tyndale New Testament Commentaries, Twenty Volumes, Wm. B. Eerdmans Publishing Company, Eighth Printing, July 1980.

Teachout, Raymond L., *Breaking Down the Walls…and the Gospel,* EBPA Publications Second Printing, 1999.

Tenney, Merrill C. and Steven Barabas, *The Zondervan Pictorial Encyclopedia of the Bible, Volumes One through Five,* Zondervan Publishing House, 2009.

Thomas, David, *Acts of the Apostles-Expository and Homiletical,* Kregel Publications, Published 1980.
Gospel of John- Expository and Homiletical, Kregel Publications, Published 1980.

Thomas, Major W. Ian, *The Saving Life of Christ,* Daybreak Books, Published 1961.

Tillapaugh, Frank R., *Unleashing the Church-Getting People Out of the Fortress and Into Ministry,* Regal Books, Copyright 1982.

Torrey R.A. and Charles Leach, *Our Bible-How We Got It and Ten Reasons Why I Believe the Bible is the Word of God,* Fleming H. Revell Company, Copyright 1898.

Unger, Merrill F., *The Baptizing Work of The Holy Spirit,* Van Kampen Press Inc., Copyright 1953.
The Baptism & Gifts of The Holy Spirit, Moody Press, Copyright 1974.
The New Unger's Bible Dictionary, Moody Press, Copyright 1988.
Unger's Survey of the Bible, Harvest House Publishers, Reprinted 1981, Third Printing, March 1985.
Zechariah: Prophet of Messiah's Glory, Zondervan Publishing House, Twelfth Printing, 1982.
Volume II Unger's Commentary on the Old Testament, Moody Press, 1981.

Van Doren, W.H., *Gospel of John,* Kregel Publications, Copyright 1981.

Van Gorder, Paul R., *The Church Stands Corrected,* Victor Books, Copyright 1967.

Vincent, Marvin R., *Word Studies in the New Testament,* **Three Volumes,** Wm. B. Eerdmans's Publishing Co., Seventh Printing, 1980.

Vincent, Milton R., *Word Studies in The New Testament-Volume IV,* WM. B. Eerdmans Publishing Co., Seventh Reprinting, 1980.

Walton, Arthur B., *The Heartbeat of Paul-The Book of 2 Corinthians,* Regular Baptist Press, Copyright 1978.
Marks of A Mighty Church-First and Second Thessalonians, Regular Baptist Press, Copyright 1982.

Walvoord, John F., *The Rapture Question,* The Zondervan Corporation, Second Printing, 1976.

Walvoord, John F. and John E. Walvoord, *The Rapture Question, Revised and Enlarge Edition,* The Zondervan Corporation, Seventeenth Printing, 1980.
The Holy Spirit At Work Today, Moody Press, Second Printing, 1973.
Daniel The Key To Prophetic Revelation, Moody Press, Paperback Edition, 1989.

Warfield, Benjamin Breckinridge, *The Inspiration and Authority of the Bible,* The Presbyterian and Reformed Publishing Company, Sixth Printing, 1970.
Revelation and Inspiration-Volume I, Baker Book House, Reprinted 1981.
Biblical Doctrines-Volume II, Baker Book House, Reprinted 1981.
Christology and Criticism-Volume III, Baker Book House, Reprinted 1981.
Studies in Tertullian and Augustine-Volume IV, Baker Book House, Reprinted 1981.
Calvin and Calvinism-Volume V, Baker Book House, Reprinted 1981.
The Westminster Assembly and Its Work-Volume VI, Baker Book House, Reprinted 1981.
Perfectionism Part one-Volume VII, Baker Book House, Reprinted 1981.
Perfectionism Part two-Volume VIII, Baker Book House, Reprinted 1981.
Studies in Theology-Volume IX, Baker Book House, Reprinted 1981.
Critical Reviews-Volume X, Baker Book House, Reprinted 1981.

Weisiger, Cary N. III, *Preacher's Homiletic Library-Proclaiming the New Testament, 1ˢᵗ Peter to Revelation Vol. 5,* Baker Book House, Copyright 1961.

Weiss, Christian G., *Insights Into Bible Times and Customs,* Back to the Bible Publication, Copyright 1972.

Welch, Wilbert W., *Conduct Becoming Saints-The Book of 1 Corinthians Part 2, Chapters 9-16,* Regular Baptist Press, Copyright 1978.
A Charge to Keep-The Book of First Timothy, Regular Baptist Press, Copyright 1982.

Wesley, John, *Sermons-Volume II,* Eaton & Mains, 1985.

Whitcomb, John C., *Everyman's Bible Commentary-Daniel,* Moody Press, 1985.
Everyman's Bible Commentary-Esther, Moody Press, 1979.

Whitcomb, John C. and Donald B. Deyoung, *The Moon-It's Creation, Form and Significance,* John the Baptist Printing Ministry, 1978.

White, John, *Arise and Build! Ezra and Nehemiah,* Regular Baptist Press, 1979.
Song of the Saints-A Study of Selected Psalms, Regular Baptist Press, 1980.

Wiersbe, Warren W., *Be Faithful-1-2 Timothy, Titus, Philemon,* Victor Books, 1981.
Walking with The Giants-A Minister's Guide to Good Reading and Great Preaching, Baker Book House, Copyright 1976.
Listening to The Giants, Baker Book House, Copyright 1980.

Williamson, G.A. (Translator), *The History of The Church-Eusebius,* Dorset Press, 1984.

Winter, Ernst F. (Translator and Editor), *Erasmus-Luther Discourse on Free Will,* The Continuum Publishing Company, Copyright 1961.

Wood, Leon J., *Downfall and Deliverance-The Book of Judges,* Regular Baptist Press, Copyright 1975.
Wood, Leon J., Revised by David O'Brien, *A Survey of Israel's History,* Zondervan Corporation, Copyright 1986.

Wuest, Kenneth S., *The New Testament-An Expanded Translation,* Wm. B. Eerdmans Publishing Company, Three Volumes, Twelfth Printing, July 1980.
Philippians, In the Greek New Testament for The English Reader, Wm. B. Eerdmans Publishing Company, Copyright 1942.

Young, Edward J. Young, *The Book of Isaiah, Three Volumes,* Wm. B. Eerdman's Publishing Co., Reprinted November 1992.

Zodhiates, Spiros, *The Behavior of Belief,* Wm. B. Eerdman's Publishing Co., Fourth Printing, 1973.
The Church in Prophecy, Zondervan Publishing House, Sixteenth Printing, 1980.

www.ingramcontent.com/pod-product-compliance
Lightning Source LLC
Chambersburg PA
CBHW051511150726
47997CB00001B/199